The Devil's Guide to Hollywood

"Along with the straight advice . . . Eszterhas provides the kind of insight that only a veteran with fifteen movies to his name can supply."
—*Houston Chronicle*

"Great fun. Eszterhas is a writer, and always will be." —*Bay Area Reporter*

"The antithesis of boring, a hell of a funny read." —*The Plain Dealer*

"The new showbiz Bible . . . *The Devil's Guide to Hollywood* is an absolute must-have for screenwriters, both aspiring and established, as well as anyone else desiring a raw, inside view of the so-called Hollywood dream machine."
—Todd David Schwartz, CBS

"Accessible, perceptive, passionate, and funny, delivered in the author's characteristic no-holds-barred, visceral, profanity-strewn prose . . . Joe Eszterhas, we need you!" —*The Sunday Times* (London)

"Eszterhas's tips on screenwriting are relatively brief, discerning, and recommended." —Bookslut.com

"Hundreds of sound-bite-sized anecdotes, definitions, and quotes . . . a rollicking . . . macro-rant against anyone and anything that would obstruct a writer's path to success, power, and respect." —*Los Angeles Times*

Hollywood Animal

"Absolutely first-rate—painfully, poignantly heartfelt . . . a compelling . . . [and] brutally truthful book." —*Los Angeles Times Book Review*

"The story about Mr. Eszterhas's father, buried at the heart of *Hollywood Animal,* is a powerful and affecting one. . . . A story about guilt and betrayal and forgiveness." —*The New York Times*

"[Eszterhas] is an engaging writer, and he isn't too proud to dish about himself. . . . The most outrageous . . . movie-biz memoir of all time." —*People*

"By turns entertaining, heartbreaking, funny, and outrageous . . . The details are lurid, and Eszterhas doesn't spare himself criticism. . . . Hard to put down."
—*Houston Chronicle*

"Eszterhas writes movingly about his ups and downs, including bouts with such scary monsters as cancer, divorce, and Michael Ovitz, the agent who once had Tinseltown in his grasp and was one of Eszterhas's mortal enemies. This tell-all is abrasively honest stuff."
—*The Washington Post*

"Meaty . . . Moving . . . He hardly ever spares himself. . . . There are real surprises here."
—*San Francisco Chronicle*

American Rhapsody

"Eszterhas . . . trains his well-turned phrases on the White House intern scandal. . . . The guy can write, and he is viciously funny."
—*Library Journal*

"If there's one thing writer Joe Eszterhas knows how to do, it's how to push the envelope. If you like dish served on a big, flat, silver platter, look no further."
—*Playboy*

"It's a hilarious and scandalous book, part fact, part fantasy, about a serious subject: Washington observed through the prism of Hollywood and vice versa."
—*The Observer* (London)

THE DEVIL'S GUIDE TO HOLLYWOOD

THE SCREENWRITER AS GOD!

JOE ESZTERHAS

ST. MARTIN'S GRIFFIN ✠ NEW YORK

www.stmartins.com

Design by Phil Mazzone

Library of Congress Cataloging-in-Publication Data

Eszterhas, Joe.
    The devil's guide to Hollywood : the screenwriter as God! / Joe Eszterhas.
       p. cm.
    Includes index.
    ISBN-13: 978-0-312-37384-9
    ISBN-10: 0-312-37384-8
    1. Motion picture authorship. 2. Motion picture industry—California—Los Angeles—Anecdotes. I. Title.

PN1996.E88 2006
808.2'3—dc22

                                        2006043919

First St. Martin's Griffin Edition: October 2007

10 9 8 7 6 5 4 3 2 1

For Jenö Máté, Hungarian actor,
who played bit parts in John Wayne westerns,
and who sponsored my family's immigration
from the refugee camps of Austria to the
United States of America . . . and for Naomi, Sunlight.

"In the beginning was the Word . . ."
—John 1:1

CONTENTS

ACKNOWLEDGMENTS

For their help along the long and winding road, I thank: Guy McElwaine, Sam Fischer, Gerry and Gale Messerman, Patricia Glaser, Irwin Winkler, Norman Jewison, Craig Baumgarten, Ben Myron, Jim Morgan, Ed Victor, Alan Nierob, Richard Marquand, Paul Verhoeven, Costa-Gavras, Adrian Lyne, Alan Pakula, Steven Spielberg, Arthur Hiller, Ray Stark, Don Simpson, Jim Robinson, Dawn Steele, Arnold Rifkin, David Greenblatt, Jim Wiatt, Jeff Berg, Skip Brittenham, Bob Shapiro, Kevin Bacon, John Candy, Marsha Nasatir, Gene Corman, Patrick Palmer, Mike Medavoy, Barry Hirsch, Robert Wallerstein, Steven Bochco, Steve Roth, Richard Roth, Andrew Vajna, Mario Kassar, Lee Rich, Tony Thomopoulos, Michael Sloane, Peter Bart, Liz Smith, Army Archerd, George Christy, Michael Fleming, Lori Weintraub, Claudia Eller, Lynn Nesbit, Jerry Bruckheimer, Marty Ransohoff, Bob Bookman, Jann Wenner, Michael Viner, Alan Ladd, Jr., Frank Price, Robert Evans, Charles Evans, Sherry Lansing, Brandon Tartikoff, Jon Peters, Sylvester Stallone, Whoopi Goldberg, Debra Winger, Hunter S. Thompson, Pete Hamill, Jane Scott, Gary Kress, John Reese, Ted Princiotto, Vern Havener, Chris Matthews, Sonny Mehta, Jim Silberman, Jack Mathews, Bill Gross, Tova Leiter, Ira Levin, Tom Hedley, Scott Richardson, Gary G-Wiz, Father Bob Stec, Ron Rogers, Bob Landaw, Marshall Strome, Doug Hicks, Vernon Alden, L. J. Horton, Sue Mengers, Michael Marcus, Tom Wolfe, Philip Noyce, Karel Reisz, Bob Rafelson, Guy Ferland, Roseanne, Sam Kinison, Zelma Redding, Nelson McCormick, Paul Wilmer, Herb Caen, Bob Ranallo, Richard Rosman, Father John Mundweil, Alan Smith, Doug Buemi, Jeremy Baka, Rodman Gregg, Don Granger, Elizabeth Beier, and Matt Drudge.

Special thanks to Naomi and to my children—Joe, Nick, John Law, Luke, Steve, Suzanne Maria Eszterhas, and Suzanne Maria Perryman.

Finally, no *Devil's Guide to Hollywood* would be complete without the diabolical wit and wisdom of the players quoted in this book, some captured by me and some by others. I thank all of those people and especially the insights of my fellow Hungarian, my secret adolescent crush, *dahling*, the magnificent, the regal, Zsa Zsa Gabor.

PREFACE

They're out there by the dozens, telling you how to write screen-plays, when they don't know how to do it themselves.

Robert McKee is the most famous of them, and while it is true that he has *sold* some scripts, he has had only one feature-length film produced on cable television.

McKee's Web site points out that, at the University of Michigan, his creative writing professor was "the noted Kenneth Rowe, whose former students include Arthur Miller and Lawrence Kasdan." This is, of course, success by association, McKee elevating himself to the same creative peak where stand Miller and Kasdan by saying that he once attended the same school (which admits more than twenty thousand students each year) and had the same teacher.

McKee is a former actor who, his Web site says, "appeared on Broadway with such luminaries as Helen Hayes, Rosemary Harris, and Will Geer." He thus elevates himself to the same peak where stand those *acting* luminaries. Lo and behold, McKee miraculously turns *himself* into a *luminary*. He implies that he is as good an actor as Helen Hayes, the same way that he implied he was as *luminary* a writer as Arthur Miller.

It is a great act, brought to life by an actor who barnstorms the world doing a one-man, three-day, thirty-hour show (like Hal Holbrook doing a marathon Mark Twain): Robert McKee playing the part of successful screenwriter, the actor reciting the same lines over and over again. "It is the same fundamental lecture I have been giving for twenty years," McKee told the *Melbourne* (Australia) *Herald Sun.* "It never gets old."

Reviewing the act, *Movieline* magazine wrote, "He storms the stage like

George C. Scott in *Patton*." *The New Yorker* wrote, "McKee, who used to be an actor, rarely speaks a sentence that does not call for a word so stressed that he bares his teeth."

McKee performs in L.A., Vegas, Miami, New York, Paris, London, and Singapore "from a script that barely changes a word from one performance to another," *The New Yorker* wrote. And McKee himself told *The New Yorker*, "I am an old actor and this is thirty hours of performance to a captive audience. It's very satisfying."

In that same interview, McKee said, "Warner Brothers said, 'Bob, we want *Jagged Edge* goes rock and roll for Cher. I wrote a thing called *Trophy,* for an embarrassing amount of money, about a rock star who murders her husband and gets away with it. They loved it. Loved it."

But alas, as much as they may have "loved it," Warner Bros. didn't make it. Nobody has made it.

I was amused to read that Warner Bros. told McKee to write "*Jagged Edge* goes rock and roll," since *I'm* the guy who wrote the original *Jagged Edge*. In other words, the great screenwriting guru, who tells the world how to write scripts, was assigned by Warner Brothers to sit down and *imitate me*. And imitate me he did: "A rock star who murders her husband and gets away with it" is how he described *Trophy*. That is a resounding echo of *Jagged Edge*'s theme of a prominent socialite who murders his wife and gets away with it.

I am led then to this conclusion: If you want to know about screenwriting, you might be better off listening to the guy who wrote the original than the guy who imitated it.

What you will read in this book is what I've learned in thirty-one years of writing screenplays.

I have written fifteen films: *F.I.S.T., Flashdance, Jagged Edge, Big Shots, Hearts of Fire, Betrayed, Music Box, Nowhere to Run, Basic Instinct, Checking Out, Sliver, Showgirls, Jade, Telling Lies in America,* and *An Alan Smithee Film: Burn Hollywood Burn*. I am now working on my sixteenth and seventeenth.

My films have grossed over $1 billion at the box office, and in 1992, *Basic Instinct* was the number-one movie of the year worldwide. I have been paid many millions of dollars for my scripts, more than any other screenwriter in Hollywood history: $4 million for a four-page outline of *One Night Stand;* $3.7 million for *Showgirls;* $3.7 million for an unproduced biography of John Gotti; $3 million for *Basic Instinct;* $2.5 million for *Jade,* and lesser seven-figure amounts for *Betrayed, Music Box, and Flashdance*.

I have been called "the rogue elephant of screenwriters" (the *Los Angeles Times*); "the Che Guevara of screenwriters (*Daily Variety*); "a living Hollywood legend" (ABC's 20/20); and "a force of nature" (*The New York Times*). My favorite quote about myself, of course, and one I use shamelessly to infuriate my critics, is a quote from *Time* magazine: "If Shakespeare were alive today, would his name be Joe Eszterhas?" (No, I will reluctantly admit that I am not Shakespeare; I am a refugee street kid from the West Side of Cleveland, in love with his wife, his children, movies, baseball, and America.)

I lived for twenty-two years in Marin County in northern California; a year in Kapalua, Maui; eight years in Malibu's Point Dume; and, for the past four years, back home in Ohio, where Naomi and I have decided to raise our four boys (so they, too, will grow up to be in love with their wives, children, baseball, and America).

But while I've lived in all these places, in my head I've lived in Hollywood all this time, beginning my days by reading *Daily Variety* and *The Hollywood Reporter*—and *then The New York Times* (starting, like George W. Bush, with the sports pages).

The lessons that I am about to pass on to you were learned in many and varied places: in so-called (and oxymoronic) studio creative meetings; on tension-laden sets; on luxurious Learjets headed for European locations; in limos moving like bulletproof armored vehicles down Sunset Boulevard in the L.A. night; on family vacations to movie-family vacation spots like the Kahala Hilton on Oahu and, later, the Four Seasons on Maui; at poker games in the Hollywood Hills and in Bel Air; at craps tables at Caesar's Palace, the Mirage, and Bellagio in Vegas; at innumerable parties in Aspen, Malibu, and the Hamptons; and at myriad power breakfasts, lunches, and dinners at Morton's, the Ivy, Elaine's, the Four Seasons Grill Room, Spago, Crustacean, Frida's, Citrus, Orsini's, the Friar's Club, the Daisy, Ma Maison, Café Rodeo, the Swiss House, Scandia, the Brown Derby, Palm, Patrick's Roadhouse, Michael's, the patio of the Bel Air Hotel, the bar at the Four Seasons Hotel and the Peninsula, the lobby bar at the Chateau Marmont, the Sky Bar, the Monkey Bar, On the Rox, La Dolce Vita, Jimmy's, La Scala on Little Santa Monica and La Scala at the beach, Nicky Blair's, Granita, Eureka, Dan Tana's, the Padrino Room at the Beverly Wilshire, the Polo Lounge at the Beverly Hills Hotel, the Grill on Dayton Way, and Nobu in L.A. and in New York.

In the world of Hollywood, the true battlefields are restaurants and bars in L.A. and New York. I have fought many battles in those places and have learned some hard-won, hilarious, and painful lessons.

I pass them on to you because my creative life has been dedicated to the belief that we screenwriters are not "schmucks with Underwoods" (as Jack Warner once called us) but that through hard work, strength of will, treachery, God's help, and big balls, we can write good scripts, protect them from being mutilated on-screen, make millions, and live lives that are self-respectful and fulfilling.

I am convinced the day will come when screenwriters will no longer be at the bottom of the Hollywood totem pole; the schmucks with laptops will be kicking ass.

Hollywood has often been a hellish place for screenwriters, but I think that with my *Devil's Guide* in hand, you'll feel less pain.

—Joe Eszterhas
Bainbridge Township, Ohio

PART ONE

PURSUING
YOUR DREAM

LESSON 1

They Can Snort You Here!

Why do you want to be a screenwriter?
The answer I get from most young wannabe screenwriters is, "Cuz I want to be rich."

I tell them what Madonna says: "Money makes you beautiful."

And I tell them that I've made a lot of money but that I'll never be beautiful.

Why do you want to write a screenplay?
Screenwriter/novelist Raymond Chandler (*The Blue Dahlia*): "Where the money is, so will the jackals gather."

You, too, can be a star.
My biggest year was 1994. I wrote five scripts in one year. I made almost $10 million. I had houses in Tiburon and Malibu, California, and in Kapalua, Maui.

I made half a million dollars for writing a thirty-second television commercial for Chanel No. 5 perfume.

I fell in love. I got divorced. I married my second wife. Our first child was born.

I had the best tables at Spago and the Ivy and at Granita, Postrio, and Roy's. I had limos in northern California, in Malibu, and on Maui.

I ate more, I drank more, I made love more, and I spent more time in the sun than I ever had. The world was my oyster.

I became the screenwriter as star.

"Ben Hecht," his friend Budd Schulberg wrote many years ago, "seemed the personification of the writer at the top of his game, the top of his world, not gnawing at and doubting himself as great writers were said to do, but with every word and every gesture indicating the animal pleasure he took in writing well."

Robert McKee makes money, doesn't he?

When a student interrupted a McKee seminar with a question, McKee roared, "Do not interrupt me!"

A few minutes later, McKee shouted to the student, "If you think that this course is about making money, there's the door!"

I'll say this right up front: *This book is about making money.*

Money is not the best thing about screenwriting.

The best thing about screenwriting is this: I sit in a little room making things up and put my conjurings down on paper. A year and a half later, if I'm lucky, my conjurings will be playing all over the world on movie screens, giving enjoyment to hundreds of millions of people.

For two hours, the lives of hundreds of millions of people will have been made better by something that *I* conjured up in a little room out of my own heart, gut, and brain.

By then, my conjurings will have become a megacorporation employing thousands of people—from gaffers to makeup people to ticket sellers.

And it will all have begun with *me,* with *my* imagination and *my* creativity, literally communicating with the whole world.

That's the best part of screenwriting.

The money (almost) doesn't matter.

Screenwriter Jack Epps (*Top Gun, Legal Eagles*): "You do it because you love the movies. The money gets in the way. I think that if you're a good writer, the money will follow. But if you're writing for money, I don't think it's going to work. I think that very few people can make that happen." I'll say this right up front: *This book is about making money. Without losing your soul.*

Ben Hecht is no role model.

Wrote Ben: "The fact that the movie magnate is going to make an enormous pile of money out of my story and that I am therefore entitled to a creditable share of it seldom, if ever, occurs to me. I am, to the contrary, convinced that my contribution is nil. The story I will provide will be a piece of hack work, containing in it a reshuffling of familiar plot turns and characterizations."

TAKE IT FROM ZSA ZSA

Actress and famed Hungarian femme fatale Zsa Zsa Gabor: "Money is like a sixth sense that makes it possible for you to fully enjoy the other five."

Getting to the Tit

An old Hollywood expression for making some big money.

If you sell a script, you'll be part of a fun and glamorous business.
When he got back to London after the *Lawrence of Arabia* shoot, screenwriter Robert Bolt told the London *Sunday Times* that the shoot had been "a continuous clash of egomaniacal monsters wasting more energy than dinosaurs and pouring rivers of money into the sand."

Dream Street

Hollywood legend: If you walk down Dream Street and somebody notices you (or buys your script), you can be a star overnight.

We have no role models.
When asked by reporters why he was a screenwriter, Ben Hecht, the most successful screenwriter in the history of Hollywood, said, "Because I was born in a toilet."

Screenwriter William Goldman *(Butch Cassidy and the Sundance Kid, All The President's Men)* described himself in the twilight of his career this way in his book *Hype and Glory*: "Couldn't walk, couldn't read, couldn't do a goddamn thing but stare the night away and block out the past."

His big brother, screenwriter James Goldman (*The Lion in Winter*), wrote this to director Joe Mankiewicz: "I need your help to write this thing. If this letter sounds prosy and dull, it's because I've been reading my script."

Screenwriter Charlie Kaufman, in *Adaptation*: "Do I have an original thought in my head? Maybe if I were happier my hair wouldn't be falling out. . . . I'm a walking cliché. Why should I be made to feel that I have to apologize for my existence?"

In the movie *Tales of Ordinary Madness*, written by Charles Bukowski about himself, a prostitute was trying to get Ben Gazzara (playing Bukowski) to stop writing and make love to her.

Watching the movie in the back of a Hollywood theater, the real Bukowski yelled, "If that were me, I would have stopped typing long ago."

Somebody in the audience told him to shut up.

"Hey," Bukowski said. "I'm the guy they made the movie about. I can say anything I want to say!"

Somebody yelled, "Oh yeah? Then shut the fuck up!"

Bukowski yelled, "Oh yeah? Fuck you!"

Cops were called. They handcuffed Charlie Bukowski and dragged him out of his own movie and locked him in jail.

You're certainly in good literary company.

William Faulkner, F. Scott Fitzgerald, Truman Capote, Alberto Moravia, Carson McCullers, John Steinbeck, John O'Hara, Dorothy Parker, Jim Harrison, Joan Didion, Ken Kesey, William Kennedy, Norman Mailer, Ayn Rand, Jay McInerney, and Hunter S. Thompson were all screenwriters at one point or another.

Faulkner even took a meeting with Sammy Glick.

After he won the Nobel Prize for Literature, William Faulkner did rewrites of these scripts: *The Left Hand of God* and *Land of the Pharaohs*. He took meetings with actress Julie Harris and producer Jerry Wald, Budd Schulberg's model for agent Sammy Glick in *What Makes Sammy Run?*

Robert McKee is an artist . . .

McKee: "People today don't respect screenwriting as an art. People didn't think this way in the 1930s, 40s, and 50s. But it takes real genius to do it beautifully."

Don't ever refer to yourself as an artist.

Novelist Sherwood Anderson said to Ben Hecht, "You let art alone . . . she's got enough guys sleeping with her."

The Revolt of the Assholes

Screenwriter John Gregory Dunne's definition of a writer's strike.

Faulkner was a mensch.

A producer, who'd begun as a press agent for studio czar Harry Cohn in the 1930s, wanted to demonstrate his knowledge of American "literatoor" for me.

"Fitzgerald?" he said. "His wife, that crazy bitch Thelma, told him he couldn't get her or any other woman off because it was too small. And that hotsy-totsy Brit gossip *kurva* he was living with out here, what was her name? Graham, that's it. *Heather Graham.* She said Fitzgerald was so ashamed of it, she never saw him with his clothes off. And then after the poor putz died, she said she'd rather make it with the size of a chimpanzee than the size of a horse. That was almost as ugly as the stuff Sally said about Burt in Playboy . . . that *fageleh* stuff that everybody talked about. Anyway. Hemingway? His bullfighting friend, that American, that gay guy, Sidney, Stanley, whatever. Stanley said Hemingway was always worried about his size. Sidney said it was the size of a thirty-thirty shell. And then there was that gay-bashing thing where Ernest sees a guy across the street who's flaming and goes across the street and beats the *fageleh* up. Faulkner? He schtupped that little secretary in town for almost twenty years. Liked her to put on little skimpy white dresses. Took her out to the beach in Santa Monica so the other guys could look through those white dresses, too. She told everybody he was a wild man—three, four times a night. Faulkner liked it here, kept coming back for the money and the pussy, just like the rest of us. Faulkner was a *mensch.*"

You don't have to be smart to be a screenwriter.

Screenwriter Sylvester Stallone was thrown out of fourteen schools in eleven years.

Be proud that Rocky is your colleague.

Sylvester Stallone even had himself photographed for a cover of *Writer's Digest*. He even sat in front of a typewriter. He even wore horn-rimmed glasses. He even said he was more a writer than an actor.

Then he stopped writing for thirty years and became an action figure and a windup toy.

But . . . at one point during those thirty years, he even smoked a pipe for a while.

He had himself photographed smoking his pipe, too, though he didn't wear his horn-rimmed glasses at the same time.

You don't want to turn into Sylvester Stallone . . . or do you?

Thirty years after Rocky, Sly and I were talking about writing.

"I used to love writing," Sly said. "I don't know what happened."

I said, "I do. You became a movie star. You've had your head in pussy all these years."

Sly said, "You're probably right."

You've got a good shot to make it.

Less brains are necessary in the motion picture business than in any other," producer Lewis J. Selznick, David's dad, told a congressional committee.

A Hollywood High:

To be overjoyed at the prospect of something great happening . . . something that will turn into shit the next day.

Maybe you might need a brainguard, too.

Producer David O. Selznick felt that a good idea was worth a million dollars, so he hired a guard to stand in front of the room where his company's scripts were kept.

He called this guard "the Brainguard."

Let's hope you get it kissed.

Legendary studio boss Harry Cohn: "I kiss the feet of talent and I kick the ass of those who don't have it."

Everybody wants to be a screenwriter.

Alice Sebold, author (*The Lovely Bones*): "We are living in the shadow of Hollywood where I teach, at UC Irvine. I was stunned at how students talked about movies when we went out to dinner, when I was expecting them to talk about novels. There is big money in Hollywood and it lures away really good minds."

David Benioff, screenwriter (*Troy*): "Thirty years ago, students probably wanted to be the next great novelist. Now many want to write the next great screenplay. Film is something young writers think about."

Jim Shepard, instructor, UC Irvine: "If you go into a classroom and ask who's read Michael Cunningham's *The Hours,* half the students will raise their hands and say they've seen the movie. All of these students are interested in writing books. But more and more are finding it hard to keep their eyes off the brass ring that film represents."

Paul Schrader, screenwriter/director (*Taxi Driver, American Gigolo*): "More literature is being written to be film-friendly. When I was a student, the writer Robert Coover said the goal should be to write a novel that cannot be adapted to film. I doubt any student aspires to that today."

Screenwriter/novelist William Goldman: "When I was a kid, novels were important, theater was important, movies were our secret pleasure. Now, movies are the center of our culture."

Screenwriter/director Nora Ephron (*When Harry Met Sally*): "Movies are the literature of this generation and all subsequent generations."

Norman Mailer: "Movies are more likely than literature to reach deep feelings in people. . . . People who can't read are quite able to reach profound reactions in the dark of a theater."

Because everybody but everybody goes to the movies.

In 1991, during the Gulf War, Iraqi airplanes dropped leaflets on our troops that said, "Your wives are back at home having sex with Bart Simpson and Burt Reynolds."

Even Richard Russo wants to be a screenwriter.

The Pulitzer Prize–winning author (*Empire Falls* and *Nobody's Fool*) has written three teleplays and an original screenplay and has also adapted Scott Phillips's novel, *The Ice Harvest,* starring Billy Bob Thornton.

Even FDR wrote a treatment.

Yes, Franklin Delano Roosevelt, as a young man, pitched a story about John Paul Jones to Jane Wells of the Paramount Famous Lasky Corporation.

Ms. Wells liked the future president's pitch and asked him to send her an outline. He sent her a twenty-nine-page treatment.

Everybody *is a writer.*

Disney Mogul Michael Eisner wrote a play called *To Metastasize a River*; famed attorney to the stars Bert Fields writes thrillers under the pseudonym D. Kincaid; ex–Beverly Hills mayor Robert Tanenbaum writes mysteries under his own name; former L.A. mayor Richard Riordan has written several unproduced screenplays; assistant U.S. attorney Dan Saunders has written a play entitled *The Death of William Shakespeare.*

Even the swamis write screenplays.

Writer Anthony Haden-Guest: "It was a crisp fall morning in 1971. Two swamis were down by the desk of the Chateau Marmont. They wore long swami hair and filthy swami robes, but the swami with blond hair was fiddling with amber worry beads in an un-guru-like fashion. 'Get this, Al,' he said apologetically. 'I can let you have a script by Thursday.'

"The other swami dropped his key on the desk with a metallic clatter. His occult pendant jangled.

"'I don't want *a* script,' he declared coldly. 'I want *the* script.'"

Robert McKee owes his success to me and to Shane Black.

Ian Parker, writing in *The New Yorker:* "McKee became part of a great boom in screenwriting instruction which had its roots in the end of the studio system and the subsequent rise of the American auteur director: a screenwriter being one step from a director, and a director being God. The boom was further propelled by public knowledge of the multimillion-dollar fees paid to writers like Joe Eszterhas and Shane Black."

Will this be you?

Actress Hedy Lamarr discussing screenwriter Gene Markey (*Meet Me at the Fair, A Lost Lady*): "I had never been close to an American screenwriter before and I felt Gene was an individualist, one of a kind. He was bright and amusing, often brittle and superficial but at other times deep and confused. I have since learned that most screenwriters are this way. I don't know what came first, the chicken or the egg—whether they try to live up to the reputation writers have or whether their work makes them like that."

Perk of success: this is what you're working for

When my son Steve was twelve years old and the greatest Oakland Athletics fan in the world, he was desperate to meet his hero, the slugger Mark McGwire.

I called the A's publicity office, identified myself as the screenwriter of Flashdance, and the next thing I knew, Steve and I were in the A's dugout, talking to McGwire, and McGwire was telling us how much he loved Flashdance and asking me if Jenny Beals was as hot as she looked.

When my son Joe was eight years old and the greatest Cleveland Indians fan in the world, he was desperate to meet some of the players.

I read an interview in the newspaper with an Indians rookie pitcher named Roy Smith, who was quoted as saying he wanted to be a screenwriter.

I called Roy Smith and told him that if he got Joey into the Indians' dugout, I'd buy him lunch and that at that lunch he could ask me anything he wanted about screenwriting.

Roy picked out a date on which Joey could meet the Indians, but two days before the date, Roy was traded to the Oakland A's. He called me from Oakland and said Joey could meet the Indians and the A's the next time he came to Cleveland with the A's.

A week before the A's arrival in Cleveland, Roy Smith was cut by the team and sent down to the minors. I haven't heard from Roy since, but I am certain I will hear from him again if he ever gets back to the majors.

You can even turn priests on.

Through the years, a great many people have told me, like Mark McGwire, how much they loved *Flashdance.* Hundreds of women have viewed me more kindly the moment they found out I wrote (actually cowrote) the movie; some of these women even took me to bed to demonstrate to me their enthusiastic and wholehearted endorsement of the movie.

My wife Naomi's OB-GYN told me how much he loved *Flashdance* as Naomi was in her twenty-second hour of labor—sweating and nearly purple with our firstborn. He asked me, like Mark McGwire, "Is Jennifer Beals as hot as she looked?" even as Naomi groaned in pain in the background.

And my parish priest, Father Bob Stec, told me how much he had loved the movie—for other reasons, though, than McGwire and Naomi's OB-GYN. Father Bob loved the line "When you give up your dream, you die!" and said he had lived his life by that line since he'd seen the movie as a teenager.

I gave him a *Flashdance* poster and wrote that line on it and signed it.

Life-Affirming

New Age studio exec–speak for "Will it make a hundred million dollars?" It began to be used extensively after the success of *Forrest Gump*. Dreamworks chieftain Jeff Katzenberg begins each pitch meeting with a writer by saying, "Tell me how this movie you're about to pitch will be life-affirming."

What ever happened to FDR's treatment?

I t's probably still up on the shelf at Paramount.

Twelve years after he wrote that treatment, when he was president of the United States, FDR asked a lieutenant in naval intelligence to the Oval Office. The lieutenant was a former Paramount executive.

"You know why I asked you up here, don't you?" the president asked.

The lieutenant said, "Of course. It's *John Paul Jones*."

"Whatever happened to my treatment?" the president of the United States asked.

"It's on the shelf," the lieutenant said. "Paramount hasn't rejected it, but they haven't decided anything on it yet."

Then the treatment went into storage. It now lies in a sealed locker inside a mountain in Missouri, where the studios jointly own a vast storage area of old treatments and scripts.

You, too, can be in FDR's shoes.

I certainly am.
  These scripts of mine were all bought by Paramount and are still, like FDR's *John Paul Jones,* inside that mountain in Missouri: *Nark* (1981); *Dieshot* (1982); *Beat the Eagle* (1984); *Male Pattern Baldness* (1996); *Reliable Sources* (1997); *Land of the Free* (1998); *Other Men's Wives* (1999).

What are movies?

Screenwriter Dalton Trumbo: "Movies are an art that is a business and a business that is an art."

Movies are sausages.

Producer Mike Medavoy: "Getting films made is like watching sausage be produced: the finished product is great, but the process of putting it together is often messy."

Movies are selling sausages.

Director Phillip Noyce: "I realized that the Hollywood system—based as it is on the employment of branch offices all over the world promoting and selling movies—is totally dependent on a continual flow of product, and it's been set up to promote that product into the hearts and minds of people all over the world. In essence, movies represent marketing opportunities for Hollywood."

Without you, there is nothing.

I know that in theory the word is secondary in cinema," said director Orson Welles, "but the secret of my work is that everything is based on the word. I always begin with the dialogue. And I do not understand how one dares to write action before dialogue. I must begin with what the characters say. I must know what they say before seeing them do what they do."

You are more important than the director.

It all begins in the script," says director Milos Forman. "If what's happening is interesting, it doesn't matter where you shoot from, people will be interested to watch. If you write something boring, you can film from mosquitoes' underpants and it will still be boring."

Hollywood will hate you.

"The relationship between Hollywood and the writer is basically adversarial," says writer Jim Harrison. "The film business acts as if it wishes it could do without writers, but it can't, and it has accepted the fact without grace."

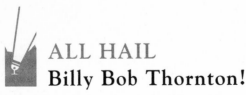

ALL HAIL
Billy Bob Thornton!

A hard-nosed screenwriter (*Sling Blade*) who went to the wall with several studios that wanted to change his scripts, he even jumped atop a studio head's desk once. . . . Billy Bob is the realization of all of our dreams: He became a movie star; he became a rock and roll star; he married Angelina Jolie.

Tony Kushner is no role model, either.

Kushner: "I didn't write *Angels in America*. The actors wrote it, the directors wrote it, we all wrote it." Can you break your Pulitzer Prize into little pieces, then, Tony, and share it with all the others?

This is you.

Screenwriter Milo Addica (*Birth*): "The writer is the lowest man on the totem pole, but potentially he has the most power. He comes up with the idea; he makes it work. You can't make a building without the blueprint; you can hire the labor and buy the material, but to make a building, you need a blueprint—which means someone has to sit at a table, rack their brain, and figure it out. That's what a writer does."

You ain't nothing but a Hessian to them.

John Gregory Dunne: "Screenwriters are regarded in the industry as chronic malcontents, overpaid and undertalented, the Hollywood version of Hessians, measuring their worth in dollars, since ownership of their words belongs to those who hire and fire them."

How about sleeping with the screenwriter?

Hedy Lamarr: "The ladder of success in Hollywood is usually agent, actor, director, producer, leading man; and you are a star if you sleep with each of them in that order. Crude but true."

These are the rules of the game.

Old Hollywood adage: "In the beginning, when he is writing the script, the screenwriter has the gun. When he turns his script in, he turns the gun over to the producer. When the producer hires the director, he hands the gun over to the director. When the director turns in his final cut, he hands the gun over to the studio. The studio then takes the gun and shoots the writer, the producer, and the director. The studio then hands the gun to the stars of the movie, who are going out to publicize the film. In rare cases like *Heaven's Gate,* the studio turns the gun on itself and blows its own brains out."

The Oscar

Woody Allen: "An inanimate statue of a little bald man."

You're not in Kansas anymore, sweetie.

Mike Medavoy: "The movie business is probably the most irrational business in the world . . . it is covered by a set of rules that are absolutely irrational."

Nobody knows anything.

This is Bill Goldman's famous (and accurate) phrase, but its flip side is: *"Everybody thinks he knows everything there is to know about writing."*

Which includes the cabbie, the waitress, the director, the traffic cop, the producer, the sanitation engineer, the studio head, the massage therapist, and the star.

Scott Fitzgerald didn't know anything, either.

He did an uncredited rewrite on *Gone with the Wind.* This is what he thought of the book: "I read it—I mean really read it—it is a good novel—not very original. . . . There are no new characters, new technique, new observations—none of the elements that make literature—especially no new examination into human emotions."

He thought it was a good novel, though, right?

Poor, poor Scott Fitzgerald . . .

Can you imagine Scott Fitzgerald's pain as he rewrote Margaret Mitchell?

Fitzgerald to his editor, Maxwell Perkins: "I was absolutely forbidden to use any words except those of Margaret Mitchell, that is, when new phrases had to be invented one had to thumb through it as if it were Scripture and check out phrases of her's which would cover the situation!"

These are words Hollywood lives by.

Keep your friends close to you, but keep your enemies closer."

These words of advice were first given to me by a woman producer who still occasionally slept with her ex-husband, also a producer, even though she had remarried and was "absolutely in love" with her new husband.

Her ex-husband had beaten her, sold naked photos of her to a Web site, told the court she was a "whore and a druggie" in a custody fight, put a .45 Magnum into her mouth and pulled the trigger, and tried to blackball her in the industry.

She loathed and feared him but slept with him whenever he wanted to "keep him close" and neutralize him.

Over the years, I heard the same advice from studio head Sherry Lansing, superagent Michael Ovitz, and producer Ray Stark.

If you get reamed, take him or her out to lunch.

Mike Medavoy: "Breaking bread with them that wronged you is as common as air kissing in the movie business."

The key to winning in Hollywood is to let them think they won.

I admit there are people in Hollywood who are much better at this than I am.

Among them is director Phillip Noyce (*Sliver, The Quiet American*): "My own directorial style can be described as 'nudging'—nudging people. I don't believe much is achieved by confrontation, except resentment. I mostly get exactly what I want. But the secret of doing that in movies is to allow the other person to think what *you* want is what they really want."

Barry Diller knows what he's talking about.

The studio head and corporate mogul said, "People get corrupted. They don't lose their brains. God knows, they don't lose their talent. But part of the process of success and what it does, it corrupts in the way that it removes their objectivity, it *removes their instincts.*"

Most of what you've heard about Hollywood is true.

Screenwriter William Goldman: "Understand this: all the sleaze you've heard about Hollywood? All the illiterate scumbags who scuttle down the corridors of power? They are there, all right, and worse than you can imagine."

God bless us everyone.

Producer Robert Evans: "In this town everybody's a whore. Everybody can be bought."

You'll need to be a really good liar.

Screenwriter Dalton Trumbo: "The art of lying is the art of the practical. It ought never be indulged in for the pure pleasure of the thing, since over-usage dulls the instrument, corrodes the character, and despoils the spirit. The important thing about a lie is not that it be interesting, fanciful, graceful or even pleasant but that it be believed. Curb, therefore, your imagination. Let the lie be delivered full-face, eye to eye, and without scratching of the scalp. Let it be blunt and forthright and so simple that you can repeat it in detail and under oath ten years hence. But let it, for all of its simplicity, contain one fantastical element of creative ingenuity—one and no more—designed to capture the attention of the listener and to convince him that, since no one would dare to invent the improbability you have inserted, its mere existence places the stamp of truth upon everything you have said. If you cannot tell a believable lie, cling then to truth which is always our secret succor in times of need, and manfully accept the consequences."

It's all good news, all the time!

What absolutely no one does in Hollywood is tell you bad news. If someone doesn't like your script, they won't tell you that. You'll simply never hear from them. If somebody doesn't like your movie, they'll tell you they haven't seen it yet.

Hold out for the fifty cents.

Marilyn Monroe: "Hollywood is a place where they'll pay you a thousand dollars for a kiss and fifty cents for your soul. I know, because I turned down the first offer often enough and held out for the fifty cents."

To Do a Begelman

To commit suicide, like agent and studio head David.

Don't live in L.A.

Everyone in L.A. wants somehow to get into the movie business or has a friend or a relative who wants to get into the business. Everyone is a wannabe, already in star training.

All the wannabe screenwriters you meet will quote you classic movie lines, which you are better off not hearing and certainly not remembering.

Lines like "I will not be ignored, Dan"—written by James Dearden in *Fatal Attraction*.

And "When you give up your dream, you die"—written by Joe Eszterhas in *Flashdance*.

And "It's turkeytime, gobble gobble"—written by Martin Brest in *Gigli*.

And "How does it feel not to have anyone comin' on you anymore?"— written by Joe Eszterhas in *Showgirls*.

You don't want to live in a tabloid, do you?

Actress Jessica Alba (*Sin City*): "Literally the whole town is a tabloid. At every restaurant, every hotel, everywhere you go, people are looking at the door to see who walked in. It seems like no one is ever satisfied with their jobs or their lives, everyone is always sort of maneuvering for something else, something better."

Just another Hollywood burnout . . .

Screenwriter/novelist Jim Harrison: "I was driving on the Hollywood freeway, crossing the hill over toward Burbank, when we stopped in traffic. I looked up at the apartment buildings stacked against the wall of the canyon and on a deck a young man was standing in an open robe, whacking off and looking down at the freeway."

Forget everything you've heard about networking.

It is *not* who you know in Hollywood. If you write a good, commercial script and start sending it out—*someone* will recognize that it is good and commercial.

It is a town that runs on greed, filled with desperate people who will do anything to make money.

If they think your script will make them money, they will option or buy your script.

You can write your script anywhere. I suggest that you write it anywhere but in L.A.

You won't be able to write real people if you stay in L.A. too long.

L.A. has nothing to do with the rest of America. It is a place whose values are shaped by the movie business. It is my contention that it is not just a separate city, or even a separate state, but a separate *country* located within America.

Real Americans live in Bainbridge Township, Ohio.

If you have to go to L.A. for a meeting . . .

Do it as former Orion Pictures head Eric Pleskow advises: "Only as needed, like taking medication."

And Truman Capote gave this advice to Dominick Dunne: "Remember this—that is not where you belong, and when you get out of it what you went there to get, you have to return to your own life."

It's still bedlam.

After two weeks of writing scripts in L.A., screenwriter William Faulkner wrote home: "I have not got used to this work. But I am as well as anyone can be in this bedlam."

Don't wind up weeping into your beer.

Norman Mailer, writing to a friend in 1949: "Hollywood stinks. I'll probably stay here the rest of my life and weep into my beer about what a writer I used to be."

REELSPEAK

A *Lanzman*

A Yiddish term for a fellow Jew, it is used in Hollywood now to describe a good and loyal friend—being a *lanzman* is one rung above being a *mensch* (good people).

They can snort you there.

Producer Bert Schneider took care of an ill friend for two years. When she died, he held a party and the guests snorted her ashes up their noses.

Save the horses.

Screenwriter William Faulkner bought a horse for his daughter in Hollywood. When he realized the mare was going to foal, he drove her home to Mississippi. "I'd be damned," he said, "if I let a Faulkner mare foal in Hollywood."

This isn't the kind of place where you want to raise your kids.

I noticed our six-year-old, Joey, staring out the window of our Malibu house one sunny morning. Curious, I looked at what he was looking at.

On the patio of the house next door, a gorgeous naked young woman was with another gorgeous naked young woman.

Joey said, "What are they doing, Dada?"

I thought about it and said, "Saying hi, I guess."

Joey said, "Like doggies."

I smiled and said, "Yup."

Take it from Zsa Zsa

Do you want neighbors like this?

Actress and Hungarian femme fatale Zsa Zsa Gabor: "Vera Krupp used to live next to me in Bel Air and they say that she got $25 million from her husband, the German armaments king, Krupp. With it, she bought the most unbelievable diamonds. Vera wasn't in the least bit overwhelmed by any of her diamonds and used to wear them while gardening or doing the dishes. But Vera lost all her money when she went to Las Vegas, fell in love with a croupier there, married him, and gave him her entire fortune. When she died, she had her four black Great Danes cremated and buried in the coffin with her."

You'll meet some mighty odd folks in L.A.

Agent Swifty Lazar: "Now, as everyone knows, I have a legendary fear of germs. The problem isn't really germs, it's the proximity of dirt that annoys me, especially someone else's dirt. Howard Hughes, on the other hand, did have a germ phobia. So that night, as I always do when leaving a public toilet, I reached for a paper towel to use on the door handle so I wouldn't have to touch it. Alas, there were none left. A few seconds later, Howard made the same discovery.

"So there we were, two germ freaks, both walking toward the door with dripping hands. I lingered, hoping to force Howard to deal with the door. But Howard saw that gambit and stepped aside, leaving me right in front of the door. Was I going to grab that germ-ridden handle? Not on your life. So we were at a standstill. Luckily, another man entered, giving us a chance to duck out before the door swung shut again."

See a proctologist often.

Playwright/screenwriter David Mamet: "Writing for Hollywood is a constant trauma."

You'll need to get yourself some Kaopectate, too.

Screenwriter William Goldman: "I bought a bottle of Kaopectate as soon as I reached the hotel. No joke. For the first several years, whenever I was in Los Angeles, I went nowhere without a bottle of Kaopectate hidden in a brown paper bag."

For almost twenty years while I was a screenwriter, I lived in Marin County in northern California and commuted to Los Angeles for meetings.

If I had a noon meeting in L.A., I'd be sitting at the bar of the terminal in San Francisco sipping two glasses of white wine at nine in the morning.

I'd have two Bloody Marys on the plane.

Upon landing, I'd go to the bar of the terminal in L.A. and drink two more glasses of white wine. Then I'd be ready for my meetings. I guess maybe Bill Goldman is smarter than I am. He limited himself to Kaopectate.

In Shallow Waters the Dragon Becomes the Joke of the Shrimp

Studio executive Dore Schary's famous line, originally applied to a down-on-his-luck David O. Selznick. Later applied to Orson Welles, producers Allan Carr, David Begelman, Dan Melnick, and directors Michael Cimino, Francis Ford Coppola, and David Lynch, among others.

If you have to be in L.A., stay at the Chateau Marmont.

Screenwriter L. M. Kit Carson: "There's several ghosts at the Chateau. The ghost would come at 3:30 in the morning. Regularly. It would wake me up and make me go to work. It was a *writing ghost.*"

If you have to rent a car in L.A.

Screenwriter and novelist Jim Harrison (*Wolf*): "Certain actors and producers are spectacularly good drivers. I'm so lousy in traffic. Having only one eye doesn't help. In fifty or so trips to L.A., I tried to drive from the airport in a rental car only once, a shattering experience. After rush hour I could drive locally, though not well, in Beverly Hills and environs, though other cars would beep at me for driving too slow. . . . A number of times I asked studios to have a five-year-old brown Taurus station wagon sent to my hotel, but they were never able to deliver."

Beware of medical help in Los Angeles.

I was hoarse. I went to see a couple of highly respected ear, nose, and throat guys in Los Angeles. They examined me and said I had a benign polyp that was wrapped around my vocal cord. They scheduled outpatient surgery at a hospital, to take place six weeks later.

My hoarseness got worse. I went to the Cleveland Clinic in Cleveland, Ohio. They told me I had throat cancer. I had surgery and lost 80 percent of my larynx.

When the head of the ENT practice read that I had throat cancer, he called my agent at William Morris, Jim Wiatt. He didn't call *me*; he called my *agent*. A doctor—calling not his patient but his patient's *agent*.

He told my agent it wasn't *his* fault. The doctor who'd first examined me was no longer with the firm, the head doctor told Jim Wiatt.

He told Jim Wiatt to wish me good luck.

Jim passed it on to me.

Beware of nurses in Los Angeles.

A young nurse who worked at a hospital in Los Angeles showed me her photo album.

It was filled with photos of delighted nurses cuddling with their famous patients. The nurses were wearing nifty little goodies from Victoria's Secret, and their patients, mostly rock stars, were niftily naked. The nurses were smiling coyly, lasciviously, joyously, teasingly, ironically, daringly, contentedly, triumphantly.

The stars in the hospital bed with them were anesthetized . . . in postsurgical comas . . . blasted out of their gourds . . . an IV sometimes still sticking in their arms.

If you're going to be in L.A. working on a script, don't take your cell phone.

The director, producer, studio execs, and any or all of their assistants, gofers, and secretaries will be bugging you all the time if you've got a cell phone.

Tell everyone that you left your cell phone home so your significant other could use it. Then tell everyone that you always shut the phone off when you're writing.

If you're Catholic, don't go to Our Lady of Malibu church.

When we lived in Point Dume, our church was Our Lady of Malibu. We'd heard of Our Lady of Lourdes and Our Lady of Guadalupe and Our Lady of Fatima . . . but we'd never heard of Our Lady of Malibu.

Lourdes and Guadalupe and Fatima were places of miracles, but we didn't know about Malibu. What had Our Lady of Malibu done? Appeared at a bonfire on the beach to tell three quaaluded surfers the secrets of the perfect and holy wave?

We went to Mass there one Sunday and I was sure the Beach Boys were making an unheralded benefit appearance, pounding out "Help Me Rhonda" to help the missions of "the Dark Continent" (as the sisters in grade school used to say).

But it wasn't the Beach Boys. It was a local Malibu group doing "Kyrie Eleison" surfer-style.

If you're staying in a hotel in Beverly Hills, don't go for a walk at night.
The cops will arrest you and take you to jail.

Nobody walks at night in Beverly Hills. Read Ray Bradbury's short story "The Pedestrian," which is about a man who goes for a walk in Los Angeles and is taken to a mental institution. Bradbury wrote the short story in *the 1950s*!

If you're writing in L.A. . . .
Drive down to the Formosa Café and get a whiff of what Hollywood used to be like. Elvis used to hang there; so did Robert Mitchum; so did Tuesday Weld. You'll run into some people if you're lucky.

The last time I was there, I ran into Sean Young, no longer a movie star but still a fine woman who likes to drink beer.

And stay away from the Rose Café. . . .
It's where all the wannabe screenwriters hang out, exchanging ideas, talking about movies, popping their pimples, sharing their dreams.

It is a stultifying, suffocating place fueled by ambition, greed, and envy.

If you share your dream with anybody here, chances are it'll be ripped off and wind up in a script that will never be sold.

Take it from Zsa Zsa

Don't buy any parrots in L.A., either.

Actress and famed Hungarian femme fatale Zsa Zsa Gabor:
"On my way to the kitchen, I passed Caesar's cage. Our eyes met and the parrot fixed me with what, at the time, seemed to be an evil eye . . . and in the clearest voice possible pronounced the words 'Fuck you!' I fetched a piece of orange for Caesar, careful to avoid his eyes. In silence, he ate it. I breathed a sigh of relief. Prematurely. Because from that moment on, all Caesar would say to me, and to anyone who crossed the threshold of our house, was 'Fuck you!'"

Go shake Bob Walker's hand.

Drive out to Malibu and check out a little gallery in the Cross Creek Center called TOPS. It's owned and managed by Bob Walker, also known as Robert Walker, Jr., who was going to be a big movie star—until one day he just left it all behind and decided to live like a human being. If you're lucky, you'll run into him and can shake his hand.

Everything in L.A. is so inbred.

Robert Walker, Jr., is the son of the actors Robert Walker (*Strangers on a Train*) and Jennifer Jones (*Duel in the Sun*).

ALL HAIL
Bob Towne!

Yelling that he was being cheated by Warner Bros., screenwriter Robert Towne drove to Warner head Terry Semel's house in the mideighties and screamed obscenities outside his bedroom window.

The Auteur Theory

It will be the bane of your existence as a screenwriter and is the biggest single reason why movies are so awful today.

In France, where directors also write the scripts they direct, they are viewed as "the authors" of their films. They own the film's copyright and distributors can only release their films, not interfere with them.

American directors—who mostly don't *write* their films—began viewing themselves as "auteurs" in the seventies, looking for the same kind of critical canonization French directors were getting.

A generation of American film critics—some of them failed screenwriters like Roger Ebert and Pauline Kael and Janet Maslin—supported these American directors and extended the "author" label to them.

The auteur theory is hypocritical and corrupt—*unless the film's writer and director are the same.*

Try not to "go Hollywood."

Screenwriter William Faulkner, a good ole boy from Oxford, Mississippi, took to wearing sunglasses while he wrote his scripts in his studio office in Hollywood.

And I, the street kid from Cleveland, allowed myself to be talked into putting blond highlights in my hair—which I grew to mid-back length—while I lived in Malibu on a bluff overlooking the sea.

I shopped at the same market as Tom and Nicole for recently arrived fresh truffles and got a black Dodge Ram pickup truck the same month that Steven Spielberg and David Geffen got theirs.

I had Sunday brunch at Wolfgang Puck's Granita, listening to violinist David Wilson play his boulevardier chansons, avoiding eye contact with the likes of Gwyneth Paltrow, who kept staring at me one day.

Her stare said, There's that misogynist, sexist asshole who wrote *Showgirls* and *Basic Instinct*.

I did *not*, however, wear sunglasses while I wrote my scripts—though I did wear them everywhere else . . . even, to my first wife's great annoyance, in airports at night.

Don't piss off the most powerful man in Hollywood.

He's not a star or a studio head. He's not a director or producer. He's a lawyer. And he's over seventy years old.

His name is Bert Fields. He's the most powerful man in Hollywood because if he sends someone a letter threatening to sue, the recipient of that letter is better off simply giving Bert what he wants, instead of going to court to argue with him. He is a brilliant litigator, maybe the best in America. He's also a writer (of thrillers) and a Shakespearean scholar. (Didn't I tell you *everyone* in Hollywood, *even the most powerful man in Hollywood,* wants to be a writer?)

Patricia Glaser is the second most powerful person in Hollywood. Don't piss her off, either.

She, too, is a lawyer. She, too, is a brilliant litigator, maybe the best in America. Behind her honeyed West Virginia drawl is a stone-cold killer (whose childhood dream was to succeed Mickey Mantle in the New York Yankee outfield).

Patty Glaser doesn't fear Bert Fields; she jousts with him publicly. She told *The New York Times* that a letter from Bert Fields was "a B.F. letter." The whole town knew that "a B.F. letter" meant a "big fucking letter" and not "a Bert Fields letter."

If you get a threatening letter from Bert Fields, hire Patty Glaser immediately.

Forget Bert Fields and Patty Glaser. Don't ever—ever—piss these people off. . . . These are the most powerful people in Hollywood.
Scientologists.

Studios are terrified of them because they represent a lot of big stars.

Other people are terrified of them because they have a reputation of not tolerating anyone who, they feel, is *trying to piss them off.*

And no, I am *not* trying to piss them off!

PERK OF SUCCESS: YOU, TOO, CAN WEAR SUNGLASSES AT NIGHT

I was wearing the hottest thing in town. Spielberg had one . . . and Geffen . . . and I got mine before Jeff Katzenberg did.

They cost four hundred dollars a pair, but they were in such short supply that some people were offering a thousand dollars for them.

They were the best pair of sunglasses Chrome Hearts on Robertson had ever made—but that's not why everyone (me, too) wanted them. They wanted them because—if you rubbed the glass—ingrained in the glass very delicately, facing out, so you could see it if you really looked, were these words: Fuck you.

PERK OF FAILURE: YOU DON'T WANT TO WEAR THIS HAT

I saw two screenwriters recently at the farmer's market in L.A. wearing ball caps that said DON'T SHIT ON MY HEAD.

A Hollywood parable . . .

ARwandan tracker who appeared in *Gorillas in the Mist* was invited to attend its New York premiere by the producers.

The tracker had never been on an airplane. He had never been in New York. He had never been in America. He had never been out of the Rwandan mountains.

But he somehow got to New York.

And there was no one at the airport waiting for him.

He *walked* from Kennedy Airport to Park Avenue, where the producer who'd invited him lived.

The doorman turned him away. The producer was out of town.

The producer got back the next day and found the tracker waiting for him—squatting beneath the emergency stairway at the back of his apartment house.

Don't contemplate your navel.

Producer Sean Daniel, after superagent Michael Ovitz left the Creative Artists Agency: "First the fall of the Soviet Union and now the fall of CAA."

If you have to live in L.A., you simply have to have a pool.

California has, like, half the swimming pools in the whole USA," said actress Drew Barrymore. "After you're successful, you can't *not* have a pool. Here, a house without a pool is like a neck with no diamond necklace."

Look out! The pool underneath you is empty.

Jim Harrison: "My friend the novelist Tom McGuane used to compare the whole Hollywood experience to being on a high board, mostly at night, and possibly the pool beneath you was empty. I habitually think of it as being stuck on a shuddering elevator, always caught between one floor or another, always in transition up or down."

You don't want to leave a suicide note like this one.

Actor George Sanders left this suicide note: "I am leaving because I am bored. I feel I have lived long enough. I am leaving you with your worries in this sweet cesspool. Good luck."

I probably shouldn't mention that he was once married to Zsa Zsa Gabor.

And I certainly shouldn't mention that after their divorce, he married one of her sisters.

The Movie God

The explanation for all the insane, inane, moronic, crazy, surreal, hilarious, tragic things that happen daily in Hollywood.

As in: "There is nothing to explain it except the movie God."

PART TWO

LEARNING THE BUSINESS

LESSON 2

Use Your F-Bombs!

Want money and fame?

Producer and studio head Mike Medavoy: "Don't *do* something to be remembered; it is the things you *do* that are remembered."

There are some good reasons to want to be famous.

Comedian Bobcat Goldthwait: "Fame is like a big eraser. It's strange, now that I'm famous, in my parents' opinion, all the shitty things—all the wreckage of my past—is erased. . . . Now it's like I was never the kid who got arrested—now I'm the wonderful son."

You will be world-famous!

William Goldman: "There hasn't been a truly famous writer since Hemingway died. At a Knicks game last year, Norman Mailer was introduced to the crowd and half a dozen people around me said, 'Who?' and one guy went so far as to ask, 'Who did he play for?'"

Bullshit, Bill. When I walk down the street people ask me for my autograph. In L.A., I can't even stand in theater lines or in restaurants without being bothered. I've done the *Today* show half a dozen times; I've done *Good Morning America* and CNN's morning show and a whole half hour of *Hardball* and Deborah Norville and Greta Van Susteren and . . . More people went to see *Showgirls* because of my name than because of anyone else associated with the movie.

And no matter what you say, Bill, you're famous, too.

Nowdays, you can be famous.

UCLA screenwriting professor Richard Walter in his novel, *Escape from Film School*: "Back in the 60s, there was not a single screenwriter—not one—I or anyone beyond the industry had ever heard of. It was not that there were no great screenwriters—quite the contrary; it was merely that none had ever been heard of. Screenwriters wrote; they were not written about."

Are you really sure you want to be famous?

One of the most famous screenwriters in the world is Laura Hart McKinny, who teaches screenwriting at North Carolina College of the Arts.

She is one of the most famous screenwriters in the world, but she has never written a screenplay that has been made into a movie.

The reason she is one of the most famous screenwriters in the world is because of her former boyfriend.

His name is Lt. Mark Fuhrman, formerly of the Los Angeles Police Department. Laura was going to collaborate with Mark on a screenplay about L.A. cops, so she made a lot of tape recordings with him about his true-life experiences. Her tapes wound up smack-dab in the middle of the O. J. Simpson murder trail.

There's a lot to be said for not being famous.

Actor Paul Newman: "I stopped signing autographs after I was asked to sign one while standing at a urinal in a restaurant. I was already quite cool about the idea after being asked for about the thousandth time, 'Can you remove your sunglasses so we can see your blue eyes?' I started saying, 'I'm so sorry, but if I take off my glasses, my pants fall down.'"

Actor Robin Williams: "The paparazzi follow me into the men's room. They say, 'Robin, can you hold it up? Could you make the puppet talk? Oh, you're having a bowel movement? Oh, great! It's *Live-Stools of the Rich and Famous!*"

You better stay forever young . . . or else!

Mike Medavoy: "This is a business that eats its elders instead of its young."

Are screenwriters the victims of ageism?

There has always been the issue of ageism directed toward screenwriters, directors, producers, and actors in Hollywood.

An agent sets up a meeting for a screenwriter with a studio executive.

The agent says, "How old are you?"

The screenwriter says, "I'm twenty-eight."

The agent says, "Let's make it twenty-three."

How do you define success?

Director Richard Quine (*Sex and the Single Girl*): "The definition of success is to be doing better than your best friend."

If you make it, you won't have any friends.

In direct proportion to how successful one is, that's how much the need is to chop him or her down," said actor/producer Michael Douglas.

Producer Bernie Brillstein: "You're no one in Hollywood unless someone wants you dead."

Marilyn Monroe: "It's funny how success makes so many people hate you. I wish it wasn't that way. It would be wonderful to enjoy success without seeing things in the eyes of those around you."

Question: What things, Marilyn?

Mike Medavoy: "Friendships are a funny thing in Hollywood. Everyone talks about what good friends they are with everyone else. In truth, most people in the entertainment industry have many acquaintances and few friends, at least in the way I define friendship. In a movie script, you can create a fifteen-year friendship in fifteen minutes. In real life it takes fifteen years."

Some canaries make it and some don't.

My fellow Hungarian, actor Tony Curtis: "The Mocambo was on Sunset Boulevard in the middle of the Strip. It had a bar, a dining room, and a dance floor with a small stage, and along one long wall were cages with yellow canaries. We'd go there on weekends for an evening on the town, and I was always intrigued how those canaries were able to survive in that smoke-filled, noisy club. One night I found out. I happened to look over when one of the canaries toppled off its perch and fell to the bottom of the cage, dead. A waiter standing nearby just whipped out a fishnet from his pocket, opened the cage, and scooped it up. Another waiter came up instantly and replaced the poor dead canary with a live one. Nobody noticed it but me. So that was the mystery of the dead yellow canary. Some make it in Hollywood, and some don't."

Audience-Attuned

If you write movies that make a hundred million dollars each, you're audience-attuned. Otherwise, you're just another dumb schmuck writer.

You, too, can enjoy their pain.

Producer Peter Guber: "As I was to learn and experience in Hollywood, it's not so much your own success that is relished, but more your friends' failures."

How to make it in Hollywood . . .

Legendary light-heavyweight champion Billy Conn: "He was a nice fellow. I hit him in the balls and knocked his ass through the ropes in the thirteenth round. You're supposed to do everything you can to win. Hit 'em on the break, backhand 'em, do all the rotten stuff to 'em. You're not an altar boy in there."

Studio head L. B. Mayer: "There's only one way to succeed in this business. Step on those guys. Gouge their eyes out. Trample on them. Kick them in the balls. You'll be a smash."

To Do an Ovitz

To commit an act of homophobia in public; like agent Michael, who, some said, committed such an act in the pages of *Vanity Fair*.

They lie, they cheat, and they steal.

Studio executives do not like to deal with honest men," said screenwriter/novelist Raymond Chandler.

Hire a good accountant.

Accountants," said screenwriter Dalton Trumbo, "are the most important people in the world."

Let your accountant be your rabbi.

My accountant said to me, "In Hollywood, you only get ripped off by your friends and the people you trust."

Invest wisely.

A well-known director in his sixties made millions of dollars and invested much of it years ago in a ranch in Wyoming. He visits his ranch three or four times a year but says he doesn't really like to go there.

"Every time I'm there," he says, "I think this is what my career amounted to—millions of dollars of horse shit."

Save your money.

Sugar Ray Robinson, boxing champ, years after his retirement: "Do I still own a flashy Cadillac? No more. The car I drive now is a little red Pinto. *But I've been there.*"

TAKE IT FROM ZSA ZSA

Tips to save money in Hollywood . . .

Actress and famed Hungarian femme fatale Zsa Zsa Gabor: "When you open a new five-pound can of Beluga caviar and you are not able to eat it all right away, put what's left over back into the refrigerator, where it will keep for five days, then you will always have nice fresh caviar handy. . . . Another hint to save you a lot is to never throw away any truffles. If, for instance, you open a can and you don't use them all in the pheasant Souvaroff or whatever you're making, don't throw them in the disposal for garbage, but freeze them and they will be as good like new later."

One good way to avoid writer's block . . .

Advice to legendary producer David O. Selznick from his father: "Spend it all. Give it away. Throw it away. But get rid of it. Live expensively. If you have confidence in yourself, live beyond your means. Then you'll have to work hard to catch up. That's the only fun there is: hard work."

The Three Cs

The "Three Cs" are what old-timers say Hollywood was once all about: "cocktails, cards, and cunt."

Schtup Music

An old producer's term for romantic music.

If you make it, you're going to need an accountant.

If you don't get one, you're going to spend all your time book-keeping and worrying about taxes—not writing.

You have to pick your accountant carefully, because some people have been robbed blind: Allen Funt, the creator of *Candid Camera*, lost everything he had to an unscrupulous accountant. Your fellow screenwriter Sylvester Stallone lost millions, too, to an accountant.

But for a set figure each month, based on what you've earned, you can get full-scale protection . . . the kind of protection where you won't even receive your own bills, since everything will go to the accountant.

Just make sure you get a weekly cash-flow report, *signed* by your accountant.

You, too, can be addled by accountants.

Jim Harrison (*Wolf, Revenge, Legends of the Fall*): "Entering a bank made me sweat, lawyers frightened me, and accountants addled me so that I couldn't write for a day or two. Despite learning how to make money I couldn't quite figure out that I had to give half to the government."

Perk of success: my accountants almost killed me.

The day after I had my first meeting with accountants, I had a full-blown anxiety attack that was initially misdiagnosed as a heart attack.

Your accountant may fire you.

This is especially true if you have gotten behind on paying your taxes. The good accountants in L.A. all have excellent relationships with the IRS.

The IRS knows that if you are being represented by an accounting firm it's done business with, the odds are very good that you won't be cheating on your taxes—which makes an audit of your returns a waste of time. So it won't audit you if you are represented by one of these firms.

But if you can't pay your taxes, your accounting firm will worry that your problems will affect its relationship with the IRS, and its other clients, so it will quickly rid itself of you.

Sometimes the accounting firms get rid of a client too quickly and regrets it. Sharon Stone's accounting firm got rid of her the year before she starred in *Basic Instinct*. They made a big, big mistake.

Congealed Snow

What screenwriter Dorothy Parker called Hollywood money.

Hire a good lawyer, too.

Peter Guber: "In business, you don't get what's fair. You get what you negotiate."

Be sure to hire a damn good lawyer.

John Gregory Dunne: "The attitude studio business affairs attorneys seem to take toward writers is that a writer's time is nowhere near so valuable as that of a director, producer, or star; that the writer always needs money; and that stalling is a tactic that will ultimately cause the writer who is a little short on the do-re-mi to cave in."

You're going to need an agent, too.

There's no heart as black as the black heart of an agent," my longtime agent, Guy McElwaine, once told me.

You need an agent right now, right this minute.

The playwright Brendan Behan sold the rights to all of his plays at the pubs where he drank—sometimes to customers, sometimes to bartenders, sometimes for as little as a couple of drinks.

It's still the same old story.

Sixty years ago, studio head Howard Hughes sent his executives a memo saying he only wanted to make movies "about fighting and fucking."

It's always been a meat market.

Marilyn Monroe: "Expensive cars used to drive up beside me when I was standing on a street corner or walking on a sidewalk and the driver would say, 'I could do something for you in pictures. How would you like to be a Goldwyn girl?' I figure those guys in those cars were trying for a pickup and I had an agent so I could say to those fellows, 'See my agent.'"

It is still the same old meat market, too.

Producer Brian Grazer and I were driving back to town after a meeting in the Valley, when Brian spotted a gorgeous young woman walking down the street.

He pulled over, got out, and said, "Hi, I'm Brian Grazer, the producer. Has anyone ever told you you should be in movies?"

She gave Brian a dazzling smile and said, "Thank you. My agent tells me that all the time. I'm represented by CAA. Here's my agent's card."

Don't be too sure.

Well, that's the last cock I have to suck," said Marilyn Monroe after she signed her first big studio contract.

You see what I mean?

I crawled the hill of broken glass and I sucked and I sucked until I sucked all the air out of my life," Sharon Stone told me after she became a big star.

It helps to be Hungarian, though.

I am Hungarian-born. I dallied with the star I created, Sharon Stone. André de Dienes was Hungarian, too. He dallied with the star he photographed, Marilyn Monroe. The famous William Morris agent Johnny Hyde was part Hungarian (Ivan Haidabura). He also dallied with the star he created, Marilyn Monroe.

But it's not enough to be Hungarian.

In the early days of the film business, there were so many Hungarian filmmakers in L.A. that there was a sign at the MGM commissary that read "IT'S NOT ENOUGH TO BE HUNGARIAN. YOU STILL HAVE TO PAY FOR THE CHICKEN SOUP."

The Panic List

Allegedly kept by the studios, it is a list of those who badly need money and will work cheap. The only time I heard direct mention of it was in a studio meeting with a Paramount executive, who suggested hiring a well-known director for one of my scripts and said, "He's on the panic list. He just bought a house on Martha's Vineyard and needs to go to work."

ALL HAIL
Hail Paul Rudnick!

He not only has put together a lengthy and successful career as a screenwriter but, as columnist Libby Gelman-Waxner in *Premier* magazine, he has also wickedly trashed most of the town's heavyweights and gotten away with it.

Don't gamble.

Gambling is part of ancient Hollywood tradition, going back to David O. Selznick losing much of what he made. David Begelman, agent/studio exec/embezzler/suicide was addicted to gambling.

I saw producer Don Simpson lose thirty thousand dollars in fifteen minutes at Caesar's Palace in Las Vegas.

If you're successful, you'll be invited to industry poker games—some are legendary. Don't do it.

I was even introduced to a little man who was the industry's bookie to the stars. He was very rich and knew the works of George Bernard Shaw inside out.

TAKE IT FROM ZSA ZSA

Don't marry a writer.
*Actress and famed Hungarian femme fatale Zsa Zsa Gabor:
"Even though painters and sculptors and composers and writers have a romantic reputation all over the world, in my opinion they are worthless as ex-husbands, or as husbands, or as anything else you may have in your mind to do with them, except if you want to have a beautiful nude statue made of you. Honestly, no woman, even if she is the most alluring creature that ever existed, can win out when she is competing for a man's attention with his precious muse. Artists spend all their time thinking about imaginary beauty. . . .*

"Let's face it, nine times out of ten intellectual men would rather go to bed with a good book. Which just goes to show how unintelligent an intelligent person can be."

If you get married, do it in Portofino.

This, too, is an old Hollywood tradition. David O. Selznick was married there . . . and I had an agent who was married there— at the Splendido Hotel—three times to three different women.

I stayed there once, when I was already married to my first wife, Geraldine, and happened to arrive the first day that the Splendido opened for the season. In the dining room that night, Gerri and I found ourselves surrounded by German couples in their seventies and eighties.

"All Nazis," our American waiter told us. "They came here to hide after the war, and on the first day that the hotel is open each year, they flock here to celebrate surviving another year without capture."

Always let them pick up the check.

Only pick a check up if you're out with another screenwriter . . . and if you're doing better than he/she is.

Agent Swifty Lazar, describing gossip columnist Walter Winchell: "He had a great way of not reaching for a check. He'd feign a move toward it, but if someone made the slightest protest, he'd redirect his hand and pick up his water glass. In all the years I knew him, I never saw him pay for a meal."

You're dealing with horribly spoiled people.

Actress Hedy Lamarr: "If a man sends me flowers, I always look to see if a diamond bracelet is hidden among the blossoms. If there isn't one, I don't see the flowers."

I sent Sharon Stone a hundred red roses once. She sent me a card thanking me.

I sent her a gold bracelet. She called and asked me to dinner.

Everything you've ever heard about Hollywood parties is true.

Actress Hedy Lamarr: "At one magnificent party (for which I bought a gown that cost me two weeks' salary) I excused myself to fetch a scarf that was in the sleeve of my fur coat. I couldn't find a maid, so I went into the darkened master bedroom, where many furs were laid out on the bed. And when I got into the room I could see and hear that wasn't all that was laid out on the bed. A man and woman were right on top of all the furs, taking desperate advantage of the occasion. I merely said, 'Excuse me,' reached under the young girl, and pulled out my green scarf. They never stopped for one moment. Later on I saw the two of them formally dressed, sipping champagne cocktails. They knew it was me, but they didn't seem the slightest bit embarrassed. Nor was I."

Avoid Hollywood parties.

Screenwriter/novelist Charles Bukowski wrote this after getting home from a Hollywood party: "Sitting naked behind my house, 8 a.m., spreading sesame seed oil over my body, Jesus, have I come to this? I once battled in dark alleys for a laugh, now I'm not laughing."

F-bomb the world!

Tom Tapp, the editor of *VLife* magazine, published by *Daily Variety*: "Among moguls, crude language is part of routine business. In turn, the executives who work under them don't exactly censor themselves. One network honcho is so well-known for his foul mouth that it's become a calling card. Such language is not necessarily derogatory. It's a colorful patois that can often be complimentary. Everyone understands this."

Even Mel Gibson, *The Passion of the Christ* director and a devout Christian, described the man in charge of distributing the movie as "a very smart fucking guy."

Bill Clinton belongs in Hollywood.

Producer David Geffen took his boyfriend to meet Bill Clinton in the Oval Office.

Clinton said, "Is that a fuckin' reporter?"

"No, he's with me, Bill," Geffen said.

"Oh," Clinton said, "I thought he was a fuckin' reporter."

If you want to sound like a real Hollywood pro . . .

Always refer to MGM as "Metro" and Twentieth Century–Fox not as "Fox" but as "Twentieth."

Dirt Sandwich

Popularized by Sharon Stone's reference to a boyfriend as such, it's an old Hollywood term for someone who rips you off, someone who leaves a bad taste in your mouth.

Be nice to the Godfathers.

I met Sidney Korshak, mob lawyer and Hollywood Godfather, in producer Robert Evans's screening room moments after a young woman in her twenties had finished going down on him. Sidney was in his late seventies.

I'd stumbled into the screening room (literally) as the young woman was leaving and as Sidney was getting his pants up off his ankles.

I introduced myself and said it was a pleasure to meet him, and Sidney said likewise, reached out a hand, shook mine, and finished zipping himself up.

I went into the nearest bathroom and washed my hands just as the same young woman was coming out of it. A bottle of mouthwash was on the sink.

As I spent more time in Evans's house, I realized there were bottles of mouthwash everywhere.

Hey, Sidney, I liked Estes Kefauver.

Sidney Korshak once blackmailed Senator Estes Kefauver, the head of a Senate rackets committee, by showing him a photograph of a naked young woman going down on the senator in a Chicago hotel room.

Take it from Zsa Zsa

Don't ask a Hungarian to help you.
The young Zsa Zsa Gabor went to see an old Hungarian friend, the producer Alexander Korda, when she got to Hollywood. She asked him to help her get an acting career started.
He said, "Take your clothes off."
She fled.

Remain philosophical.

An angry housekeeper who arrived and found a disastrously messy house said to the producer who owned it, "There's shit everywhere."

The producer said to her, "There's shit all over the world."

Think Yiddish, Dress British

A saying of Harry Cohn–era studio heads.

And William Morris was Jewish, wasn't he?

William Morris agent David Wirtschafter described the industry's perception of the agency this way: "In the minds of our competitors, we're still a lot of old Jews dropping dead in our offices."

But Walt Disney was a schmuck.

Everybody argues about who is entitled to call it "my film."

Screenwriters hate it when a director or producer refers to "my writer."

And during an interview with a reporter involving a financial question, Walt Disney said, "Before answering, I'd like to ask *my Jew* to come over and help me on this one."

Unelectric

Uninspired, flat, dull, benighted—the opposite of producer Peter Guber, known in the industry as "the Electric Jew."

The Blue in the Toilet Bowl

An old-time studio term for a successful WASP in Hollywood.

Never underestimate how scared everybody else in town is.

I said this on ABC's *20/20*: "People in Hollywood pee themselves the moment their feet hit the floor in the morning."

Don't count on anything.

Actress Hedy Lamarr: "That's how it always is in the entertainment industry, your feet are always treading Jell-O. From one minute to the next everything changes."

Take this to heart.

Producer Ray Stark gave me this advice: "Don't let anyone push you around, do what your heart tells you to do, and don't borrow any money."

To Cut Down on Your Cream

To stop living excessively, to save for a rainy day.

Do what Sharon does.

Sharon Stone keeps a large punching bag in her garage and pounds on it every day.

I created a monster.

Actress Sharon Stone: "I've got the biggest balls in Hollywood. It's good that they're scared of me. The longer they stay scared, the longer I keep my job."

If you don't like your own writing, do something else for a living.

William Goldman: "Since I don't much care for my writing, *Princess Bride* is the only picture of mine I can look at without embarrassment."

Why does your butt hurt after you've taken Robert McKee's course?

The New Yorker wrote: "McKee, who is sixty-two, and likes to wear dark shirts with two buttons undone at the neck, suggesting a career in extortion, lit a cigarette, then walked down the street while listening to an agitated young man say that the last time he had heard McKee speak the effect had been so overwhelming that he had fallen ill. 'All the stuff you don't want to face, which is to say emotional truth, the stuff of good story telling, it was coming out!' the young man said, very fast. 'It was coming out in such a way that it caused this pain in my back, because subconscious growth is such a painful process.'"

I shouldn't be telling you all these things.

Screenwriter Dan O'Bannon (*Alien*): "Most of what is written on how to write a screenplay is written by people who don't know how. . . . There aren't that many who do know how, and those who do know how tend not to tell. For the very obvious reason: they don't want to train their own competition. These are not unknowns, but it's on the level of the mortuary trade—it's passed on by word of mouth."

The Screenwriter's Lament

"The fucking you get isn't worth the fucking you get."

LESSON 3

Don't Let 'Em Fart at Your Ideas!

If you're nineteen years old and writing your first script, know this: Life will get easier.

Paddy Chayefsky (*Network, The Hospital*): "Nineteen-year-old writers want more out of their writing than mere satisfaction. They want approbation, to change the world and many other things. Besides, at nineteen, he doesn't know his ass from his elbow."

Don't be a screenwriter; be a writer who just happens to write for the screen.

Don't spend all of your time in dark theaters watching movies. Live. Love. Immerse yourself in the messy entanglements of *real,* not *reel,* life.

Listen to human beings talk, not characters created by other screenwriters who spend all their time in dark movie theaters.

Use the events and the human beings of your everyday life to create a fictional world that *real* people, not *reel* people, will recognize, understand, and be moved by when they see what you have created.

You scare the living shit out of the studios.

Paddy Chayefsky: "When the studios hire a director, they can see him direct, or an actor act, or a typist type, but they can't see a writer think, and that frightens them."

Darling and Honey

These are two of Hollywood's most meaningless and overused words and greatest clichés. In the past few decades, there has been a trend away from using these words, although longtime Paramount head Sherry Lansing insisted on calling everyone "darling" and "honey," perhaps as a homage to Hollywood's Golden Age.

Robert McKee and I agree about one thing.

McKee: "Movie-making is a collaborative endeavor—requiring great skill and talent by the entire cast, crew, and creative team—but the screenwriter is the only original artist on a film. Everyone else—the actors, directors, cameramen, production designers, editors, special effects wizards, and so on—are interpretive artists, trying to bring alive the world, the events, and the characters that the screenwriter has invented and created."

You're the storyteller, not the director.

The director takes your story and characters and translates it and them to the big screen.

If anybody in your presence refers to the director as a "storyteller," deck him (or her).

In musical terms, *you* are the composer; the director conducts the orchestra.

The director is passé.

William Goldman: "There is a theory put forward by some (Gore Vidal for one) that the true influence of the director died with the coming of sound. In the silent days, Griffith could stand there and, with his actor's voice, he could talk to Lillian Gish or whomever and literally mold the performance with long, heated verbal instructions *while the camera was rolling*. Not anymore. Now the director must stand helpless alongside the crew and watch the actors work at their craft."

You are more important than the director.

Sometimes even directors admit this. Famed director Akira Kurosawa (*Rashomon*): "With a good script a good director can produce a masterpiece; with the same script a mediocre director can make a passable film. But with a bad script even a good director can't possibly make a good film. For truly cinematic expression, the camera and the microphone must be able to cross both fire and water. That is what makes a real movie. The script must be something that has the power to do this."

Aren't you worried about your next job, Bill?

Screenwriter William Goldman: "Directors—even though we all know from the media's portrayals of them that they are men and women of wisdom and artistic vision, masters of the subtle use of symbolism—are more often than not a bunch of insecure lying assholes."

You're the asshole responsible.

Screenwriter Robert Towne: "Until the screenwriter does his job, nobody else has a job. In other words, he is the asshole who keeps everyone else from going to work."

They all know you're the asshole responsible.

Actress Barbara Stanwyck: "The performer can't work miracles. What's on paper is on the screen. If it isn't there, it isn't on the screen."

Without you, nobody gets paid.

Mike Medavoy: "Writers get directors. Directors get actors. And the right combination of all three gets the money."

Don't let 'em fart at your ideas.

Producer Bert Schneider could fart whenever he wanted and farted often during story meetings with screenwriters at ideas he didn't like.

Like I said, damn it, don't let 'em fart at your ideas.

Screenwriter Robert Carson was summoned to producer David O. Selznick's house to pitch a script.

Selznick was in the bedroom, lying down, in pain from an attack of the stomach flu.

Carson said, "David, I don't think you're really in any shape to listen to a story."

Selznick said, "That's all right—go ahead."

Carson told his story.

Selznick listened in bed as he groaned, strained, and passed gas.

The next day, he informed Carson that he was passing on his project, too.

The War Zone

Beverly Hills, Bel Air, the Palisades, north to Malibu and Point Dume and Carbon Beach . . . where most of the industry's wealthiest and most powerful "player" warriors live.

Haunt streets, saloons, and whorehouses.

Ben Hecht: "I haunted streets, whorehouses, police stations, courtrooms, theater stages, jails, saloons, slums, madhouses, fires, murders, riots, banquet halls and bookshops. I ran everywhere in the city like a fly buzzing in the works of a clock, tasted more than any fit belly could hold, learned not to sleep, and buried myself in a tick-tock of whirling hours that still echo in me."

Live your life fully so you can write fully.

Screenwriter Michael Blake (*Dances with Wolves*): "Characters do come out of the thin air. I think writers acquire characters by living a life in which something is risked. It's only by being defeated, rejected, exalted, by going through all the peaks and valleys, that you can acquire anything worth writing down."

Don't see a movie; read a book.

Director Akira Kurosawa: "In order to write scripts, you must first study the great novels and dramas of the world. You must consider why they are great. Where does the emotion come from that you feel as you read them?"

See some good movies.

Screenwriter Michael Blake: "My approach to learning how to write screenplays was to watch the best movies. I tried not to watch lousy movies, because I didn't think I could learn anything from them. I didn't take any classes. I just kind of dreamed it."

Don't see too many movies.

Novelist Charles Bukowski: "People who hang around celluloid usually are."

Don't turn into a film geek.

It's okay to see movies, but it's not okay to get caught up in movie trivia if you want to write screenplays—that is, to become a film geek who can tell you the name of the DP on the movie *Two-Lane Blacktop,* directed by Monte Hellman . . . or the name of the character in Jack Nicholson's first bit part.

Knowing these things will clutter up your brain. Knowing these things won't help you become a screenwriter.

Knowing too much about movies can be hazardous to your creativity. Put that energy into learning about real life and the loves, hopes, aspirations, guilts, failures, and dreams of the human beings around you.

There's hope for you; Faulkner couldn't write screenplays, either.

Jim Harrison: "A good screenplay takes a sizable measure of talent and I hadn't yet studied the genre. Later on at Warners when I read a half dozen of William Faulkner's screenplays I was appalled and amused by how terrible they were."

To Do a Joe Eszterhas

To get out of town and live somewhere in flyover country, in some town no one has ever heard of.

Put a piece of paper up above your writing desk.

Mine says, "The first thing a writer must do is protect his own ass."

Novelist/screenwriter Jim Harrison's says, "You're just a writer."

Novelist Mickey Spillane's used to say, "Fuck 'em if they can't take a joke!" After he was born again, Mickey replaced that with "Oh Lordy! Oh Jesus!"

Repeat to yourself: "I've got nothing to lose."

That's what screenwriter Callie Khouri kept telling herself as she wrote her first screenplay. "I've got nothing to lose. I've got nothing to lose. I've got nothing to lose!" She was writing a groundbreaking and original script, which won the Academy Award for Best Screenplay: *Thelma & Louise.*

Exempt yourself from shit.

Novelist/screenwriter Harlan Ellison has a typewriter emblazoned with "I am an artist and should be exempt from shit."

ALL HAIL
Harlan Ellison!

The screenwriter/novelist did an interview with a magazine and posed for the photograph accompanying it. He was nude.

The caption read, "The writer at work; naked and unashamed."

"Fuck You" Money

You know you have "fuck you" money when you tip the bathroom attendant ten bucks for handing you a towel and then, after he looks at you quizzically, you hand him another ten and smile as you walk out the door.

Sit on your damn butt.

What's the key to being a successful screenwriter?

I say it's "*sitzfleisch*"—a German term that means the ability and the strength to sit on your ass.

According to my writer/producer friend Bill Froug, it's "the seat of the pants to the seat of the chair."

Ego is good.

Paddy Chayefsky: "The most impure motives are useful to a beginning writer. Just to get your name in the papers is not an improper motivation for a writer, when you're a kid, when you're young. The need for fame and notoriety, I think, is part of the package that brings you into show business."

When Paddy was at the height of his fame, he was the only screenwriter to get his picture—of him beating away at his typewriter—on the posters for his movies.

I tried like hell to equal that but couldn't do it. I did get the line "From Joe Eszterhas" splashed across the poster for *An Alan Smithee Film: Burn Hollywood Burn*. I also got the same words onto the T-shirts made to promote the movie, which, alas, was a critical and commercial disaster.

Hollywood is the kingdom of greed.

It doesn't matter if you are a convicted child molester; it doesn't matter if you once pissed on a studio executive's new Tibetan rug; it doesn't matter if you bitch-slapped David Geffen at the Ivy; it doesn't matter if you told the press how Sherry Lansing saved the best Paramount scripts for her husband to direct.

All that matters is that someone who reads your script believes that money can be made making it into a movie.

Be polite at all times.

My fellow Hungarian, actor Tony Curtis: "Universal sent me to Chicago on tour for a picture. I made an appearance at a theater, and while I was there I met a beautiful girl who worked in the Universal distributing office, and I asked her if she'd go out with me after I finished the tour that day. She said yes, so we had dinner, and I took her up to the hotel room. We necked on the couch and got semi-undressed, and she started to go down on me. About the fourth stroke, she stopped and looked up at me and said, 'If my mother could only see me now.' I said, 'Darling, it's not polite to talk with your mouth full.'"

When speaking to people in the industry, try to put things in Hollywood terms.

Producer Robert Evans to director Larry Kasdan: "I'd give up a blow job to direct this picture."

Practice humming.

You, too, can sound authoritative.

Producer Robert Evans says his deep baritone is a result of many years of practice.

Humming, Evans says, deepens the voice.

Evans hums all day, every day.

Never stand anyone up for a meeting.

I had a breakfast scheduled with agent John Gaines, but I got back to my hotel at five o'clock in the morning, after extensive late-night research. I knew I'd never make the breakfast. So I called to cancel. At five in the morning. To cancel an eight o'clock date.

John said, "I've never had anyone call me at five in the morning to cancel breakfast."

I said, "I didn't want to be rude and stand you up," then hung up . . . and laughed myself to sleep.

Always treat superstar actors with the proper respect.

When screenwriter/novelist Charles Bukowski met Arnold Schwarzenegger, he said, "You're a piece of shit."

You, too, can be Jack Nicholson's bodyguard.

Screenwriter/novelist Jim Harrison: "Several times when traveling with Jack Nicholson, I suppose partly because of my poor tailoring and thickish appearance, I had been mistaken for his bodyguard."

TAKE IT FROM ZSA ZSA

Don't let yourself get horsewhipped.

Zsa Zsa Gabor: "Once she arrived in America, my sister Magda also started acting, winning parts in several plays. Then she married an Irish screenwriter. Unfortunately, though, he was continually drunk. Magda complained to Father, who promptly horsewhipped the screenwriter and arranged for Magda to divorce him."

Your time is more precious than theirs.

A producer sent me a two-page outline of a story he wanted me to write. To each page was attached a thousand-dollar bill.

I read the two pages and then, just to be fair to the man, reread the two pages.

I didn't like the story and wrote him a note telling him that . . . and also thanking him for the "beer money."

You, too, can be Robert Evans's writer.

Robert Evans took two writers with him to the island of Maui, where they all stayed at the Ritz-Carlton, which overlooked the sea, and helped Bob write his autobiography.

One "writer" was sixteen, the other seventeen. They looked like corn-fed farm girls. During the day sometimes, while Evans slept, gathering his energy, they enjoyed manicures and pedicures in the hotel salon.

Evans introduced them to everyone they met as "my writers."

A Mush Pit

A place where a lot of women looking to become stars hang out to meet powerful men in the industry—to get a knee up the ladder. Producer Robert Evans's house is a well-known Hollywood mush pit.

You won't get a Land Rover, either.

On *Lethal Weapon 3,* the studio gave the director, Dick Donner, and the star, Mel Gibson, gift Land Rovers.

Shane Black, the screenwriter who invented the entire franchise, didn't get one. He didn't even get to write the sequels.

If you make it, they'll ask you to steal from yourself.

Mike Medavoy: "The natural instinct of studio executives is to pigeonhole creative people and ask them to repeat themselves."

I got pigeonholed.

I had a meeting with Cuba Gooding, Jr., about playing soul singer Otis Redding in my script *Blaze of Glory.*

I wrote it after *Showgirls* and *Jade* and was happy that since the critics had clobbered me for excessive sexuality, there was no sex in this script.

"I want to talk to you about that," Cuba said. "You're the guy who wrote *Showgirls* and *Jade*. That's what you do—I mean, can't we put some sex in this script?"

PERK OF SUCCESS: YOU DON'T HAVE TO GET YOUR TEETH FIXED

"I could never be attracted to a man who had perfect teeth," Marilyn Monroe said. "A man with perfect teeth alienates me. I don't know what it is, but it has something to do with the kind of men I have known with perfect teeth. They weren't so perfect elsewhere."

Learn all you can about modern art.

Steven Spielberg has an extensive collection; the real reason producer David Geffen and once-superagent Michael Ovitz hate each other is because they are jealous of each other's art collections; and—get this—director Arne Glimcher (*Mambo Kings*) was an art dealer (Ovitz's) when he began directing movies.

Don't write an adaptation of The Great Gatsby.

Gatsby has been filmed four times. It has failed at the box office four times. Being assigned to adapt *Gatsby* for the screen is the filmic equivalent of what city editors on newspapers used to do to rookie reporters: assign them to interview the mother of the Unknown Soldier.

Don't let your urine rise to your head.

It's an old industry saying.

When the agent Michael Ovitz told me his foot soldiers would put me into the ground, he was letting his urine rise to his head.

When I told the director Arthur Hiller he was a "doddering old fuck," I was letting my urine rise to *my* head.

Other urine risings:

The director Paul Verhoeven saying to me, "I am the director, ja? You are the writer. You will do what I tell you to do."

And me saying to Paul: "If you use that tone of voice with me again, I'm going to come across this fucking table at you."

(Notice how artfully I used my f-bomb in that last sentence.)

Choose your projects wisely.

In the 1980s, "the Polish Prince," crooner Bobby Vinton, asked me to write the screenplay of his "true life story."

It was a tortuously tough decision . . . but I turned the Polish Prince down.

Fartland

What Hollywood executives call the Midwest, the heartland.

Mel Brooks caused the impeachment of Bill Clinton.

The former president of the United States, William Jefferson Clinton, watched *Blazing Saddles* in the White House screening room twenty-four times.

I wonder if Mel Brooks feels responsible for what happened with Monica.

Writing during a Writers Guild strike can be extremely lucrative.

The Guild strike had been going on for several weeks when the producer flew up to see me at my home in northern California.

If I rewrote the script that would soon go into production, he said, he would pay me $200,000.

He would put the money into a bank account in Dubrovnik, in what was then Yugoslavia.

No one would ever know, he said. Not the IRS and certainly not the Writers Guild, which forbids doing any writing during a strike.

Did I do it?

Ha! What are you—nuts?

If you live in L.A., don't get involved in Writers Guild politics.

Don't join any committees or go to too many meetings. The people who get involved in Writers Guild politics are people who don't, or can't, write all that much—or all that well, or all that well anymore.

They'll pay you for writing nothing.

I made a deal with ABC Films in the early eighties to write a script about the wheat harvesters who travel from state to state in the summer.

I was to be paid $350,000.

I went off to Nebraska and Iowa for two weeks to interview the harvesters.

When I got back, ABC informed me that their marketing people had concluded while I was doing research that a film about wheat harvesters wouldn't be commercially successful.

So ABC wanted me to write a film instead about Ross Perot.

My agent said not a chance—the deal we had made called for me to write a script about wheat harvesters.

ABC Films paid me the full fee—$350,000—for what amounted to two weeks' research.

Don't buy the mink coat yet.

This advice was given to me by *F.I.S.T.* producer Patrick Palmer after everyone involved loved my first-draft screenplay.

He was right. The movie went into turnaround; then forty pages had to be cut from the script; then $7 million had to be cut from the budget; then Robert De Niro wouldn't respond to the studio's offer to star in the film; then Sylvester Stallone played the lead instead of De Niro; and after all that, the movie failed both critically and commercially.

With a mentor like this, you, too, can cowrite Predator.

Robert McKee was the closest thing I've had to a mentor," said screenwriter Jim Thomas on McKee's Web site. Thomas is listed as the cowriter of *Predator, Executive Decision,* and *Mission to Mars.*

A screenwriter got JFK elected president.

The day of the West Virginia primary, which decided the Democratic nominee in the 1960 race, John Fitzgerald Kennedy was relaxed and in the best of humor.

He told reporters he'd watched a movie the night before and had gone to bed early.

He didn't tell them it was a porn movie called *Private Property.*

He didn't tell them he hadn't gone to bed alone, either.

My point is this: Someone wrote *Private Property.* Did he know that he would one day relax and perhaps inspire the future president of the United States?

TAKE IT FROM ZSA ZSA

Don't go to bed with Hungarians.

Zsa Zsa Gabor: "Tony Curtis is also Hungarian and we were cast in the same movie. We got on very well. We shot our love scene at the studio. The script called for me to be in bed with Tony and I was seminude through most of it. After one take, the director said, 'Let's do another take!'

"Whereupon Tony ruefully admitted, 'But I can't retake it. That would be impossible.'"

Don't step on any big toes accidentally.

I wrote a script about a man who kills his wife, and the film's producer told me that if I wanted to get it made at *this* studio, I'd have to change the ending: It would have to be an innocent man falsely accused of killing his wife.

"Why won't they make it the other way?" I asked.

He told me why: The studio head was a venerable and truly respected former producer, now a very wealthy man. But he hadn't always been wealthy. He'd come to Hollywood as a penniless wannabe screenwriter and met a wealthy, socially elite widow. He married her and some years later she committed suicide and he inherited all of her money.

Then he met another wealthy, socially prominent widow and married her, too. And she, too, committed suicide some years later and he inherited all of *her* money, as well.

Demand your payment on time.

Screenwriter Dalton Trumbo to producer Sam Spiegel: "Listen, I have a gun and I will shoot you if I don't get my money today."

To Spiegel

To manipulate, flatter, seduce, cajole, con, like producer Sam.

Spiegelese

A line of BS that sounds terrific and is designed to take advantage of you, it was originated by Sam Spiegel, producer, but perfected by David Begelman, who spoke perfect Spiegelese and became a top-ranked agent and then a studio head and then (flat broke) a suicide. "How *cheesy,* wags said, to commit suicide at the Century Plaza, of all places, not at the Bel Air, the Chateau Marmont, or a bungalow at the Beverly Hills Hotel."

Three's Company, but Four Is an Orgy

Old Hollywood rule, allegedly first said by Mae West, then later by Zsa Zsa Gabor.

Learn to recognize bullshit when you hear it.

A director called and told me he'd read my script and was interested in directing it. He said, "I don't want to exploit your script. I want to pay homage to it."

I hung up on him.

If you want to sell your script, be capable of anything.

Actress Sigourney Weaver was in the middle of her gynecological exam when the doctor said, "I have written a screenplay. Could you possibly read it?"

Move to the Midwest.

Discussing a script, producer Sam Spiegel said to screenwriter Harold Pinter, "They won't understand it in the Midwest."

Pinter said, "Fuck the Midwest!"

Spiegel said, "Do you want to fuck the *whole* of the Midwest?"

It's okay to live in your car.

Michael Blake did before he sold *Dances with Wolves.*

I was so poor before I sold my first script that I was working as a bartender and going through my pockets looking for forgotten change.

L.A. has lots of places where you can work all day without paying too much—the Rose Café, the Farmers Market, in the company of other screenwriters.

And many young screenwriters swear that the El Pollo Loco diet is healthy, too, besides being filling.

Forget playing video games; watch Tracy and Hepburn instead.

The old Tracy and Hepburn movies are a dialogue treat, as are the films of Preston Sturges and Woody Allen. They're fun to watch, and good dialogue exercise, too.

It's okay to have literary influences.

Screenwriter William Faulkner referred to his penis as "Mr. Bolton," a play on the name of a character from D. H. Lawrence's *Lady Chatterley's Lover.*

Don't have an affair with a script girl.

Screenwriter William Faulkner did; he had a lengthy affair with a script girl. After he died, she wrote a book about him. She wrote that for most of his life he was impotent. She even wrote that he ran the water in the bathroom so no one could hear his bodily functions and that he took a bath before they made love. He had the "prettiest little feet," she wrote, and always kept a handkerchief around in case he coughed.

Don't have an affair with an actress, either (heh-heh-heh).

Sally Field did an interview for *Playboy* magazine in which she said "there were always" men around Burt Reynolds. It came at the same time that Reynolds had lost a lot of weight, thanks to a broken jaw. The Field interview led to rampant and false rumors that Reynolds was gay and dying of AIDS.

There are many in Hollywood who think that single Sally Field interview destroyed Burt Reynolds's career.

Never lie to yourself.

Michael Moore, after his famous Bush-bashing acceptance speech for *Bowling for Columbine,* asked Academy president Frank Pierson, "Did I make an ass out of myself up there?"

To Do an Eric Red

To flip out and lose it suddenly. Red, the talented screenwriter of *The Hitcher* and other action-noir films, drove his car one day into a bar full of people in Westwood.

If you want to be a movie star, write a screenplay.

Sylvester Stallone wrote *Rocky.* Billie Bob Thornton wrote *Sling Blade.* Matt Damon and Ben Affleck wrote *Good Will Hunting.*

Then they stuck to their guns and said they wouldn't sell their scripts unless they could play the star parts.

Producers argued with them and offered them vast sums of money not to act in their films. They turned the vast sums of money down . . . and became movie stars and multimillionaires by holding firm.

Don't try to figure out the next trend before you write your script.

There was an investor who thought *Heaven's Gate* was going to be such a big hit that dozens of other Westerns would be made, so he *bought all the horses* used in *Heaven's Gate,* thinking he'd make a fortune renting movie-trained horses out to other film companies.

Well, after *Heaven's Gate* became one of the biggest disasters of all times, he was stuck with all these unemployable horses.

What did he do with them?

Well, they shoot horses, don't they?

It doesn't pay to go out to lunch with other screenwriters.

Ben Hecht: "Would that our writing had been as good as our lunches."

The Cocaine Highway

Sunset Boulevard in Los Angeles.

If you need drugs to write.

The valet parkers at a lot of "hot" Hollywood restaurants will be able to help you.

For many years, the valet-parking guys at a famous Sunset Strip restaurant had the best coke in the business, until they all got busted. Some people said the real reason people ate there was for the coke, not the food.

ALL HAIL
Peter Viertel!

The author, who wrote the screenplay of *The Sun Also Rises*, had a reputation for "looking great in bathing suits" and for coaxing "everyone" to be "naughty."

TAKE IT FROM ME: IT'S OKAY TO DEVELOP SOME SCHOLARLY INTERESTS

My lifelong scholarly interest has been Zsa Zsa Gabor.

There is a story that I just can't get out of my head about Zsa Zsa, who is a fellow Hungarian, a story that I'm fixated on. It's a true story.

Zsa Zsa and Marlon Brando are on The Tonight Show *with Johnny Carson. Zsa Zsa is saying something—they are on the air—and Marlon interrupts her rudely and says to Johnny, "I don't know why Zsa Zsa has to talk so much. With those boobs she really doesn't have to say anything! Do you want to know what I want to do with that girl, Johnny? I want to fuck her!"*

Then Marlon turns to Zsa Zsa and says, "A man can only do one thing with you, Zsa Zsa—throw you down and fuck you!"

Call yourself on the phone.

If you want people to think you're important, have yourself paged by friends at the Polo Lounge or at the pool of the Beverly Hills Hotel.

Producer Robert Evans once took a phone call from director Roman Polanski while being interviewed for ABC's *20/20*. An ABC staffer picked an extension up and found Evans speaking to dead air. Bob had faked the call from Roman.

Your script can burn.

Screenwriter/novelist Charles Bukowski: "Usually what the greatest actor of our day and his friends do after eating (if the night is cold) is to have a few drinks and watch the screenplays burn in the fireplace. Or after eating (on warm evenings) after a few drinks the screenplays are taken frozen out of cold storage. He hands some to his friends—keeps some—then together from the veranda they toss them like flying saucers far out into the spacious canyon below. Then they all go back in knowing instinctively that the screenplays were bad."

Don't work in a studio office.

Screenwriter William Faulkner: "It's like a hospital prison corridor. Those damned gray walls, those damned wide corridors, all those closed doors. And everything so damned hushed and still. I hate it."

Believe in God-incidence.

As a young journalist at the Cleveland *Plain Dealer,* I did an interview with soul singer Otis Redding after a concert at a place called Leo's Casino. Otis and I hit it off and I found him a generous and truly soulful man.

The next afternoon, he got on a little plane in Cleveland and the plane crashed at a lake in Wisconsin and Otis Redding died.

My interview with him was his last.

Nearly thirty years later, listening one afternoon to one of his songs, I thought back to that interview with Otis and I heard a voice telling me to write his story.

The next day, I sat down and called his widow in Macon, Georgia, did a month's worth of research, and started writing.

In Hollywood, sometimes even God can't help you.

Otis's widow loved the script so much that she kept it under her pillow for a month and prayed that someone would make it.

Eight years later, no one has made it.

Don't write any personal pet projects.

Look what happened to Oliver Stone: *Alexander.* Kevin Spacey: *Beyond the Sea.* Martin Scorsese: *Gangs of New York.* Bill Murray: *The Razor's Edge.* Francis Ford Coppola: *One from the Heart.* And Joe Eszterhas: *Telling Lies in America.* All personal pet projects. All box-office disasters.

Everything in moderation . . .

Novelist and screenwriter Dominick Dunne: "Drunk, I once set my room on fire in the Volney Hotel in New York, where I was living. Another time, I was in the closet with people I didn't know using Turnbull and Asser ties to find a vein to shoot cocaine. One of the strangers died. I ran. Then, when I was stoned again, a crazed psychopath beat me, tied me up, put a brown grocery bag over my face, and dropped lighted matches on the bag. I lived."

Try to write a "fuck film" like Love Story.

According to Paramount's research people, that's what *Love Story* was.

Why? A guy took his date to see *Love Story*. They held hands and cried when she died at the end. Then they went back to his place and vigorously showed their appreciation that *they* were alive.

Any publicity is good publicity.

The week after his eleven-year-old daughter, Marci, was abducted, Calvin Klein sold a record number of blue jeans: 200,000 in a single week.

Help those who have helped you.

I got more exposure from the *Today* show than any screenwriter in history thanks to a *Today* show producer who had befriended me.

When he told me that he wanted to write television sitcoms, I fixed him up with a TV agent.

You can make directors beg to work with you.

Director Phillip Noyce: "I liked the script of *Sliver* a lot. Or at least I liked the idea of jumping on the Joe Eszterhas bandwagon."

LESSON 4

Beware of the Back Pat!

You'll need to ward off evil spirits.

When he was a young director, Marty Scorsese wore a gold talisman to keep evil spirits at bay, as well as an American Indian pouch filled with holy objects.

The Jack Story

Superagent Jeff Berg told me this old Hollywood story in an effort to calm me down about what I saw as a potential problem.

Jeff said, "A guy is driving down an abandoned country road and gets a flat tire. He opens his trunk and finds he doesn't have a jack. He looks around, freaks, and says, 'Oh, God, what am I going to do now?' He doesn't see any houses anywhere. He starts walking down the road—angry, worried, fearful that he is in Deliverance country and anything can happen to him. He can wind up like poor Ned Beatty in that movie. He turns a corner and there's a big house in front of him. He walks up warily. Norman Bates can be in there. A beautiful woman opens the door. He asks the woman if she's got a jack. Of course she does. She walks back to his car with him. She helps him fix the tire. She asks if he wants a cold beer. She walks back to her house with him. They have more beers. She fucks him atop the kitchen table. They fall in love. They marry. They have blond, blue-eyed children. They live happily ever after."

The moral of the story: Don't turn every mini problem into "a jack story."

You've gotta be Sammy Glick.

Paul Schrader (*Taxi Driver, American Gigolo*): "No one succeeds in film if he's not hustling. The first thing you think of when you wake up in the morning is 'Who can I hustle?' And the last thing you think of before you go to bed is 'Who can I hustle?'"

Get arrested.

Screenwriter Stuart Beattie (*Collateral*): "My business manager once gave me this great advice. He said, 'If you are not kicking down enough doors to sell your script and knocking on enough windows to get arrested, you are not trying hard enough."

Beware of the back pat.

If a director or producer shakes hands with you and at the same time reaches around you and rubs your back with his left hand, run.

He's looking for the soft spot where he can best stick the knife in your back.

You, too, can give a studio head an orgasm.

Jaws producer David Brown: "The only orgasm that Lew Wasserman [the longtime Universal chieftain] ever had in his life was when he saw the opening numbers for *Jaws*."

This is what your brilliant, literary script is really about.

Producer Scott Rudin: "A movie is about two movie stars."

Avoid spending time with Sherry Lansing.

Raymond Chandler: "These Hollywood people are fantastic when you have been away for a while. In their presence any calm sensible remark sounds faked. Their conversation is a mess of shopworn superlatives interrupted by four telephone calls to the sentence. Ray Stark is a nice chap. I like him. Everybody at the brothel is nice."

They've made us settle for a Polish starlet.

Frank Pierson, screenwriter (*Dog Day Afternoon*) and Writers Guild president: "Screenwriters have accepted the idea of being third-class citizens, the industry's pain in the ass. Our position is that maybe someday we could forget the old joke about the Polish starlet. You know, she thought she could get ahead by fucking the writer."

I struck out with the Polish starlet.

I tried like hell to get Polish starlet Joanna Pacula to leave a party at Robert Evans's house with me and go back to my hotel room, but it was no-go.

These are our male role models.

Many screenwriters have bedded movie stars: Charles MacArthur teamed up with Helen Hayes, Norman Mailer with Shelley Winters, Thomas Wolfe with Jean Harlow, Paddy Chayefsky with Kim Novak, Arthur Miller with Marilyn Monroe, Pete Hamill with Shirley MacLaine, John O'Hara with Marlene Dietrich, Robert Graves with Ava Gardner, Romain Gary with Jean Seberg, Tom McGuane with Elizabeth Ashley and Margot Kidder, Tom Green with Drew Barrymore, Peter Viertel with Deborah Kerr, James Jones with Montgomery Clift, John Monk Saunders with Mary Astor.

Get in touch with your feminine side.

The only good artists are feminine," said Orson Welles. "I don't believe an artist exists whose dominant characteristic is not feminine. It's nothing to do with homosexuality, but intellectually an artist must be a man with feminine aptitudes."

Norman Mailer has a feminine side.

Said Shelley Winters of Norman: "Norman's not capable of sleeping with a starlet and using her and then just saying 'That was great, kid. Goodbye.' Unlike most men in Hollywood, he's actually a feminist. He sees women as people, not just sex objects. He reveres women. He feels there's a kind of respect they must have. He didn't treat me like a dumb starlet, he just couldn't do that. In fact, I remember times when he was in a restaurant with me and Burt Lancaster. Pretty, sexy girls would come over and sit down and be introduced to 'Norman Mailer, the writer.' And Norman would cool it. He wouldn't be rude or anything, he'd be charming and with that funny little grin of his he has, he'd flatter them and compliment them. But as far as I could see, he wouldn't make dates with them. Now maybe he tells people different, but from what I saw over the years in Hollywood, my impression—from a woman's point of view—is that he never treated a woman like a hunk of meat."

Find yourself a smart mate.

I take my wife, Naomi, into most studio meetings with me. Before he was the governor of California, Arnold Schwarzenegger relied on his wife, Maria, the same way.

Says studio head Mike Medavoy about trying to get Arnold to star in the *Sixth Day*: "Maria Shriver made notes on all the drafts of the script. She saw her role as her husband's advisor and protector. In one meeting, she was the only one who had problems with the material, so I began addressing my questions to her, as if she were the one who had to be fully sold on the material. In a way, she was. No matter how much money we paid Arnold, he wasn't going to do the movie unless both he and Maria felt comfortable with the script."

Does anyone realize that Maria Shriver is running the state of California?

We all have our own trophies.

I'm jealous that Bill Goldman has won two Oscars and I've won none.

But I bet Bill Goldman is jealous that I've bedded Sharon Stone.

Larry McMurtry says what you're doing isn't even hard work.

Screenwriter/novelist Larry McMurtry: "So much has been written about the miseries of screenwriting or, more precisely, about the miseries of the screenwriter's lot, that I, for one, am sick of reading it. I think it is time to redress the balance, to treat Hollywood fairly, and to suggest that screenwriting, far from being hard work, might actually be considered to be a form of creative play."

Perk of Success:
You Can Make Them Baby-Sit
Your Dog

Screenwriter John Milius, at the height of his success, forced producers to make side deals with him. Not only did they have to sign a contract for him to write the script; they also had to baby-sit his dog on certain days so he could write that script.

ALL HAIL
Harlan Ellison!

After he won a copyright court battle with Paramount over a TV show, the screenwriter/novelist bought a billboard just outside the Paramount lot.

It read WRITERS—DON'T LET THEM STEAL FROM YOU.

Unemployable

The biggest scare word in Hollywood—as in, "You'll never eat lunch in this town again." As in, "NO—MORE—MONEY!"

Your film can become a joke at the Oscars.

Discussing my film *Showgirls,* Whoopi Goldberg said at the sixty-eighth Academy Awards, "I haven't seen that many poles mistreated since World War Two."

Make 'em feel smart and you'll get your way.

I learned this trick from screenwriter Waldo Salt (*Midnight Cowboy*). He'd finish his script and then tear six or seven pages out of it and turn the script in to the studio.

The studio execs would sometimes—not always—notice that something seemed to be missing from a sequence and suggest that he fill it in with some scenes.

Seemingly acting on *their* suggestions, he would then put the pages that he had torn out *back* into the script.

The studio executives would then praise him for listening to, and acting upon, *their* suggestions.

When you're not writing, read stage plays.

Reading plays is great training for writing dialogue; think of it as doing push-ups for the ear.

Don't, however, read playwrights like Mamet or Pinter and Beckett, who are so stylized that their style can creep into your head and stylistically affect what you write.

Reading plays from the thirties and forties is ideal training because plays in those days were much more accessible than they are today.

Hollywood won't corrupt you, but your family might.

Screenwriter Dalton Trumbo: "I begin to realize why people believe the legend that Hollywood corrupts writers. But they're quite wrong. All Hollywood does is give them enough money so they can get married and have kids like normal people. But it's the getting married and having kids that really corrupts them."

Pay for your own drinks.

If a studio has flown you to L.A. for a meeting and is picking up your hotel bill, don't put any drinks you may have had in the bar on it.

A studio accountant will let the executive in charge of your project know how many drinks you had. If you had more than a few, the studio will decide that you have a drinking problem and will not hire you for the project.

And, obviously, don't charge to your hotel bill any hookers, sex toys, or jewelry bought in the store in the lobby, either.

See Thunder Road.

Hunter S. Thompson: "Between Mitchum and Burroughs and Marlon Brando and James Dean and Jack Kerouac, I got myself a serious running start before I was twenty years old, and there was no turning back. Buy the ticket, take the ride. So welcome to *Thunder Road,* Bubba. It was one of those movies that got a grip on me when I was too young to resist. It convinced me that the only way to drive was at top speed with a car full of whiskey, and I have been driving that way ever since, for good or ill."

PERK OF SUCCESS:
SLEEP WITH THE STAR

Even if you're married—it's worth the memory.

Don't lose your head in the process, though. Paddy Chayefsky and Kim Novak had a brief affair. "He was awestruck, really, that someone like Kim Novak would be interested in him," said a producer. "Kim had Paddy thinking he was seven feet tall, a blond, blue-eyed WASP." Said another producer: "This was a sensational-looking woman. She had a pair of tits you would not believe, and she never wore a bra."

Paddy believed his friend Irwin Shaw's dictum that "the writer only has one obligation—to stay alive and try to please himself."

But he lost his head. He told his wife that he wanted a divorce because he was in love with Novak.

His wife, luckily, said, "Don't be ridiculous!"

A week later, Novak dumped him.

So you're a little nuts, so what.

I know it wasn't really sane to tell those Disney executives to "get your hands off my dick" in the Disney conference room . . . or to send a memo to a director that caused him to suffer a heart attack.

But all writers are a little nuts. The people who know me and love me have made peace with that.

As the writer/director Garson Kanin said of his friend Paddy Chayefsky: "I think it's fair to say—and nothing against him—Paddy was a little crazy. I don't think there is any important writer who is completely sane. If he was, he wouldn't be a writer—or a painter, or a poet, or a sculptor. I don't mean clinically insane—but his reactions aren't normal, and his perceptions certainly aren't normal. And Paddy, more than most, was a little bit cuckoo."

It is not who you know.

All it takes to become a successful screenwriter is to *sell one script.*

One person has to read your script and believe that he/she can make money off of it. *They* can't begin *making* money, of course, until they pay *you* some.

Spend your time on your butt, working on that one script instead of trying to seduce people into being your friends—so they can be there to buy your script, if and whenever you finally get around to writing it.

They'll do everything they can to stop you from being a star.

It is not in the studio's interest for a screenwriter to become a star, the way directors become stars.

If a screenwriter becomes a star, studio execs won't be able to tell him what to write.

If a screenwriter becomes a star, he'll wind up in the papers and on TV, criticizing studio heads.

Everyone knows directors are controllable and they *need* the studios to be able to work.

But those crazy asshole writers—all they *need* to go to work is a piece of paper and a pencil.

Don't break your own heart.

Shane Black was the hottest young writer in town, selling original spec scripts for lots of money. He was a savvy, well-read guy with balls.

The Long Kiss Goodnight was his pet project—a brilliant script that director Renny Harlin and his wife at the time, Geena Davis, turned into a turgid and empty film.

Shane stopped writing for a long time after that nightmarish experience and tried to make it as an actor. The reason he stopped writing was that his heart was broken, but that's only half the story.

The reason his heart was broken was that he had broken it himself. He had let Renny Harlin cajole and charm him into making fatal changes to his script, the changes that ruined his own script and doomed his own movie.

After many years, Shane came back to direct his own script—one way of making sure you don't break your own heart again . . . unless, of course, he listens too closely to his producer, Joel Silver, who is, unfortunately, a friend of his and very good at cajoling and charming.

Don't write for "blood money."

Blood money" is when you're rewriting someone else's script, and you change anything and everything in the script—plot points, characters, and especially characters' names—not because the changes are creatively necessary but so you'll get screen credit and the money that's tied to you getting that credit.

There is a story, hopefully apocryphal, about a screenwriter assigned to adapt *The Great Gatsby*. The screenwriter changed the name "Gatsby" to "Farrell" and the title to "The Great Farrell" in an attempt to get screen credit and more money.

Sometimes the damn place just makes you cry.

Corky was a sweet little man who poured the stiffest drinks at the Hideaway Bar at the Beverly Wilshire Hotel.

Jack Lemmon and I would sip our drinks there on soggy or smoggy L.A. afternoons.

Corky had a laugh that made Jack and me laugh, and he told the dumbest jokes in Southern California.

One day, I walked in and there was a new guy behind the bar and Jack was floating his scotch high up in his eyeballs.

Jack told me that Corky had met a guy right there in the Hideaway Room who'd taken him home, then left his body in a Dumpster.

No more laughs and jokes. No more hiding in the afternoons at the Hideaway Bar. Jack and I both started to cry, realizing that sometimes there is simply no shelter from the town's degradations.

You don't want to get in a creative disagreement with a Scientologist.

While they're nice folks, scientologists don't like to be messed with.

I once threatened to take Sylvester Stallone on in a fistfight. I once threatened to break a studio executive's knees. I once told the most powerful man in Hollywood to go fuck himself and the foot soldiers he rode in on.

But under no circumstances would I get into a creative disagreement with a Scientologist.

Besides, I don't think the Dogon fighting stick or the Tibetan rock or the hunting knife I carry are any match for their E-meter.

You don't want to mess with that E-meter, either.

Scientologists have this machine called the E-meter. They will have someone read your script and E-meter it before one of their people commits to do the movie.

It's more than enough, in my experience, for a screenwriter to deal with a director, a producer, studio notes, a star's ego, et cetera.

Trust me on this: You don't need to deal with an E-meter.

Oscarosis

A disease whose main symptom is that the victim is willing to do anything—*anything*—to win an Oscar.

With actors and executives, act like you're a playwright, not a screenwriter.

Actress Jill Hennessy (*Crossing Jordan*): "When you're an actor working in the theater, you would never say anything to the writer, never alter the dialogue, never dream to ask for changes."

Good ideas can come from great gossip.

In *Sliver,* Sharon Stone spends a lot of time looking through a telescope at her New York apartment building neighbors. I got the idea from a friend of Jackie Kennedy's who told me Jackie loved to do the same thing.

ALL HAIL
Clifford Odets!

Agent Swifty Lazar: "Clifford Odets was a wily client. One day he called me. He was so in debt, he said, that he'd sold his art collection. But he had an idea for a movie, *Page One*. I knew he was spitballing, but I took him over to see Jerry Wald and Jerry bit. Jerry sent us out to Darryl Zanuck.

"I got Odets two hundred thousand, a small fortune for a screenplay in those days. . . . A month later, Odets invited me to pick up the script. When I walked into his cottage, he was holding a six-hundred-page screenplay—a document about five times longer than a standard script.

"Odets said, 'I'll cut it if they pay me.'

"I soon realized that Odets had planned this caper. . . . I got him some additional money. Odets started cutting away. He trimmed it down to three hundred pages, and then I had to get him some additional money to cut it to two hundred. At that point, he announced he wanted to direct the movie. . . . They let him direct the picture. . . . It was a ghastly movie that died on Pico Boulevard and should never have been released."

The word Death in a title is death at the box office.

It will bum audiences out and let them know they're in for a depressing experience. I've heard at least three producers tell me this.

Each time I've said, "Have you ever heard of something called *Death of a Salesman?*"

If you sell the concept for a script, demand a hotel suite in which to write it.

Many screenwriters claim to get in touch with their muses *best* at places like the Dolder Grand in Zurich, the Dorchester in London, the Kahala on Oahu, the Ritz-Carlton on Maui, or the relatively cut-rate Beverly Hills Hotel and Chateau Marmont in L.A.

While vacationing with my family at the Kahala once, we were sitting on the beach when we saw John Gregory Dunne and Joan Didion walking along the beach, their heads down, *matching sweaters tied around their hips,* lost in *serious thought.*

A producer and his family sat near us and I asked him what Dunne and Didion were doing here.

"What do you think?" the producer said. "Can't you tell? Writing. Working."

If you make it, directors will resent the amount of money you make.

Director Phillip Noyce: "I continued to work on a script of *The Sum of All Fears.* Paul Attanasio [*Donnie Brasco* and *Quiz Show*] wrote another draft with a lot of input from myself and, particularly, my business partner Kathleen McLaughlin. He was paid more than a million dollars to rewrite the screenplay, which, due to another commitment, he ended up doing in about ten days. Nice work if you can get it!"

You didn't write Gone with the Wind.

I was at a shop in Los Angeles in the mideighties and the store owner asked me what I did for a living. I told him I wrote movies, and when he asked me which ones, I told him my last movie was *Flashdance.*

"Hey," he said, "you must have worked with my niece." He told me her name.

I'd never heard of his niece and asked what she did on the film.

He said, "She wrote it, too."

I said, "No, she didn't."

He said, "Yes, she did."

I said, "Is her name up on-screen?"

He said, "She wrote the damn movie; that's what she told me."

I discovered that his niece had been brought in to do some "polishing" on the script but didn't do enough work on it to get any credit from the Writers Guild.

It was my first introduction to a whole subgenre of screenwriters in Hollywood: those who claim to have "written" a movie but don't have any writing credit on it.

You're a writer, not a social butterfly.

I ran into him by the pool of the Four Seasons hotel in Beverly Hills. He came up and introduced himself and told me his story.

He was a successful and well-known attorney from Chicago but had always wanted to write for television, so one day he took a leave of absence and came out to L.A. He was living at the Four Seasons.

He'd given himself six months. He'd be at the Four Seasons for six months and in that time he would have as many meetings with television producers and executives and showrunners as possible. If it didn't work out in six months, he'd go back to Chicago.

I got a note from him about a year later. He was back with the law firm in Chicago. It hadn't worked out in L.A.

"But I'll always know that I tried," he wrote. "I didn't futz around. I really, really went for it."

I remembered what I had told him when we met: "Stop running around meeting people. Go back to Chicago and write something."

I hoped that's what he was doing.

You, too, can con the MPAA.

When the MPAA ratings board saw *Basic Instinct,* they gave the movie an NC-17.

As long as Sharon uncrossed her legs, the board told us, the NC-17 would stand.

I told the studio PR people to tell the MPAA that this wasn't a sex scene; this was a confrontation scene between an empowered and liberated modern woman and her male-piggy poe/leece inquisitors.

The "empowerment" argument swayed the MPAA and saved the beaver. Paul Verhoeven only had to take a few snips from the, um, *focal point* of the scene to satisfy the ratings board.

You never know how they'll film the scene that you wrote.

I wrote an extravagant dance sequence for Jennifer Beals in *Flash-dance.*

Some studio wizard suggested cutting the sequence in half and rewriting it, but I convinced them that a big dance movie had to have a lot of dance in it.

Since Jenny couldn't dance very well and certainly couldn't do a big dance sequence, the director hired a "dance double" for Jenny named Marine Jahan.

But it still wasn't enough to convince the audience that Jenny Beals could dance, because Marine Jihan couldn't do the floor spins.

So the producers brought in someone who could do the floor spins perfectly—a guy, who had to wear a wig and shave his legs . . . but who refused to shave his mustache.

If you slow the film down and look very closely, you can see Jenny Beals spinning around, wearing leotards and a mustache.

Don't die with the wrong people.

That's what happened to screenwriter/novelist F. Scott Fitzgerald, whose last girlfriend was gossip columnist Sheilah Graham.

Graham had once been previously married to a man who was twenty-five years older and arranged dates for her with wealthy men. She and her husband lived off the gifts given to her by the wealthy men she went out with.

R E E L S P E A K

To Do a Belushi

To OD on drugs, like actor John.

Some people do, temporarily, know some things about making hit movies.

Producer Jerry Bruckheimer, producer Brian Grazer, the late producer Don Simpson, producer/director George Lucas, and producer/director Steven Spielberg all know some things.

Producer/director Ivan Reitman *knew* some things, but he has forgotten them. So has Francis Ford Coppola.

After *Flashdance, Jagged Edge,* and *Basic Instinct,* I knew some things about making hit movies, too.

But after *Sliver, Showgirls,* and *Jade,* I, like Ivan and Francis, forgot what I knew.

PERK OF SUCCESS:
YOU, TOO, CAN GET FRANKIE AVALON TO SING FOR YOU

He knew who I was, and somebody at our table, as a joke, told him that it was my wife Geraldine's birthday. So Frankie Avalon sang "Happy Birthday" for her.

It wasn't her birthday at all, but she'd loved Frankie Avalon as a teenager, and when he sang happy birthday to her, she cried. She told me after our divorce that it was one of her greatest thrills as a screenwriter's wife.

Billy Wilder was a sexist pig.

Screenwriter/director Billy Wilder had a recurring fantasy that he told friends about: He wanted to invent a mattress that would make a woman disappear after he'd made love to her.

In her place would appear three of his friends around a card table.

Wilder said that if men were forced to choose between sex with a woman and playing cards, 98 percent would choose cards. (Not me, babe.)

If they say it won't work, it probably will.

I was once told by a studio head that movies set on farms didn't sell because "dirt doesn't sell." Then the film *Witness* came out. It was set on a farm and it was a smash.

Paddy Chayefsky was told by a studio head that movies "with funeral scenes" don't sell. Then *The Godfather* came out. It had a funeral scene and it was a smash.

I was told by another studio exec that "courtroom dramas don't sell." I wrote *Jagged Edge* and it was the number-one movie in America for more than a month.

The truth is that anything that is well written, well directed, and well acted can sell.

Bull-whip every Hollywood astrologer you meet.

Author Hunter S. Thompson: "There is a ghastly political factor in doing any business with Hollywood. You can't get by without five or six personal staff people—and at least one personal astrologer. I have always hated astrologers, and I like to have sport with them. They are harmless quacks in the main, but some of them get ambitious and turn predatory, especially in Hollywood. In Venice Beach, I ran into a man who claimed to be Johnny Depp's astrologer. . . . I took his card and examined it carefully a moment, as if I couldn't quite read the small print. But I knew he was lying, so I leaned toward him and slapped him sharply in the nuts. Not hard, but very quickly, using the back of my hand and my fingers like a bull whip, yet very discreetly. He let out a hiss and went limp, unable to speak or breathe."

PERK OF SUCCESS: YOU, TOO, CAN WIN AN INDUSTRY AWARD

Screenwriter Dalton Trumbo, in a note to himself: "Develop the idea that no moderately competent hack in any field of Hollywood endeavor can spend ten years in the community without winning a wide assortment of plaques, medals, and certificates of merit."

Leave a message at 1:30 P.M., during lunch hour, on his answering machine.

Do this when you don't want to talk to that studio executive but want to make it appear that you do.

But if you get a message back on *your* answering machine during lunch hour, it might really be time to talk to him.

You're not going to be in The Dictionary of Film.

A magazine wanted to do a profile of me and assigned the job to David Thomson, the critic and author of *A Biographical Dictionary of Film,* recognized as a classic film book.

I had lunch with David Thomson, a pleasant man, at the Lark Creek Inn in Larkspur, California, and told him I wasn't going to let him do the article.

He seemed shocked. "But why not?"

I said, "Because I've read your dictionary and there are hardly any screenwriters in it; there are all kinds of actors, directors, producers, even cinematographers, but not one screenwriter."

David Thomson said, "What does that have to do with anything? Just because you're a screenwriter doesn't mean I can't write about you in a publication."

I said, "But you obviously don't believe very many screenwriters are important enough to include in *A Biographical Dictionary of Film*."

"No," he said calmly, "I don't suppose I do."

So I didn't let him do the interview—enjoying the fact that I, a lowly screenwriter, was denying him a paycheck.

Keep your name out of the trades.

Mike Medavoy: "I told my writer clients to ignore the big-splash announcements in the trades about some unknown writer getting big bucks for a script, because often these guys are never heard from again."

Don't be anybody's N word.

According to screenwriter Buck Henry, screenwriter Robert Towne became "Warren Beatty's nigger."

Don't take yourself seriously.

Producer Gerry Ayres: "Bob Towne would love to work for money on rewrites on which he got no credit, and would do it quickly. Over three weeks, he'd have a whole new script ready. But something that had his name on it would become all involved in the neurosis of completion and failure and would take forever."

Scald 'em with chicken soup.

Mike Medavoy: "I had lunch with Paddy Chayefsky. We were talking about directors for Paddy's script *Network* and Paddy asked me what I thought of Sidney Lumet.

" 'Sidney Lumet to do *Network*?' I gasped. 'What was the last funny movie he made?'

"In response, Paddy turned his bowl of chicken soup over on the table.

" 'You're right, Paddy,' I replied, 'he'd be great.' "

If you make it, don't brag about it.

My fellow Hungarian, actor Tony Curtis: "It was a miserable, rainy late afternoon, my chauffeur drives me down Forty-eighth Street, and who do I see out front, standing under the marquee, but Walter Matthau. He's got a long, heavy coat on and looks as grumpy as he's ever looked in his life . . . he's looking out at this cold miserable world he's got to live in. He hates it. I'm getting this reading as I'm sitting in my limo, warm and comfy, looking at this poor guy on the sidewalk staring into the gutter and saying to himself, 'What's ever going to happen for me? Nothin'.' You could see that on his face.

"So I say to the driver, 'See that guy standing under the awning? Drive up to him as slowly as possible, and when we're alongside of him, stop.' He says okay, so we drive up, and I see Walter watching this limousine come rolling up, and it stops right where he's standing. I roll the window down, I look at him, and I say, '*I fucked Yvonne DeCarlo!*'

"Then I just rolled that window back up and told the driver to get the hell out of there."

To Do a Hughie

To trip on your own dick, like actor Hugh Grant.

The definition of "creative differences" . . .

The producer had a reputation for having a nasty temper, so some people were surprised when he was named to take over the studio.

He soon developed a conflict with a lawyer in Business Affairs who kept questioning some of the personal expenses that the new studio head was writing off—expenses like an airplaneful of orchids sent to an actress girlfriend in Rio.

The studio head told the lawyer several times to back off. The lawyers' *friends* told him to back off.

Yet he kept after the studio head, questioning expenses in meetings—expenses like twenty thousand dollars for a party involving three girls who worked for a club in Vegas.

One day, at a meeting in a studio conference room full of executives, the lawyer nitpicked about some suspicious expense. The studio head punched him in the mouth, judo-chopped him in the throat, and kicked him in the head and ribs while the other studio executives sat there and did nothing.

The lawyer was taken by ambulance to a hospital. He recovered quickly. He left the studio and received a $5 million settlement.

Raymond Chandler, role model . . .

Producer Ray Stark told screenwriter/novelist Jim Harrison that as a young agent one of his jobs was to get Raymond Chandler off the floor of his apartment, where he sometimes slept fully dressed in a drying pool of his own vomit.

Never hug an actress on a soundstage.

You'll screw up her hair, costuming, and makeup. She'll hate you.

LESSON 5

Don't Let 'Em Bleed on You!

You're on your own.

After I sold *Basic Instinct* for $3 million to Carolco, Disney studio honcho Jeff Katzenberg wrote a memo lamenting the fact, and studio heads got together in meetings to discuss ways of keeping future script prices down. (*Daily Variety* reported both the memo and the studio meetings.)

The Writers Guild should have filed an antitrust action against the studios for conspiring to keep writers' prices down, but the Guild, great on matters of health plans and insurance and awful on matters of creative rights, did nothing.

The multimillion-dollar script frenzy ended within six months, making it pretty clear that the studios had successfully put the writers back in their places: the schmucks at the bottom of the totem pole.

In 2001, the Guild threatened a strike. One of its main demands was the elimination of the directors' possessory "Filmed by" credit.

When the Guild made progress on financial fronts, it simply—without even an explanatory statement—dropped its demands about the directors' possessory credit, and signed a new contract with the studios.

Be an outlaw.

John Milius (*Apocalypse Now, Dirty Harry*): "I liken myself to a successful outlaw. To be worth a shit in the world, you've got to blaze your own trail. Nothing else is any good. Whatever you're going to do you're going to do alone."

Even Mailer lost his soul.

Sandy Charlebois Thomas, Norman Mailer's secretary: "Something happened to him out in Hollywood. He's talked to me about being corrupted out there. He was young, suddenly very famous, and he was wined and dined. He discovered if he did the cutest little things, people just fell all over him."

Don't let 'em bleed on you.

Stanley Jaffe, producer and former head of Paramount, would yell at people with such force that blood would flow from his nostrils.

Don't do it.

Screenwriter/playwright David Mamet: "Working as a screenwriter, I always thought that 'Film is a collaborative business' only constituted half of the actual phrase. From a screenwriter's point of view, the correct rendering should be 'Film is a collaborative business: bend over.'"

Slug some more Kaopectate, Bill.

Screenwriter William Goldman: "It's probably not unwise to try to remember why movie people have kept the tranquilizer business booming; after a debacle, it's hard to get work; after two, it's hard to get television.

Can I have a slug of your Kaopectate, Bill?

Your last movie has bombed at the box office. Good luck. You're in a heap of *creative* trouble. Everyone in every story meeting or phone conference will now think that they know more than you do.

　　They may have thought that *before* your movie failed, but now that it has, *they* know that *you* know that you have to listen to their ideas.

Don't be a road map.

Screenwriter Terry George (*Hotel Rwanda*): "Film today is more and more concentrated on the amusement park element. If a writer can attach an actor or a producer who has some clout, then you can arm yourself; otherwise, a script simply becomes a road map to attract money and talent."

I've moved out of Malibu, thank you.

Screenwriter Milo Addica (*Birth*): "Most writers just want to get their movie made, and it doesn't matter how. I think I am not in that category. I like to get my movies made by the right director, so that I can have a body of work I can look back on and be proud of. Otherwise, I would not be doing anything I am doing now. I would be in Hollywood trying to make my first million and move up to Malibu."

They want to control you.

Novelist/screenwriter George Pelecanos: "When I was a kid, I used to watch *Twilight Zone,* as everybody did. The reason I watched it—although I didn't know enough intellectually then to know why I was watching it—it was written by novelists like Richard Matheson. I always wondered, Why don't they do that more? Because, damn, novelists sure could use the work; I mean, just to get that extra thirty grand or whatever the scale is for a script and a story is a huge amount of money to most novelists. I think one of the reasons they don't—actually what a producer told me one time is, 'We can't control you guys.'"

They'll spring the monster on you.

John Gregory Dunne: "A producer and writer were arguing vigorously against the changes the studio was demanding in a picture already in production. The president of the Disney division overseeing the picture suddenly demanded silence. He was, he said, forced by the writer's intransigence to 'take the monster out of its cage.'

"In the silence that ensued, the division president reached under the table, pretended to grab a small predatory animal from its lair, and then, as if clutching the creature by the neck in his fist, exhibited his empty, clawlike hand to the people around the table. He asked the screenwriter if he saw the monster. The writer, not knowing what else to do, nodded yes.

" 'I'm going to put it back in its cage now,' the executive said, drawing each word out, 'and I never want you to force me to bring it out again.' Then he mimed putting the monster back into its cage under the table. When he was done, the executive asked the writer, 'Do you know what the monster is?'

"The writer shook his head.

"The executive said, 'It's our money.' "

Don't let 'em tell you what to write.

I did what they said," Marilyn Monroe said, "and all it got me was a lot of abuse. Everyone's just laughing at me. I hate it. Big breasts, big ass, big deal."

They'll even try to take your brains.

Monroe Stahr, the producer in F. Scott Fitzgerald's final novel, *The Last Tycoon*: "I never thought I had more brains than a writer has. But I always thought that his brains *belonged* to me— because I knew how to use them."

Robert McKee taught him . . .

A young screenwriter who'd attended Robert McKee's screen-writing seminar sent me a script. It was about a young screen-writer who'd attended the Robert McKee seminar, hadn't learned anything, and wound up homeless in Santa Monica.

The script was awful.

It helps to know how to fight.

Screenwriter J. P. Miller said this about Paddy Chayefsky: "Paddy was an extraordinarily good human manipulator. He knew his way around a scrap as very few writers do. Most writers, if they get into a fight or a bad situation on a movie, call their agents. But Paddy knew Hollywood and he wouldn't back down. He would go head to head with anybody—and at the same time he had this incredible writer's sensitivity. That's a rare combination which many of us don't have. He was that rare breed of talent and fighter."

You don't ever need a job this badly.

During a script meeting, a producer suggested something that screenwriter William Goldman thought was "a moron point."

Goldman: "I wanted to scream so loud. I wanted to choke the asshole. But I was so sweet. I took notes. I grunted and nodded. I smiled when it was conceivably possible."

Kick 'em in their ass!

Screenwriter/novelist Raymond Chandler: "I don't care about the money. I just like to fight. I'm a tired old man, but it takes more than a motion picture studio to push me around."

Kicking ass can do you good.

Paddy Chayefsky: "I stormed and ranted. And the more I ranted, the more the studio people respected me."

I got into so many nasty fights with studio execs over my fifteen movies that the *Los Angeles Business Weekly* quoted an anonymous screenwriter as saying this about me: "At the heart of the Eszterhas phenomenon is titillation. There is a sense of danger about him, violence. For a lot of movie executives, who have no life experience, he's exciting, exotic. They get a sense of danger by being in business with him."

Clench your fists; throw a fit.

I once told a group of Disney executives in a crowded conference room to "get your hands off my dick and tell me the truth."

Billy Bob Thornton, back in his screenwriting days, leaped atop a studio executive's desk and threatened to strangle the man for ruining his script.

"Sometimes I find myself dealing unpleasantly with people," said Paddy Chayefsky, "talking to them as if they were animals."

A producer describes Chayefsky at a meeting this way: "When he was crossed, his entire body would tighten like steel. He'd scowl, clench his fists, glare, then the verbal avalanche would begin. He could level armies with that tongue of his if he didn't explode first, because his whole body would shake in a fit of apoplexy. For the most part, he looked like a monster child having a tantrum."

Pretend you're Clint Eastwood.

After seeing *The Outlaw Josey Wales,* Warner Bros. studio executive David Geffen said to director Clint Eastwood, "I only want to suggest one thing: I think it would be better if it was twenty minutes shorter."

Clint said to David, "I'm glad you took the time to see the picture, and I appreciate your comments. But why don't you study the picture some more and see if you have any more thoughts. When you do, give me a call over at Paramount."

David said to Clint, "Why over at Paramount?"

"Because that's where I'll be making my next movie," Clint said.

David said, "The picture is perfect. I wouldn't change one frame. Thank you very much."

Clint said, "Thank *you.*"

Don't ever quit a job.

If you've been hired to work on a script and you loathe the director and the producer and you feel that what you wrote is being truncated and transmogrified into dog shit, don't quit. Keep telling them that you are "ready, willing, and able to perform"—legalese right out of the contract that you signed.

If you are pleasantly intransigent, they will fire you. That's what you want. You'll be paid in full and the trades will report that because of "creative differences," you've left the project.

He was talking about Hemingway, honest, not about me.

Screenwriter/novelist Raymond Chandler: "He never really wrote but one story. All the rest is the same thing in different pants—or without different pants. And his eternal preoccupation with what goes on between the sheets becomes rather nauseating in the end. One reaches a time of life when limericks written on the walls of comfort stations are not just obscene, they are horribly dull. This man has only one subject and he makes that ridiculous. I suppose the man's epitaph, if he had the choosing of it, would be: Here Lies a Man Who Was Bloody Good in Bed. Too Bad He's Alone Here. But the point is I begin to doubt whether he ever was. You don't have to work so hard at things you are really good at—or do you?"

Our scripts turned Garbo into a recluse.

Screenwriter/playwright Mercedes de Acosta, an intimate friend of Greta Garbo, said Garbo's reclusiveness was caused by disappointment in herself "for not fighting harder for better scripts."

In other words, bad screenplays screwed Garbo up.

If you make an ass of yourself, don't make an even bigger ass out of yourself.

Screenwriter/novelist Anne Rice looked silly when she said the biggest movie star in the world at the time, Tom Cruise, was too short to play her character Lestat in *Interview with a Vampire*.

But she looked even sillier when, after seeing the film, she took a two-page ad in *Daily Variety* saying how much she had loved Cruise . . . and the film.

ALL HAIL
Ben Hecht!

Agent Swifty Lazar: "No one was better at beating the moguls at their own game than Ben Hecht. The deal I made for him with Sam Goldwyn certainly proves that he had Sam beat.

   " 'I get paid two thousand dollars per day—in cash,' Ben told me. 'I want it in hundred dollar bills on my desk, or I don't show up for work the next day. And, by the way, there's a very pretty girl who's a wonderful secretary. You've got to get her a contract while I'm still out here. She'll make a thousand a week. I know that sounds like a lot, but she's a great actress and a great typist—and I want her to have a part in the picture.'

   " 'Can she really act?' I asked.

   " '*She* thinks she can. *I* think she can. Nobody may agree with us, but I can tell you right now. I'll fight for her.' "

Don't join a writing committee.

The writing committee is a relatively new phenomenon, first seen when a few writers (very few) began getting more publicity on their films than the directors they were working with.

So the directors decided to bring not one writer on board a project, but *half a dozen*—on the theory that if there were half a dozen cooks in the kitchen, it would be obvious that the director was the auteur chef who told them what to do.

Don't do "quick job" rewrites.

These are rewrites done at the behest of the director or a studio days before a movie goes into production.

There is no time to write anything except what the director or studio tells you to write.

Screenwriter William Goldman has done many of them.

"I make a point of never reading anything I've written in these rewrites," he says.

Be respectful of those whose work you adapt for the screen.
I adapted Brian Moore's novel *The Doctor's Wife,* and on the front page of my script I wrote, "Screenplay by Joe Eszterhas, from the novel by Brian Moore."

The executive in charge of the project at United Artists, Marcia Nasatir, said to me, "In all my years in the business, I've never seen the screenwriter put the novelist's name on the title page of the script."

I did the same thing with Ira Levin's *Sliver.*

I did it because I knew that without their *novels,* without the story and characters *they* created, I wouldn't have this job of *translating* their work from book to screenplay.

This is what you do when you are asked to rewrite the last draft of Gone With the Wind.
Ben Hecht read the previous seven drafts, which had been done by different writers. He turned his rewrite in *three days* later. And he never read the novel.

Write original screenplays, not rewrites.
Director David Lean: "We want someone who has written original stories. We don't want a scriptwriter who has spent his time embroidering on other people's ideas."

The more writers on a movie, the worse it will be.
If a character has been rewritten by, say, six or eight or ten writers, that character will not have a distinctive and original voice; the voice will be a hodgepodge of a bunch of characters' voices, as each writer envisions the character *for himself.*

The actors aren't smart enough to realize that their lines are being homogenized, and directors feel that *their imprint* on the film will be more felt the more writers there are on it.

Even the Writers Guild is happy about all the writers employed—the wealth is spread, there are fewer unemployed writers, and they're all being paid handsome sums to fuck one another's work over.

Oh yeah? Then how come Premiere magazine named me one of the one hundred most powerful people in Hollywood?
Screenwriter William Goldman: "There are still a few lost souls who actually think that screenwriters have some authority. If only it were so. We have none. . . . There are lots of reasons. We're not, most of us, so terrifically talented. And we're so easy to fire—at

least half of the people in positions of authority in Hollywood know the alphabet. You don't fire composers often; editors are safe, too. But it's not unusual, despite what you see on the credits, to have two or three or eight writers write on one film script. As well as being inept and disposable, we're also, truly, disliked. Why? Because you can't make a movie without us. If it's going to be a decent flick, it better have a decent screenplay; directors know this and it drives them maaaaaaad."

Don't sprinkle their piss.

If, that is to say, the studio execs agree to kill the script they are asking you to rewrite.

If you can create a whole new plot with all new characters, then it's probably worth putting your creativity to work on the rewrite.

Otherwise, you're just being asked to pour the director's or the producer's or the studio execs' piss into the stew.

They piss into the bottle, hand it to you, and let you sprinkle it into the script however you want. But it's still piss—and it's *their* piss.

The Robert Towne award goes to . . .

I may not be the slickest screenwriter in Hollywood," said William Faulkner, "but I know how to fix a screenplay."

Faulkner rewrote Hemingway.

Everybody out here rewrites everybody else," said screenwriter William Faulkner as he adapted Ernest Hemingway's *To Have and Have Not*. Ironically, adapting the Hemingway book was Faulkner's greatest success as a screenwriter.

But I didn't rewrite Gore Vidal.

Vidal did an adaptation of Lucian Truscott's novel *Dress Gray,* which Paramount wanted me to rewrite.

I tried to explain to the Paramount executives that I wasn't comfortable rewriting Gore Vidal, but they didn't understand why not.

I didn't rewrite William Goldman, either, but I should have.

Bill wrote an original script about Ross Perot that ABC Films wanted me to rewrite.

I tried to explain to the ABC executives that I didn't feel comfortable rewriting Bill Goldman, but they didn't get it.

Time to retire, Bill.

William Goldman: "No matter how much shit you may have heard or read, movies are finally only about one thing: THE NEXT JOB."

He even capitalized those three words in a book to make sure you got the point.

It's time to get off our hands and knees.

Norman Mailer, writing to a friend in 1949: "We found us a house high above Sunset Boulevard in the hills west of Hollywood, and can see half of that horrible city that lies below us . . . the writers are walking around on their hands and knees, not knowing where their next job is coming from."

Sometimes you won't get any credit for what you've written.

Director Phillip Noyce: "Steve Zaillian wrote the script of *Patriot Games* that we shot. Uncredited, because the Writers Guild decides on credits, and they usually give it to the original writer. In this case, two of them: Peter Iliff and Donald Stewart—the guy who wrote *Missing*. Their names are on the credits, but eighty percent of what was shot was written by Steve Zaillian."

Don't break Milton Berle's rule.

Uncle Miltie said, "Don't tell jokes only the band laughs at."

I wrote a whole movie filled with esoteric in-jokes about the movie industry—*An Alan Smithee Film: Burn Hollywood Burn*.

No one understood the in-jokes. And no one went to see the movie.

Write an animated film.

Screenwriter Nicholas Kazan (*Reversal of Fortune*): "*The Incredibles* was the wittiest film of the year, as witty as *Sideways* and maybe more. There was a degree of verbal and visual wit that you just don't see anymore, that we saw in the films of the 1930s, 40s, and 50s—the good ones. They had a lot of great writers then who were allowed to write, and today there are a lot of brilliant writers who are not allowed to write—no one is interested in wit, except in animation."

Bill Goldman should have been a mailman.

Goldman: "In twenty-five years of movie work, I've never been late. I do crazy things to make that happen sometimes—once I called in and said I'd be late and asked for a week's extension, got it, then went into sleepless overdrive and turned the screenplay in by the original date. The work may stink, but it arrives."

You're not doing slave labor, are you?

Screenwriter James L. White (*Ray*): "When I started working on the *Ray* script with director Taylor Hackford, our workday would start at 9:00 A.M. and sometimes go until two in the morning. I was doing that seven days a week! We would go for stretches of a month and a half or two months, and in the last days I can recall two occasions where we would actually be up straight through for twenty-four to thirty-six hours."

When all else fails, those jealous of you will say your script doesn't "play."

That's after you've sold it for a lot of money and the studio is sending it around to directors and actors.

Some midlevel studio exec you've never met—but who is pushing some other script to be made—will say "Sure, it reads like it's brilliant. It makes sense why we bought it, but my gut is that it doesn't play."

If everyone passes on your script, he will say, "See, I told you so."

If it gets made and fails, he'll say, "I kept trying to tell all of you."

A successful screenwriter's writing schedule . . .

Screenwriters John Gregory Dunne and Joan Didion liked writing at the exclusive Kahala Hilton Hotel on Oahu.

Dunne: "Our schedule did not vary: a sunrise swim, breakfast, then four hours' work in the suite; an hour for lunch, then two more hours' work in the afternoon; another swim, then three more hours' work before a late dinner. After dinner, we went over the day's pages, then printed out a schedule of scenes for the next day."

The way to celebrate an option . . .

Screenwriter/novelist James Brown: "When an independent producer in New York options my third novel, I am excited but cautious. . . . I run out and buy an eight-ball of methamphetamine because it is cheaper and stronger than coke, a few cases of Budweiser, a half gallon of Smirnoff, Dewar's scotch, and Seagram's 7 and invite my friends over for a party. But most of them are busy for some reason and what few do show end up leaving early when I make an ass of myself."

If you make enough money to buy two houses, at least don't build your own road to reach them.

Screenwriter Albert Maltz on his friend and fellow screenwriter Dalton Trumbo: "There is no question that Trumbo had talent for much greater literary work than the film work that he produced. The reason he never did what he could have done was this obsession of his with making money and living in a grand manner. I never knew what made it necessary for him to have both a house on Beverly Drive and a ranch that he had to build a road to get to. It kept him writing, and writing, and writing, though. Why *do* writers write, after all?"

The deal every screenwriter should aspire to . . .

Yes, I did sell a four-page outline for $4 million, but . . .
      Paddy Chayefsky made a deal with a studio, which paid him $1 million for the script. They had a year to make the movie.

      If production didn't start within the year, Paddy could sell his script elsewhere . . . and keep the million dollars.

Don't think twice, it's all right.

Screenwriter William Faulkner, writing from Los Angeles to his New York agent: "Things are going pretty well. My father died last month, and what with getting his affairs straightened out and getting Hollywood out of my system by means of a judicious course of alcohol in mild though sufficient quantities before and after eating and lying down and getting up, I am not working now."

Maybe it's not all right.

At a script meeting with director Howard Hawks, screenwriter William Faulkner, who had been seen sipping earlier on a silver flask, said, "This is what I think, Howard."
      He smiled, raised his hand to make a point, fell on his face, and passed out.

Bob Towne is a big William Faulkner fan.

While waiting for executives Barry Diller and Michael Eisner to decide whether they would release his movie *Personal Best,* Bob Towne kept pouring scotch for himself from Diller's bar. He passed out on the couch before they came back into the room.

PERK OF SUCCESS: A NEW PURDY SHOTGUN

Screenwriter/director John Milius always demanded a brand-new Purdy shotgun as part of his screenwriting deals.

He told friends he needed the guns so he could arm a battalion in case it was necessary to overcome the government. Every studio making a deal with him complied. His friends say Milius could now arm a small army.

Words to live by . . .

Paddy Chayefsky's last words: "I tried. I really tried."

Don't buy a Hungarian dog.

Robert Towne did—a rare komondor, so big that it wouldn't fit into the back of his car. So Towne let the dog ride next to him in the front seat and put his wife in the back. Then he and his wife got divorced.

LESSON 6

Don't Take Your Clothes Off!

If you really want to learn about the industry . . .

Hide in a bathroom stall in the men's room of The Grille in Beverly Hills any weekday lunch hour, overhearing conversations. At the end of that time, you will have learned everything you need to know about Hollywood.

Don't obsess about getting rich.

Paddy Chayefsky: "You make a lot of money and you never get rich."

Research all celebrity auctions you may be involved in.

A man paid thousands of dollars at a celebrity auction to have lunch with me. He wanted to be a screenwriter and used the lunch to get screenwriting tips.

His name was Jerry George. He was an editor of the *National Enquirer*. I used the lunch to get celebrity tips. I asked him more questions than he asked me.

It's possible I learned more from Jerry George in that lunch than he learned from me. And it didn't cost me anything

Don't ever write a script for a movie-star couple who are allegedly in love.

It will fail.

Consider: *Shanghai Surprise* with Sean Penn and Madonna; *The Getaway* with Alec Baldwin and Kim Basinger; *Husbands and Wives* with Woody Allen and Mia Farrow; *Mortal Thoughts* with Bruce Willis and Demi Moore; *Proof of*

Life with Russell Crowe and Meg Ryan; *Made in America* with Whoopi Gold-berg and Ted Danson; *Eyes Wide Shut* and *Far and Away* with Tom Cruise and Nicole Kidman; *Bounce* with Ben Affleck and Gwyneth Paltrow; *Gigli* with Ben Affleck and Jennifer Lopez.

You, too, can live the screenwriter's life.

Hunter S. Thompson described his "workdays" in Hollywood as "Violence, joy, and constant Mexican music."

> **PERK OF SUCCESS: YOU, TOO, CAN GET MAXFIELD'S ON MELROSE TO SEND YOU A $150,000 SELECTION OF GOLD AND DIAMOND CROSSES**
>
> *If, that is, they know you've sold a lot of scripts for a lot of money. Then they'll send you their selection of crosses— wherever you are in the world—by FedEx by ten o'clock the next morning, and trust you to send the unbought crosses back to them.*

Help those who've helped you.

Marcia Nasatir was a studio executive at United Artists when she discovered me, in 1974. She had read a book that I had written, which had been nominated for the National Book Award.

As the years went by, my career as a screenwriter prospered, while Marcia had turned to the shaky world of independent production.

In 1991, after I wrote *Basic Instinct,* I was the hottest screenwriter in Holly-wood and Marcia was in New York, a producer trying to find hot scripts and put films together.

I asked if she wanted to produce my latest script with Irwin Winkler, one of the town's hottest producers. She was happy and grateful, but, unfortunately, we never got the movie I had written made.

My agent at the time said, "If you really want to say thank you to her for the help she was to you and pay her back, maybe next time you should give her a script that's not about the president of the United States having sex with a cow."

This industry is much more inbred than the music business.

Producer Don Simpson died of a heart attack while straining on the toilet. He was reading a book about Oliver Stone. (Elvis also died of a heart attack while straining on the toilet. He was reading a book about Jesus Christ.)

If you write a hit movie, don't write the sequel.

Your vision didn't include a sequel: your vision was for one story, which they are now asking you to stretch to two.

Remember that piece of rope can only stretch so far without snapping.

When MGM asked me to write the sequel to *Basic Instinct,* it was easy for me to pass: I'd get millions from a sequel whether I wrote it or not, according to my contract for *Basic Instinct.*

I had other incentives to pass, too. The studio executive in charge of the project, Lindsay Doran, told me she thought the original was "sexist" and "misogynistic" and said, "We have to figure out a way not to make the sequel like that."

I didn't remind her that the original had made nearly $500 million worldwide at the box office.

I didn't tell her that a French newsmagazine picked the release of *Basic* as *the* worldwide event of 1992—not in entertainment, but in world news.

I didn't tell her that, thanks to her attitude, I thought my characters Nick Curran and Catherine Tramell were in the hands of a *politically correct ideologue.* But I knew that any sequel they might make would be a disaster.

I'm glad I didn't write the sequel to Basic Instinct.

Written by Henry Bean and Leora Barish, it turned out to be the disaster of the year, getting reviews that made my reviews for *Showgirls* look terrific in comparison.

Typical was David Thomson's review in *The Independent on Sunday* (London): "Everyone now marks Sharon Stone down as the chump who enabled them to do the remake . . . And Sharon Stone, for the first time in her life, has been publicly disgraced. Now it is hard to see where she can go—except to the kind of roles Joan Collins played when television had soap operas."

Its opening weekend box office was $2 million—unfathomably abysmal— the numbers were similar all around the world.

Thanks to Henry Bean and Leora Barish, I finally got some damn good reviews for the original.

The trades wrote: "Part of this disaster is the fault of the abysmal script (I can't believe I'm saying this, but: Joe Eszterhas, we need you!).

The Toronto Star: "Missing in action in the sequel are Michael Douglas, director Paul Verhoeven, and writer Joe Eszterhas, who are sorely missed, as is any semblance of a coherent plot."

The Guardian (London): "The original *Basic Instinct* had style, of a barking mad sort; Eszterhas's screenplay had its own beady-eyed narrative drive."

The Denver Post: "With *Basic Instinct*, Eszterhas, the one-time writer for *Rolling Stone*, became screenwriter as rock star."

The New York *Daily News*: "Written as a fever dream by Hollywood bad boy Joe Eszterhas, the original introduced into the pantheon of femme fatales a wealthy thirty-year-old widow with degrees in literature and psychology."

The Independent (London): "Mounted on the different testosterone drives of Joe Eszterhas, Paul Verhoeven, and Michael Douglas (major league hard-ons)— *Basic Instinct* was a trash masterpiece, deliriously inventive, hatefully incorrect, and exhiliratingly sure of its bad taste."

The Weekly Standard: "Only once, really, did a genuinely filthy mainstream Hollywood picture strike it big, and that was the original *Basic Instinct*—a brilliantly made thriller in which a bisexual woman goes around San Francisco killing men with an ice pick. At one moment, *Basic Instinct* is the ultimate male fantasy about a completely uninhibited woman, while at the next it's the ultimate male nightmare about a woman so cold she would kill you as soon as look at you. It's lascivious and puritanical in equal measure, a movie that says sex will probably kill you and, what's more, you'll deserve it. But man, what a way to go. *Basic Instinct* became a sensation because it rides its mixed messages all the way to a daringly unrealized conclusion that leaves us in perpetual doubt as to who the real killer is. That playful trickery is entirely absent from the endless and lethargic sequel."

The Village Voice: "The original *Basic Instinct* was both a manifestation and a critique of sex panic, an effortless distillation of a late '80s/early '90s zeitgeist: the end of second-wave feminism, the peaking of AIDS anxieties, the dawn of the Clinton years. Stale and corny, *Basic Instinct 2* isn't even accidentally relevant."

On the other hand, some critics still want me dead.

Even though I had nothing to do with the sequel, the *Arkansas Times* wrote in its review of *Basic 2:* "It's the kind of movie that makes me wish Joe Eszterhas's mother had left a few more dry cleaning bags around when he was a kid."

Thanks to the sequel, I'm a director.

The Sunday Independent of Johannesburg, South Africa: "We all remember that famous scene—the flash—with Sharon Stone in *Basic Instinct*. It was trashy film, but Joe Eszterhas directed it with the flair born of knowing delight in trashiness."

If it's a bad movie and it fails—well, what the hell—blame it on George W. Bush.

Paul Verhoeven, who turned down a lot of money to direct *Basic*'s sequel, said this about the sequel's failure: "Anything that is erotic has been banned in the United States."

Did you know they paid me homage in Basic Instinct 2?

That's what a critic said, discussing a scene in the film where someone is reading a Hungarian-language primer.

I don't think that the critic knew that one of the movie's producers was Hungarian, as was the cinematographer. And the producer's girlfriend had a small part.

So the Hungarian homage may have been addressed to *all* the Hungarians making the film, an homage made by Hungarians to Hungarians, dancing merrily off the sinking ship.

I did not pleasure myself . . . , I swear I didn't. . . .

Reviewing *Basic Instinct 2* in *The Weekly Standard,* John Podhoretz wrote: "The only person who'll enjoy this travesty is the exiled Eszterhas, who'll no doubt be pleasuring himself as his pagan goddess thuds to earth."

Yeah, okay, but she's still got chutzpah.

After the failure of the sequel, Sharon Stone announced that she would direct either another sequel or a *Basic Instinct* television series.

A producer friend told me, "What happened to the sequel says nobody even wants to see her pussy anymore, let alone her movies."

Beware of quisling screenwriters.

Notice how often critics and film journalists write that such and such a screenwriter worked on a film, doing an uncredited polish or rewrite.

The critics and journalists are leaked this information by the director or the studio. The screenwriters they plug are either the director's friends or the studio's lackeys.

The reason the names of these screenwriters are leaked to the press is to take credit *away* from those writers who *really wrote* the script and who may have gotten into defiant creative disagreements with the director or the studio.

Don't take a screenwriting course in Cleveland, Ohio, either.

Bob Noll teaches screenwriting at both John Carroll University and the Cleveland Play House. His credits? Producer and co-director of the local weekly children's show *Hickory Hideout* on Cleveland's Channel 3.

He was also a child actor and worked in local theater.

His advice about how to write a good script?

"Step one: Put a character in a tree. Step two: Shake the tree and let loose ravenous animals to prowl beneath it. Step three: Get the character out of the tree—survival optional."

Sometimes everything goes wrong on your movie.

Director Phillip Noyce, on *Sliver*: "On *Sliver* I just became so tired I couldn't get off the floor. I had to have doctors constantly injecting me with vitamins. I was trying to give up smoking at the time and I don't think I was all that stable myself, as I had been inhaling up to six packs a day previously. . . . I was terribly addicted and had decided to give up before *Sliver*. This probably wasn't a good idea for my equilibrium. But every day of pressure on the *Sliver* set caused bad nicotine-induced panic attacks, so the chaos of the whole thing was not something I could blame on others. The film had become a Hollywood nightmare—with a producer [Robert Evans] who, from the beginning, had dreamt of his movie being directed by someone else, a writer [Joe Eszterhas] who had abandoned a best-selling novel to pen his own version of the story, an actress [Sharon Stone] who I couldn't communicate with and who loathed her co-star and producer, and a cinematographer [Vilmos Zsigmond] who was creating beautiful images at a snail's pace, on a set that made more noise than the actors when they spoke their lines. At night I dreamt of turning up at a schoolboy rugby match and then running onto the field only to discover I'd left my football boots at home. I'd wake with a deep sense of dread. Facing another day at the factory that filmmaking had become."

Never mind all that, the real reason Sliver failed.

Two of the key elements (screenwriter and cinematographer) were Hungarian.

Time is your best ally.

When *Betrayed* was released in 1988, the critics said it was "an unrealistic apocalyptic vision."

Just a few years later, neo-Nazi Timothy McVeigh, the spittin' image of the Tom Berenger character in *Betrayed*, blew up the federal courthouse in Oklahoma City.

When *Showgirls* was released in 1995, critics said it "maligned and libeled" Las Vegas, "a place of family values."

Just a few years later, Vegas casinos were playing topless stage shows and casino buses were taking tourists to lap-dance bars.

If you get lucky, you'll find partners.

I hooked up with three directors twice: with Richard Marquand on *Jagged Edge* and *Hearts of Fire*; with Costa-Gavras on *Betrayed* and *Music Box*; with Paul Verhoeven on *Showgirls* and *Basic Instinct*.

I hooked up with the producer Irwin Winkler (*Rocky, Raging Bull*) four times: on *Betrayed, Music Box, Basic Instinct* (he was replaced by Alan Marshall), and *Sacred Cows* (unproduced).

ALL HAIL
Harlan Ellison!

The screenwriter/author claimed that the script of *The Terminator* was a rip-off of both a novelette and a TV script that he had written. He sued and won.

After he won, he bought a full-page ad in the trades, which said, "The film acknowledges the works of Harlan Ellison."

Use Frank as your role model.

I was appearing as myself in *An Alan Smithee Film: Burn Hollywood Burn,* and Arthur Hiller, the director, did two takes and wanted to do more.

I said no, that two were enough, then got up and walked off the set.

Arthur gaped, but what could he do? I wasn't going back to do any more takes.

I learned that from Sinatra. Frank did two takes—no matter who the director was—and no more.

Can you be a person of integrity as a screenwriter?

Screenwriter/novelist Raymond Chandler: "All progress in the art of the screenplay depends on a very few people who are in a position to fight for excellence. Hollywood loves them for it and is only too anxious to reward them by making them something else than writers. Hollywood's attitude to writers is necessarily conditioned by the mass of its writers, not by the few who have what it calls integrity. It loves the word, having so little of the quality."

Keep everything close to your vest.

Producer David Merrick once got a phone call telling him his building would be blown up in two minutes. He told no one else, ran out of his office, yelled, "Take any messages!" to his assistant, then scurried to the elevator and out of the building.

Hit 'em back.

When MPAA president Jack Valenti told people that I was "desperately ill and needed immediate medical attention," I reminded people that Jack Valenti was the White House aide who briefed Lyndon Johnson in the West Wing bathroom each morning and handed him the toilet paper under the stall before he got his gig at the MPAA.

If they kick the living shit out of you, smile and say, "Is that the best you've got?"

I won the Hollywood Women's Press Association's Sour Apple Award—following in the footsteps of Norman Mailer and Howard Stern . . . for acting boorishly and believing my own publicity.

When I received the award at the Beverly Hilton Hotel, I said this:

"Mel Gibson said that if I came here to accept this award, I should wear a bulletproof vest. I've brought my wife with me instead. I pity any potential assassin who may be lurking here. Naomi keeps a riding crop next to our bed, you know.

"I know that this award is given for believing your own publicity and I thought what I'd do here today is share some of my recent publicity with you. I'm doing it, of course, so that you will have no lingering doubt in your minds that you have given this award to the right person.

"The Portland *Oregonian* said about me: 'He is an imbecilic ape of a screenwriter.'

"*Time* magazine said, 'His movie is ludicrous, he can't write.'

"*The Boston Globe* said, 'He types, he doesn't write, and if the stories about his manual typewriter are accurate, he can't type very well, either.'

"A small-town paper in Florida said, 'He is the overwriter—overweight and overpaid.'

"*The Miami Herald* said, 'It's hard to believe this is the same man who wrote *Music Box* and *Betrayed*. With age, his brains seem to have lowered gravitationally to another part of his anatomy.'

"Ladies and gentlemen, allow me to thank you. I am proud of you for giving this award to a screenwriter instead of Jim Carrey, the actor who was my main competing candidate. This is a landmark day for screenwriters! Good Lord, I have defeated the biggest movie star in the world!

"Eat your heart out, Jim. The apple is mine!"

You'll need some K-Y jelly.

Producer Robert Evans: "You've gotta scare the piss out of 'em to close a deal. You've gotta make 'em feel that if they don't do the deal, you've got somebody waiting in the wings who will. Fear is the K-Y jelly that gets the fucking done. Without that jelly, the deals don't close."

Mark Twain, Homer, and Shakespeare were in the same boat you're in.

Novelist/screenwriter Raymond Chandler: "No writer in any age ever got a blank check. He always had to accept some conditions imposed from without, respect certain taboos, try to please certain people. It might have been the church, or a rich patron, or a generally accepted standard of elegance, or the commercial wisdom of a publisher or an editor, or perhaps even a set of political theories. If he did not accept them, he revolted against them. In either case they conditioned his writing. No writer ever wrote exactly what he wanted to write, because there was never anything inside himself, anything purely individual that he did want to write. It's all reaction of one sort or another."

Thank God for television.

Mike Medavoy: "The audience certainly recognizes a second-rate product when it sees it. It ought to: it grew up watching second-rate stuff on television."

Don't become a complete cynic.

Have a touch of cynicism, but only a touch," wrote Raymond Chandler. "The complete cynic is as useless to Hollywood as he is to himself. He should be scrupulously honest about his work, but he should not expect scrupulous honesty in return. He won't get it."

Some people might begrudge you your success.

When he heard that *Time* magazine was thinking of putting producer Robert Evans on its cover, studio chief Frank Yablans said to Evans, "If you're on the cover of *Time* without me, I will make each hour of each day of each week that you're here so miserable you'll be sorry you're alive."

Help those who've helped you.

Two young guys wrote a script that was butchered by the director and the studio. The producer stuck up for the writers but couldn't protect them from the director and the studio.

The script that was butchered was called *Assassins,* starring Sylvester Stallone and Antonio Banderas. The screenwriters were Larry and Andy Wachowski. The producer was Joel Silver.

Because Joel Silver stuck up for them, Larry and Andy gave him their next script. It was called *The Matrix.*

P.S. *Assassins* was a disaster.

This can metaphorically happen to you.

At first I was shocked," Marilyn Monroe said. "I hadn't been around enough to know what was going on. He had a suit on, so I didn't think he could hurt me. When I started thinking about a new dress I wanted and couldn't afford, well ... I was pretty drunk, too, so I said okay. I still wasn't sure what he wanted to do. He asked me to take off my clothes. I thought that was a pretty good deal for fifteen dollars."

PERK OF SUCCESS: YOU, TOO, CAN GET THE BEST TABLE AT SPAGO

I do, sometimes on only an hour's notice. And Wolfgang always comes over to my table and often he even sits down. Hallelujah!

We even had dinner together while vacationing in Hawaii. He even gave me career advice: "Don't ever turn your back on Michael Ovitz! He never forgets."

Wolfgang is a good guy. He has the same respect for screenwriters that he has for directors and movie stars—as long as they've all had some hit movies.

Leni Riefenstahl smiled in her grave.

The Writers Guild gave its Best Original Screenplay award to the liberal propagandist Michael Moore for his script of *Bowling for Columbine,* a documentary.

In other words, Moore didn't write it; he interviewed people and edited what *they* said into a political polemic.

Memo to Michael Moore.

Old Hollywood saying: "If you want to write a message, use Western Union."

Don't let anyone impugn your integrity . . . not even Farrah Fawcett.

In the book *American Rhapsody,* I wrote that Farrah Fawcett pooped on the front lawn at a party she was attending. In an interview with a New York gossip columnist, Farrah denied it. I wrote the gossip columnist a note:

"I sure don't see why she's denying it. In an interview in the September *Movieline* magazine she said, 'If I'm on location in the woods and my trailer is miles away, I will go to the bathroom in the bushes. There's no way my makeup lady would do that, for instance, but that's who I am.' Farrah clearly loves nature; she is, after all, a country girl from Texas.

"Let me say in defense of Farrah that we've all been in situations like that. It's tough when nature calls so rudely. As they say in Ohio, where I'm from, 'When you gotta go, you gotta go.' I remember nearly causing an international incident once—when I asked a limo to pull over between Tel Aviv and Jerusalem and took a hike into a field.

"Also, this party where nature called Farrah so rudely was held at the agent Arnold Rifkin's house. I was at a party on another occasion at that house and I remember my wife, who was very pregnant at the time, had to use the bathroom. But the bathroom was locked. Some sniffling people were having a lengthy Hollywood conference in there. So I certainly understand the same thing could have happened to Farrah. Some sniffling people may have been having a lengthy Hollywood conference in the bathroom and Farrah couldn't get in there and nature called."

A pratfall is better than a kiss.

If you want to write a hit movie . . .

Remember screenwriter Preston Sturges's (*The Power and the Glory, Strictly Dishonorable*) eleven rules for writing a hit movie:

1. A pretty girl is better than an ugly one.
2. A leg is better than an arm.
3. A bedroom is better than a living room.
4. An arrival is better than a departure.
5. A birth is better than a death.
6. A chase is better than a chat.

7. A dog is better than a landscape.

8. A kitten is better than a dog.

9. A baby is better than a kitten.

10. A kiss is better than a baby.

11. A pratfall is better than anything.

Don't write a script set in a jungle.

Actors will avoid your script. Actor Christopher Walken: "Just a month ago I shot in a place in Hawaii where they made *Jurassic Park*. I mean, I didn't know there was a place like that: it was so pristine. . . . But I'll tell you, I would have to really need money to do another jungle movie. I'm never going back to the jungle. It's a nightmare. Getting up at night and turning on the light in the bathroom? You see lots of, you know, scary things. I'm never going back."

They were honorable hookers.

During the blacklist, screenwriters like Dalton Trumbo sometimes wrote ten scripts a year under pseudonyms for relatively little amounts of money.

Because it was so difficult for them to get work, they did what Trumbo did. Trumbo agreed to rewrite and rewrite until the producer was "satisfied"—no matter how many drafts the producer wanted him to do and no matter *what* the producer wanted him to write.

Trumbo didn't care. He just wrote what he was told to write.

Since this became somewhat common practice during the blacklist, some producers ever since have expected "their writers" to write this way. If you're ever asked to do this, tell your producer you want to check it out with your lawyer.

You're a bust-out loser if you do this.

Dalton Trumbo: "In order to earn what I do earn I have felt compelled to make a policy of absolutely guaranteeing my work. Thus I may rewrite a script three or four times. Certainly it's not worth it for the one fee involved, but the man comes back if he gets this kind of service, and thus I am assured of a continuing income."

Those old lefty screenwriters really were hacks.

Screenwriter Dalton Trumbo: "I am obliged to warn you in advance that an original screenplay, designed for sale on the local market, involves a combination of prose and conviction and sentimentality that appalls even me, who am used to it, and would appall you even more. The only thing which makes it possible for a self-respecting writer to engage in such an enterprise is that the story is never published, and is read only by Hollywood."

Those old lefty screenwriters had some big balls, too.

Dalton Trumbo: "And so it chanced in Hollywood that each blacklisted writer, after swiftly describing that long parabola from the heart of the motion picture industry to a small house in a low-rent district, picked himself up, dusted his trousers, anointed his abrasions, looked around for a ream of clean white paper and something to deface it with, and began to write. Through secret channels, and by means so cunning that they may never be revealed, what we wrote was passed along until finally it appeared on a producer's desk, and the producer looked upon it and found it good, and moneys were paid, and the writer's children began contentedly to eat. Thus the black market."

Free at last, free at last.

Blacklisted screenwriter Dalton Trumbo, writing to a friend: "Perhaps I should not be as angry as I am against the weaklings, cravens, and liars who have succeeded in banning me from motion pictures. For I feel a sense of relief and a sense of buoyancy at no longer being an employee, at no longer being under the absolute necessity of earning, say, $75,000 a year. I'm sure I should never have had the courage—or perhaps one should say foolhardiness—to have left it voluntarily. My feeling now—as of today, that is, with the hope of succeeding elsewhere still strong in me—[is] that I shall never return to films, that if Metro asked me back tomorrow with all forgiven, I should refuse. Hunger, of course, could in time alter that decision. But for the present it stands."

There are no heroes.

Said agent Ingo Preminger: "Nobody used blacklisted writers for the sake of giving them a chance, or for being interested in justice—everybody—whether it was Kirk Douglas with *Spartacus* or my brother Otto with *Exodus*—they all did it for business reasons. These blacklisted writers were bargains. You go to a bargain sale and the blacklist was a bargain."

My friend Phillip Noyce is part of a vast Commie conspiracy.

When he read the script of his novel *Patriot Games*, author Tom Clancy faxed the producer, expressing his belief that "Hollywood was under siege from Communist infiltrators."

Said director Phillip Noyce: "As soon as Clancy read the script he sent us a massive fax accusing us of running some sort of Hollywood, left-wing, liberal fellow-traveling club."

If your film wins an Oscar, they'll probably "forget" to thank you.

On *Forrest Gump,* everyone involved with the film who went up onstage forgot to thank the man whose novel it was based on: Winston Groom.

And on *American Beauty,* the director and the star forgot to thank the man who wrote the original screenplay, Alan Ball.

An Oscar is a pain in the . . .

Steven Spielberg, his Oscar in hand: "You know what gets tired? You think it's your legs that'll get tired, but it's not. It's your arm. Your arm gets tired holding it."

Listen up, Michael Moore.

Paddy Chayefsky said this when accepting an Academy Award: "I would like to say, personal opinion, of course, that I'm sick and tired of people exploiting the Academy Awards for the propagation of their own personal propaganda. I would like to suggest to Miss Vanessa Redgrave that her winning an Academy Award is not a pivotal moment in history, does not require a proclamation, and a simple 'Thank you' would have sufficed."

If you're walking down a red carpet and the paparazzi are taking your picture.

Goldie Hawn: "Just turn your head and smile, but don't stop. Never stop."

At least your script can't get flashlighted.

Until a few years ago, at Academy screenings for best documentary, committee members voted with flashlights. If, at any given point, three-quarters of the flashlights in the room were on, the documentary was stopped and shitcanned.

Make sure you've really won the Oscar before you go up there to get it.

Will Rogers, host of the 1933 Academy Awards, announced best director by saying, "Come on up and get it, Frank!" Frank Capra got up and was on his way to the stage when he realized that the award was Frank Lloyd's.

Make 'em use their rubber bullets.

The Academy Award producers have a serious contingency plan in case someone flips out up there in front of 600 million people and won't stop talking.

They begin with blinding spotlights and end with rubber bullets—really.

His nomination got Trey Parker laid.

Screenwriter Trey Parker: "I was in a strip club in Vegas at four o'clock this morning. I was pretty fucked up, but I do remember looking at a stripper and yelling, 'Hey, you wanna go with me to the Academy Awards nominee lunch tomorrow?' And she looked down and yelled 'Sure!'"

If you desperately want an Oscar . . .

Three statuettes ripped off in the late 1990s were never recovered by police. They're out there somewhere—all you need are connections.

If you win an Oscar, display it proudly.

Screenwriter Ben Hecht used his as a doorstop in his home in Nyack, New York.

If you're not nominated for an Oscar . . .

Hungarian composer Béla Bartók said, "Competitions are for horses, not men."

I've never been nominated for an Oscar, but . . .

Jon Bon Jovi asked me to fly to Budapest, Hungary, with him and introduce the band onstage in the Hungarian language. And Sam Kinison dedicated a CD to me.

It's a bird, it's a plane, it's a screenplay!

At the sixty-sixth Academy Awards, a screenwriter hired an airplane that towed a banner behind it proclaiming WORLD'S FUNNIEST SCRIPT, along with a phone number.

It didn't do him any good. The script remains unsold.

PART THREE

GETTING READY TO
WRITE THE SCRIPT

LESSON 7

Avoid the Woodpecker!

Inhale a writer you admire.

K nowing nothing about writing a play, Paddy Chayefsky taught himself playwriting by sitting down at the typewriter and copying Lillian Hellman's *The Children's Hour* word for word.

He said, "I studied every line of it and kept asking myself, Why did she write this particular line?"

WRITE WHAT YOU KNOW . . . F.I.S.T.

I grew up on the west side of Cleveland among working-class folks, many of whose parents were involved in the union struggles of the 1930s and 1940s.

The first script I wrote was called F.I.S.T. and was about a union's struggles in the thirties and forties.

Do your research . . .
BASIC INSTINCT

*When I was a police reporter in Cleveland, I knew a cop
who was also a television cameraman on his days off.
He'd been involved in several police shootings. He craved
action. He couldn't stand to be away from the scene, even
on his days off, which is why he did the cameraman gig.
He liked it too much. He got sucked too close to the flame.
I remembered him twenty years later when I wrote the
burned-out cop Nick Curran, who got sucked too close to
the flame in* Basic Instinct.

ALL HAIL
The Old Macho Bastard!

Selznick told Ernest Hemingway that, as an homage to him, he
would give him fifty thousand dollars from the profits of *A
Farewell to Arms,* even though that was not in the contract.

Hemingway wrote him a note back, telling him that since
Selznick's forty-one-year-old wife was playing Hemingway's
twenty-four-year-old Catherine Barkley, any profit on the movie
was unlikely.

But if a miracle somehow occurred and the movie did go
into profit, Hemingway told Selznick, he could change the fifty
grand into nickels . . . and shove them up his ass . . . until they
came out his ears.

High Concept

The best high-concept definition of a film I've ever heard is producer Robert Evans's description of his film *The Cotton Club*: "Gangsters, music, pussy."

Don't pitch a story; write it.

Don't sit there like Willy Loman with a roomful of imbeciles who see shoe salesmen pitching their wares all day. If you do this, you'll demean yourself and it will harm your creativity.

If you really believe in your story, believe in it enough not just to chatter about it but to sit down and *do the hard work and write it.*

It is the only honest way to sell a script. With a pitch, you're trying to convince the studio that you *will* write a good script. Instead, *just write the good script.*

If they buy it, chances are good that they will piss in it less . . . because it's all done and ready to be cast and produced.

And, too, if it's already written and ready to go, they will pay you more for it than as a "pitch"—especially if you can get other studios interested in buying it.

One of the reasons I've made so much money on my scripts through the course of my career is that most of my sales have been scripts I just sat down and wrote and then sold . . . instead of "pitching" them to the imbeciles.

Real writers sit down and write: wannabe writers sit around and talk.

In a town full of cons, writing a spec script is an act of integrity.

It's the honest way to go for both you and the studios you are trying to sell it to.

As a spec script, something that you have already written in toto for no compensation, it's right there in front of your potential buyers. You're not selling them a hustle: your promise in a pitch meeting that you'll write and your promise *how* you'll write it.

You're selling the thing itself—boom!—it's right there on the table, take it or leave it.

It's the most honest way for you to deal with *you,* too. You can sell it to a whole *bunch* of possible buyers in a script auction instead of the one or two you'd pitch it to. If you get two or more wannabe buyers bidding against each other, the sky is your limit.

I sold *Basic Instinct* for $3 million because every production entity in town except one was bidding on it.

The greatest fun in screenwriting is *not* getting paid a lot of money . . . and it's certainly no fun trying to hustle the Neanderthal who doesn't even read and barely watches movies into being impressed with your pitch; the great fun in screenwriting is writing your first draft without anyone else's ideas cluttering or polluting it. Just you and your muse and the empty page or blank screen. Creating. Playing God.

Why would you turn down being God for playing Willy Loman selling his shoes to an imbecile studio exec?

Pitching your script can hurt your writing.

Director David Lean: "These American screenwriters really frighten me. They talk so well and write so badly. I have now worked with five of them, and not one has come along with a big original idea. We *need* an original idea. Hence my fright."

There is no risk to writing a spec script.

Not selling it is not a risk.

I didn't sell several—*Magic Man, Blaze of Glory, Platinum*—but by writing each one I got better at writing scripts; I learned form and structure on each one. It was like going to school.

And even though no one bought those unsold-at auction scripts, a lot of people read them and admired them—which is how many years later I sold *Magic Man* (I retitled it *Telling Lies in America*). A producer who'd read it during the failed auction recommended it to a young director, who fell in love with it.

Ron Bass is Willy Loman.

Screenwriter Ron Bass (*Rain Man*): "I was sitting with David Madden [a studio executive] and I was pitching him. At the beginning, I used to have fifty different ideas, a carpetbag; I would go and I would pitch six or eight things at a time. I pitched him, over the course of a day, about six or seven ideas and two different main ideas. . . . I work in this very strange way where I book myself way, way, way ahead. I'm usually booked for two or three years in advance; that's the way I work. I have a lot of things going at the same time. I'm usually writing six or seven things at the same time, different drafts at different stages."

Here comes the woodpecker!

One studio exec gave writers three minutes to pitch their stories. He had an aluminum pole in his office with a woodpecker on top of it. When the writer began the pitch, the exec prodded the woodpecker and it made its way down the pole—hammering away loudly with its beak—as the writer chattered on about his idea. The woodpecker got to the bottom of the pole exactly three minutes later, when the writer had to finish his pitch.

You don't want to do your work at a urinal.

Ben Hecht walked into a restaurant rest room and found Sam Goldwyn standing at a urinal. Ben stood at the next urinal and pitched Sam a story. Goldwyn had prostate problems, so Ben had a long time to pitch. When Sam finally shook off, he told Ben he'd buy it for $125,000.

Don't become "a good meeting."

John Gregory Dunne: "Screeenwriters known in Hollywood as 'good meetings' are those with the gift of schmoozing an idea so successfully—as if getting that idea down on paper was only a matter of some incidental typing—that studio executives pressed development funds on them."

Don't listen to morons like this.

In his book *Screenwriting from the Heart: The Technique of the Character-Driven Screenplay* (the reading line of which describes it as "An Indispensable Guide to Developing Dramatic and Passionate Screenplays Based on Compelling Characters"), Professor James Ryan writes: "To begin a pitch you should first lure someone with a tease, such as 'Did you ever think what it must be like to have sex with someone in your office? It doesn't just happen in the Oval Office. Maybe your girlfriend has dumped you and you are hurt and vulnerable, or maybe you found out that your lover is two-timing you.' The pitch then continues to the story.... You may notice that I tied the tease to the current events of that time in the Oval Office.... However trite it may seem, it's good strategy. Giving a pitch ... is about being simple and *shameless* in your effort to grab the listener's suggestion."

Always go to a pitch meeting with a witness.

Try to convince your agent or your agent's assistant to accompany you. If you can't convince them, go with a friend, whom you should call your "writing partner."

They will be less likely to rip you off if they know you had a witness in the room—and if they do rip you off, you can go to court with a chance to win.

Who is this goofball?

Professor James Ryan in *Screenwriting from the Heart*: "A pro-ducer asked me to take the concept of the film *The Man Who Came to Dinner* and change it into *The Woman Who Came to Din-ner*. He had a producing deal with a well-known actress and thought this screenplay would provide an excellent vehicle for her talent. Written by the Epstein Brothers, *The Man Who Came to Din-ner* was based on the Kaufman-Hart play about a pompous New York critic, Monty Wooley, who accidentally slips on ice, breaks his leg, and is forced to stay with a midwestern family during his re-covery, driving them crazy with his arrogance and grandiosity. At the time we were pitching this project in Hollywood, *Jurassic Park* had just opened and everyone was taken with its blockbuster suc-cess. When we sat down to discuss the project with a studio execu-tive, my producer introduced me in this way: 'James has a really great story to tell you. Just like *Jurassic Park*, this story is about a di-nosaur that descends upon an unsuspecting midwestern town.'"

Take notes for yourself after a pitch meeting.

Describe what you pitched, what you said, and what those in the room said to you. Be very detailed about everyone who was in the room.

Then mail these notes to your lawyer, keeping, of course, a copy for yourself.

Bill Goldman and I agree on something.

William Goldman: "I have only tried one 'pitch' in my life and that was for friends, and I was so awful I quit halfway through."

Send those that you've pitched an e-mail.

The e-mail should begin by saying how much you enjoyed the meeting, and end by detailing everything that you said and that they said.

Yes, of course they will know why you sent the note, but it will make it less likely that they will steal your ideas.

Pukeheads

A studio exec's term for those screenwriters who are nervous doing a pitch.

WRITE WHAT YOU KNOW . . .
MUSIC BOX

As an immigrant kid in Cleveland, I played with kids whose fathers were raving anti-Semites and whom other Hungarians in Cleveland were calling "war criminals."

Many years later, I wrote a script called Music Box about a Hungarian-American lawyer who defends her father against criminal charges for activities back in Hungary during World War II.

DO YOUR RESEARCH . . . BASIC
INSTINCT

One night when I was a young man, I was with a girl I'd picked up at a go-go bar in Dayton, Ohio. She was one of the dancers.

We went to a hotel and, after what we'd done what we went there to do, she pulled a cute little .22-caliber revolver on me and asked if I had any real good reason why she shouldn't pull the trigger, considering the way her life was going and considering how used she felt at that moment.

She told me I wouldn't be the first guy she'd pulled the trig-
ger on, and I believed her . . . and somehow talked her out of
pulling it on me.

When I was writing Basic Instinct *many years later in a*
little room of my house in San Rafael, California, I remem-
bered the girl in that hotel room in Dayton, Ohio.

If you've pitched a story and they want you to give them an outline . . .

Fudge. I do this all the time. I explain in the first paragraph of the outline that it isn't an outline. It is a document containing "notes in the direction of a story."

This wording gives you a legalistic out in case your script doesn't reflect what is in the outline that isn't an outline.

Don't talk your story away.

Keep what you're writing to yourself. Don't expend the energy you'll need to write it by talking your story instead, telling friends in bars, restaurants, and beds what you're working on.

I've heard too many good stories from screenwriters who talked but never wrote them. I've come to the conclusion that your characters get angry at you if you speak about them . . . and stop you from giving birth to them on the page in revenge.

Remember: Real writers sit down and write; wannabe writers sit around and talk.

Screenwriter Robert Towne is famous in Hollywood for talking terrific scripts that never get written. Towne even had an agent once who heard so many brilliant and unwritten scripts from Towne that he started writing their plot summaries down. He proposed to Towne that they form a production company together and assign the unwritten Towne stories to other writers. Towne, horrified that his agent was taking notes about what he was telling him, fired the agent instead.

There is another reason not to tell anyone what you are writing. It isn't as likely that you'll be ripped off if you stay mum. Rip-offs are common in Hollywood; some of the town's most successful writers have plagiarized. A screenwriter won an Academy Award by ripping off a novel written by one of his college professors; the studio paid a hefty six-figure sum to settle the suit.

Write your script; don't schmooze your producer.

Producer David Geffen, discussing screenwriter Robert Towne: "Bob was a very talented writer, although an extraordinarily boring man. He always talked about himself. He used to go to Catalina to write and would describe to you in endless detail watching the cows shit."

She wouldn't have liked Bob Towne.

Hedy Lamarr: "In my experiences with writers, I found that those who talk less are more talented. I sat a whole evening with Otto Preminger and Tennessee Williams and Mr. Williams said just ten words."

It's okay to plagiarize yourself.

Ben Hecht based his 1958 film, *The Fiend Who Walked the West,* starring a young Robert Evans, on his 1947 hit film, *Kiss of Death*, starring Richard Widmark.

I based my 1983 film, *Flashdance,* on the Dutch film *Spetters,* directed by Paul Verhoeven. Then I based my 1995 film, *Showgirls,* directed by Paul Verhoeven, on *Flashdance.*

It might be fair then to say that my friend Paul Verhoeven was the creative spark behind both *Flashdance* and *Showgirls.* I'm certainly happy he didn't direct *Flashdance,* though, because he probably would have had an affair with Jennifer Beals, and Lord knows how *Flashdance* would have turned out.

You can rob yourself blind.

Raymond Chandler did it all the time, turning sketches into short stories, stories into novels, and novels into screenplays.

As he said, "I am the copyright owner. I can use my material in any way I see fit. There is no moral or ethical issue involved."

Chandler was once lambasted for plagiarizing himself—by a reader named E. Howard Hunt who, twenty years later, was one of the burglars involved in the Watergate break-in.

Hunt obviously didn't have any issues with someone stealing from *other* people.

Eugene O'Neill plagiarized Raymond Chandler . . . or did Raymond Chandler plagiarize Eugene O'Neill?

My ideas have been plagiarized," wrote Raymond Chandler. "Throughout the play *The Iceman Cometh* O'Neill uses the expression "The Big Sleep" as a synonym for death. He is apparently under the impression that this is a current underworld or half-world usage, whereas it is a pure invention on my part. If I am re-membered long enough, I shall probably be accused of stealing the phrase from O'Neill, since he is a big shot."

I swear I wasn't influenced by reading Hungarian plays.
Orson Welles said, "Every Hungarian play is plagiarized from another Hungarian play."

Write what you know . . .
TELLING LIES IN AMERICA

I went to a Catholic high school in Cleveland, where I was the victim of a great deal of prejudice because I was an immigrant and because I was poor. I dreamed of overcoming all that animosity and becoming an American writer one day.

Thirty years later, I wrote Telling Lies in America, *the story of a kid at a Catholic high school in Cleveland who is the victim of a great deal of prejudice because he is an immigrant and because he is poor. He dreams of overcoming the marginalization and being a famous American writer someday.*

Do your research . . .
FLASHDANCE

I researched a script about pipeline welders for a script about the Alaska pipeline. The script, called Rowdy, *was never made into a film.*

Four years later, I used all the research I had done about the pipeline for the young woman that I made a welder in Flashdance.

The most important part of what you write is what will be left out.

"The hell of good film writing," Raymond Chandler wrote, "is that the most important part is left out. It's left out because the camera and the actors can do it better and quicker, above all quicker. But it had to be there in the beginning."

WRITE WHAT YOU KNOW . . .
CHECKING OUT

In my midthirties, I suddenly began experiencing panic and anxiety attacks, during which I felt I was going to die. I wrote a script—Checking Out—about a man who begins having anxiety and panic attacks and is convinced he is going to die.

After I wrote the film, I stopped having the attacks. I had cured myself with my own writing.

When the movie failed both critically and commercially, I had a couple more attacks.

The "asshole guy" might read your script.

By writing screenplays for Hollywood production, you are writing for studio executives who don't read anything, except maybe their readers' summaries about scripts.

Oh, they might skim through *Vanity Fair* to see the new chichi Prada and Dolce ads. But they don't read books or scripts. They are about as illiterate as most people who want to write scripts . . . as illiterate, maybe, as *you*.

Some go to the greatest lengths to avoid reading. I know a studio exec who gives the comedies his reader says he should read to his wife's gynecologist and the dramas to his own proctologist.

I know another illiterate exec who's made everyone believe that he's got dyslexia; consequently, he has his assistants tape a script (even then he will sometimes fast-forward through it).

The fact that most studio execs don't read books or even scripts isn't good news . . . if you want to write a literate and literary script that the critics would praise but no one would see.

If, however, you want to write a script of a movie that everyone would see, like *Basic Instinct* and *Jagged Edge* and *Flashdance*, then these semi-illiterate and illiterate studio execs might be your perfect first audience.

Write what you fear . . .
BIG SHOTS

While I was having my panic attacks, I worried what would happen to my ten-year-old son, Steve, if I died. So I sat down and wrote a script called Big Shots, which is about a ten-year-old boy who loves his father very much and whose father dies.

When they were about to film the script, the producer met my son Steve and wanted to cast him in the film as the kid whose father dies. I stopped it because I was afraid that if Steve played the kid whose father died, then I might die.

When Steve graduated from high school, I gave him the Rolex Submariner that I always wore, and which was featured in the movie. It was the watch that the fictional kid always wanted and which he got after his father died.

I felt odd giving Steve the watch . . . since I was very much alive.

You'll probably be rewritten.

In some ways, this has always been the case in Hollywood. Witness what F. Scott Fitzgerald said during his Hollywood years: "If one writer on a picture is good, ten are ten times better."

I was very fortunate in this regard: Of my fifteen films, I had sole credit on nine.

Francis Ford Coppola caused the carpet bombing of Cambodia.

The night before American fighters carpet-bombed Cambodia, Richard Nixon watched *Patton* in the White House over and over again.

Paddy Chayefsky got Arnold elected.

Thanks to his line—"I'm mad as hell, and I'm not going to take this anymore!"—Arnold Schwarzenegger was elected governor of California.

James Cameron has blood on his hands, too.

"H asta la vista, baby!" Cameron wrote in *The Terminator*. It, too, became a slogan of Arnold's gubernatorial campaign.

WRITE WHAT YOU KNOW . . .
BETRAYED

I attended every one of my son Steve's Little League games and found racist and anti-Semitic epithets carved into some of the grandstands—in liberal Marin County, northern California.

I wrote a script about the rise of neo-Nazis in America, Betrayed.

It was filmed in Lethbridge, Canada, and one day during filming, missing Steve, I wandered down to a local field and watched some Little Leaguers play a game. And I noticed that the grandstand I was watching the game from had the same kind of anti-Semitic epithets on it that I had seen in Marin County.

Don't try to discover the hot new thing.

M ike Medavoy: "I'm always suspicious of the hot new thing. You can really get burned attempting to make films like the ones that worked last month or last year."

Write what your heart tells you to write.

I t might lead you nowhere. I've always loved old-timey honky-tonk country music . . . Ernest Tubb and Hank and Ray Price and George Jones.

I decided one day that I was going to put my love of real country music up on the big screen. I wrote an old-timey country musical, called *The Honky-Tonk Opera,* which was more a stage musical than a movie. Once I had the script written, I didn't know what to do with it. For one thing, somebody would have to write the music—all I had were the words.

I sent the script to Tom Ross, who had been the head of CAA's music division. He loved it. He said he could envision stage versions of *Honky-Tonk* produced in places like Nashville, Vegas, and Houston after the movie's release.

Tom felt we needed "a country music partner," so we made a trip to Nashville, trying to convince country-music record executives Tony Brown, Joe Galante, and Mike Curb to come aboard as coproducers. Curb, the former lieutenant governor of California, went for it. He was a huge name in country music—among his artists at Curb Records were Tim McGraw, Faith Hill, and Jo Dee Messina.

With Ross and Curb attached to the project, my agents went out to sell the script. They got nowhere. Potential buyers didn't know what to do with it. Old-timey Hank Williams country music? Say what? A tear-jerking celebration of love and America? *Huh?* By the guy who wrote *Basic Instinct* and *Showgirls?* Oh boy. Where was the sex? (There was no sex.)

I went to David Geffen, who'd produced both films and plays, and asked him to read the script and tell me his opinion. He read it and told me that it was "unproducible."

I thanked him and put *The Honky-Tonk Opera* into a drawer. It's still there . . . where my heart had led me.

Only shitheads do shitwork.

Oscar-winning screenwriter Bill Goldman: "Screenwriting is shitwork. Brief example: *Waldo Pepper. Waldo* was basically an original screenplay of mine. I say 'basically' because the pulse of the movie came from George Hill, the director, and we worked for ten days on a story. . . . Okay, we open in New York and three daily papers are split—two terrific, one pan. In neither of the laudatory reviews was my name even mentioned. But you better believe I got top billing in the pan. I had screwed up George Hill's movie. Nothing unusual at all about that—it's SOP for the screenwriter. That is simply the way of the world. You do not, except in rare, rare exceptions, get critical recognition."

The moral of the story: Don't work with any director for ten days trying to come up with a story. Don't let the screenplay be "basically" yours. Make sure the "pulse" of the movie comes from you and not the directing.

If you do all those things, you won't be doing shitwork.

Do your research.

Ben Hecht: "The producer wanted my script to top all the other gangster pictures. So I had my secretary go out and see all the gangster pictures playing. She scouted up all the dead people in each picture. In one film nine people were bumped off, so I went to the producer and said, 'We're going to kill twenty-five people!'"

LESSON 8

Ideas Are Poison!

Go outside the box.

Screenwriter/director Jean-Luc Godard: "A film should have a beginning, a middle, and an end, but not necessarily in that order."

Violate everyone's privacy.

To write the way real people talk, *listen* to the way real people talk. Pretend you have a scanner in your head and, as people talk, imagine their words running across the screen, complete with punctuation marks, to "see" the words more clearly.

A friend of mine who is a screenwriter taped his own phone calls but felt after awhile that his conversations were becoming stilted because he knew he was taping them. So he put a tiny microphone into a flowerpot near a table at a bar and listened to the conversations at that table while he sat across the room with a tiny transmitter in his ear.

I have another friend, a phone repairman in L.A. He sits atop a telephone pole for hours every day listening to strangers' conversations. He wants to be a screenwriter.

Perk of success: you, too, can get a free Lexus

When I wrote An Alan Smithee Film: Burn Hollywood Burn, I wrote several Toyota Land Cruisers into the script.

I got a call from a Lexus representative, who told me that if I changed the Toyotas in the script into Lexuses, I'd get a free Lexus delivered to my house in Malibu.

In what was probably the most stupid move of my life, done for obviously perverse reasons, I turned my free Lexus down.

Write what you know . . . reliable sources

When I was a young newspaper reporter, I covered a hostage situation where a gunman was holding his ex-girlfriend hostage.

Twenty-five years later, I wrote the story as Reliable Sources and sold the script to Paramount for $2 million.

Don't write a Western.

The odds are overwhelming that it won't be made, and that if it is, it will fail. Almost every year or so, there is a failed attempt to do a Western—some, like Larry Kasdan's *Wyatt Earp,* have been especially good, but the public doesn't seem interested.

A producer said to me, "A Western in space, yes, a hip-hop Western, yes, but a Western with horses, absolutely not."

A Tender Love Story

That, according to director Jim Cameron, is what *The Terminator* was.
Cameron used the very same words to describe *Titanic*.

"The worst thing that could happen" is the worst thing you can do.

A lot of screenwriters write scripts this way!

A man is happily married and has three beautiful children. What's the worst thing that could happen to him? His wife dies. Okay. *Now* what's the worst thing that could happen? His kids die, too. Okay. *Now* what's the worst thing that could happen? He falls in love with the wrong woman. *Now* what's the worst thing that could happen? She steals all of his money. *Now* what's the worst thing that could happen? He becomes a homeless person. *Now* what's the worst thing that could happen? He finds himself asleep at night atop his wife's grave. *Now* what? He gets pneumonia. *Now* what? He dies. *Now* what? The person who receives the kidney that he left to medical science rejects his kidney and dies, too.

And on and on and on.

Do not allow that sentence—What's the worst thing that could happen?—to enter your thoughts as you write.

No more Travis Bickle . . .

If you want to sell your script, give your main characters lots of friends, extended families to cheer him/her on.

Studios love this—studio execs feel that if an audience sees a lead character being cheered on-screen, then the audience will automatically like him.

Studio research on *Top Gun,* for example, discovered that audiences weren't cheering the movie at its end. The studio inserted a scene that had been shot earlier, which showed all the other pilots cheering on-screen at the end.

After that scene was inserted, audiences everywhere cheered the ending of the movie.

DO YOUR RESEARCH . . . AN ALAN SMITHEE FILM

A director came to have lunch with me at my home in Malibu. His name was Stuart Baird. He was formerly a film editor and he had just directed his first big action hit. He was a Brit who'd worked with Ken Russell and was dressed all in khaki. I liked him and we talked for hours.

A couple of weeks later, I sat down to write An Alan Smithee Film: Burn Hollywood Burn, *which is about a former film editor who directs his first film. My lead character, the director, Alan Smithee, is a Brit who has worked with Ken Russell and dresses in all khaki.*

When the film was released, Stuart Baird went to the producer and said, "That bloody Hungarian—he stole my whole life in one bloody lunch."

You're better off getting the rights.

My movie *F.I.S.T.* was about Jimmy Hoffa. But United Artists didn't have the rights to Hoffa's life and didn't want to pay to acquire the rights, either; so throughout the writing of the script, I had to be careful not to get too close to the details of Hoffa's life (even though I knew and the studio knew that I was writing about Hoffa).

It was a nightmare because I had to be as concerned about what the lawyers would think as what the director, producer, and studio executives would think.

Angie Dickinson inspired Basic Instinct, Sliver, Showgirls, *and* Jade.

I was staying overnight in a producer's guest house in Beverly Hills and dreamed all night about sex.

I don't dream often about sex, but on this night I kept having a vision of endless coupling with women whose faces I didn't recognize.

The dreams were only of the act itself—without tenderness or feeling—sporting, athletic, as though I were riding a mechanical bull.

I awoke worn-out, drenched in sweat, and with the kind of painful erection I'd had when I was thirteen years old.

The producer asked me how I'd slept, and I lied and said fine. Then he told me that his guest house had been the place where JFK trysted with Angie Dickinson when he came to town.

A couple weeks later, as I was waiting for a cab in the portico of the Beverly Wilshire Hotel, I watched as a little Mercedes convertible pulled up and a stunning older woman got out and walked toward me into the hotel.

As Angie Dickinson passed me, I couldn't help winking at her, and she gave me a knowing, dazzling smile.

Be nice to those you've wounded.

Don't try to take credit away from the first writer, who thought the basic concept up. After I rewrote *Flashdance,* there wasn't much left of Tom Hedley's original script except the title and the concept of a working-class girl wanting to be a ballet dancer.

It was enough, though.

In its arbitration, the Writers Guild ruled that the credit should be: Screenplay by Hedley and Eszterhas, story by Hedley.

While in my heart I felt that I should have had story credit along with him, I understood that without him, we would've had nothing. So, after the arbitration was announced, I called Tom Hedley and congratulated him.

ALL HAIL
Nunnally Johnson, Charles MacArthur, and Joel Sayre!

Told by Dave Chasen one night that his restaurant was about to close, the three screenwriters picked Chasen up, took him outside, came back in, and locked the door.

Do your research . . . an Alan Smithee film

In my film An Alan Smithee Film: Burn Hollywood Burn, the lead character, Smithee, has two props that he carries throughout the film: his Dogon fighting stick and his Tibetan rock. They are his talismans, holy objects he carries for luck.

Stuart Baird didn't carry those things around, but I did. I keep those holy objects near me—even now, as I write this.

I made my holy objects famous! I put them up on the big screen!

You're not writing children's books.

Professor Andrew Horton, of Loyola University, in his book *Writing the Character-Centered Screenplay*: "Want to get a good feel for writing screenplays? . . . Check out an armful of children's books from the library. I'm serious. Comic books do much the same thing—after all, they're written in 'frames' with speech bubbles. But children's books have become incredibly inventive and VISUALLY IMAGINATIVE JOURNEYS for kids."

Avoid writing about living people.

In my Otis Redding script, *Blaze of Glory,* I wrote about Zelma, his wife, and his friend and manager, Phil Walden.

Zelma loved the script and her depiction and had no problems. Initially, neither did Phil Walden, who publicly said he loved the script.

But after a couple of weeks, he changed his mind. While both Phil and one of his brothers had managed Otis, in my script, for reasons of dramatic tension, I showed only Phil (no brother) representing Otis.

Understandably, Phil's brother didn't like being left out of the script, and Phil, no doubt not wanting to make his brother unhappy, turned against the script—one reason it hasn't been made in all these years.

WRITE WHAT YOU KNOW . . .
FLASHDANCE

When I was nineteen years old, I dated a twenty-four-year-old woman from the West Side of Cleveland who worked for Republic Steel as a welder. She'd once dreamed of being a ballet dancer and went to every ballet performance in the city.

Twenty years later, I wrote the story of the young woman who wants to be a ballet dancer and works as a welder—Alex, in Flashdance.

Expose all your family secrets.

You know all the family secrets—how Uncle John used to dress up as a woman on weekends and how one of his kids spotted him getting out of a car downtown; how Aunt Emily disappeared at the wedding reception for forty minutes with the best man.

Change all the names, of course, and if you sell your script and Uncle John sees himself on-screen, pretend that it has nothing at all to do with him. Chances are he won't confront you because *he won't want* the comparison to be made by anybody.

If someone in the family asks you how you came up with that particular story, just smile and say that your writing has nothing to do with you, that there's a twisted little person inside you who makes all this stuff up.

Your toys can inspire you.

An African Dogon hatchet that I bought at an antique fair became the murder weapon in *Jade.*

My favorite antique manual typewriter became the McGuffin in *Jagged Edge*—the clue that gives Jeff Bridges away as the murderer.

Compounded irony: I actually wrote the script of *Jagged Edge* on the very antique manual typewriter that was the McGuffin in the script.

If you're good in the sack, you can make 'em laugh.

Comedian Jay Leno: "No one thinks they're a bad lay. Everyone figures 'I may be fat and acne-riddled or stupid, but I know, in the sack, I'm the greatest thing in the world' . . . and it's the same thing with comedy. Telling someone they have no sense of humor is like telling someone they're bad at sex."

If you want to win an Oscar . . .

Paddy Chayefsky gave this advice to Gore Vidal: "If you want all the prizes, you gotta write shrill."

"He had a point," said Vidal.

Winner's Walk

The passageway at the Academy Awards between the stage and the press room—the route taken by all Oscar winners.

If you want to win an Oscar, fight the good fight.

A Holocaust-related film was, for many years, a good bet to be nominated for an Oscar; in later years, it was a film about civil rights and black empowerment.

Today's hot Oscar subjects are gay rights and gay empowerment.

An Oscar-winning producer said to me, "The Holocaust battle has been won. We're winning on women's empowerment, too. The best indication of that is the record number of copies sold of Hillary's book. The real door-to-door political street fighting is about gay rights and gay marriage now. Those are the movies the Academy wants to reward, and there are a lot of shrewd people in this town who always figure out what the Academy wants to reward, before they sit down and go to work."

POWs

Past Oscar winners.

If you write this script, you're probably a sure bet for an Oscar.

The script is about a saintly black man with a newly discovered mental illness who was abused by white foster parents as a child, and who has surgery now to become the woman he's always wanted to be, so she can help other black children abused by white foster parents.

In the first half of the movie, he's played by Denzel Washington. In the second half, the starring role is played by Halle Berry.

They both win Oscars—for Best Actor and Best Actress, respectively—as does Michael Moore for Best Director.

Trophy Girls

Bimbos who carry the statues at awards shows.

Or, if you want to win an Oscar, try writing about . . .

A saintly heroic woman, a saintly heroic gay man or woman, a saintly heroic black man or woman, a victimized woman, a gay man or woman, a black man or woman . . . *who frees him or her,* or *himself and herself* from *victimization* and *empowers* any of the above gender/color combos, as well as anyone with autism, Tourette's, or, best of all, a bizarre new neurological disorder that only Oliver Sachs knows about.

Don't write any John Wayne–type parts.

With the exception of Russell Crowe and Mel Gibson, there are few stars able to play supermacho parts today. Many of Hollywood's top male movie stars are either bisexual or gay. If they're not bisexual or gay, their feminine sides overpower their manhood. Look at how Orlando Bloom and Colin Farrell and Brad Pitt failed, respectively, in *Kingdom of Heaven, Alexander,* and *Troy.*

Are My Nipples Even?

The greatest concern of starlets who appear on awards shows.

Another surefire formula for a quick script sale . . .

Write a script about a young woman battling cancer, whose best friend is a gay man and who has an adopted black daughter and a mutant but cuddly and ugly dog.

If you want to sell your script, don't kill off your lead character.

John Wayne made over two hundred movies; he died in only eight of them, including his last one, *The Shootist.*

Sylvester Stallone had a full-scale hissy fit when my script of *F.I.S.T.* called for him to die. Studio lawyers had to force him to die.

If you write a real man's man . . .

Do to him what Jim Brooks did to the Jack Nicholson character in *As Good As It Gets.*

Turn him inside out. Show him to be the asshole that he is and, at the end, show him reborn as a touchy-feely man who has great disdain for the way he used to be—cure him of his psychic, spiritual cancer and show how happy he is to be healthily reborn.

Or do to him what Marty Brest did to the Ben Affleck character in *Gigli*: "It's turkeytime," and he gobble-gobbles and maybe he'll even stop calling that poor kid "a fucking retard," as he's done through the whole movie.

To simplify this: If you have an old-style man's man in the beginning of the movie, castrate him gradually in the second and third acts—and at the end, show how happy he is about his gelding.

Write strong and independent female characters.

Your women have to be smart, tough, streetwise, courageous, heroic, and good. They have to be smarter than their male costars and they have to have women friends they bond with. It helps if they have gay friends—male or female—and it's not even harmful to have *them* be subtly bisexual.

While they may kiss men on-screen and condescend to them and patronize them and make love to them (in darkly shot scenes), there should be something in their persona that says, *All men are assholes.*

If you're male and trying to write a female character . . .

Screenwriter/director Ron Shelton (*Bull Durham*): "Write a woman's character as a man, then change any specifics, and you'll find there're very few things you have to change."

Write a buddy movie about two women.

You'll sell the script, though the movie might fail.

Director/screenwriter Anthony Minghella, discussing *Cold Mountain*: "I wanted to make a movie about . . . the joy that occurs when men are away and women find each other and help each other. The relationship between Ruby and Ada, the wit of it, and the idea that there could be this exchange of gifts between people, that you could help somebody else and they could help you and you would grow with them and laugh at them and laugh with them. Such a relief not to have made a movie in which the two women are fighting over the same guy."

You can get away with trashing straight white males.

There is no male counterpart for the National Organization for Women (thankfully). There are no male lobbying or pressure groups. And, as a group, straight white males have been so beaten down by their wives and girlfriends (and by media coverage, especially TV ads) that many believe they really *are* and *have historically been* villains and/or assholes.

Redeeming Social Values

The values (liberal, progressive, or elitist—that's your choice) shared by most Hollywood studio heads, producers, directors, stars, screenwriters, and all those others who want to work in this town again.

Too Ethnic

A story that is too Jewish or too black.

I don't shoot my villains.

Screenwriter Herman Mankiewicz (*Citizen Kane*): "In a novel a hero can lay the girls and marry a virgin for a finish. In a movie this is not allowed. The hero, as well as the heroine, has to be a virgin. The villain can lay anybody he wants, have as much fun as he wants cheating and stealing, getting rich and whipping the servants. But you have to shoot him in the end."

Orson Welles agrees with me: He said, "Most heavies should be played for sympathy."

No Denzel in bed with Gwyneth . . .

After *Monster's Ball,* it's possible to get a movie made that includes torrid sex between a white man and a black woman—but the reverse won't fly.

Denzel Washington or Jamie Foxx in bed with Gwyneth Paltrow or Charlize Theron (or even the dark-hued Angelina Jolie)? Forget it.

Hollywood executives are secretly still afraid there would be riots, lynchings, and God knows what else in the streets.

Richard Pryor and Margot Kidder got it on in a movie called *Some Kind of Hero* many years ago; the footage was so hot that it can still be seen at certain producers' parties, along with Mickey Rourke and Carrie Otis in *Wild Orchid* and, for comic relief, Sharon Stone and Billy Baldwin in *Sliver.*

Don't be afraid to write sex scenes.

Nothing risqué, nothing gained," said Jayne Mansfield, sexy actress.

Showing a little flesh won't hurt your movie.

Actor James Coburn: "A little titty never hurt anyone."

Swimming pool scenes are fine.

Louis B. Mayer: "You'd be surprised how tits figure in a hit movie."

But write genteel sex scenes.

Consider Louis B. Mayer *leching* with Hedy Lamarr: "If you like to make love—fornicate—screw your leading man in the dressing room, that's your business. But in front of the camera, gentility. You hear? Gentility!"

REELSPEAK

"Side-Al" Nudity

The kind of nudity on-screen that is usually rated R but tries very, very hard to get a PG-13.

DO YOUR RESEARCH . . . JADE, BASIC INSTINCT, AN ALAN SMITHEE FILM

We had both come and we were smoking our obligatory cigarettes in a motel overlooking Venice Beach. A four-story mural of Morrison as the Lizard King was outside our window. Some guy down on the beach was playing his bongo drums.

I was with a producer's wife who had once wanted to be an actress. She had picked me out at a dinner party, asked for my phone number, called me, set up the date, and made the reservation at the motel under a false name.

I asked her why she was crying.

Because she came here often, she said, with guys like me.

Sometimes, she said, she cruised Pico or Ocean in her black Porsche and picked guys up, usually Latinos, right off the street and brought them here for the afternoon.

I laughed and told her not to worry about it. Vivien Leigh, I told her, used to drive to bars in Compton and pick guys up and do them in her Bentley. Clara Bow used to pick guys off the street in a red convertible roadster. Jean Harlow did cabdrivers while wearing a black wig.

"Guys cruise the streets all the time," I said to her. "What's the big deal? Women in Hollywood have always been more empowered than in other places."

She stopped crying and smiled at me. "You're really very sweet, aren't you?" she said, and we went back to doing what we'd been doing before.

The guy on the beach was still bambing away at his bongos.

They'll confuse you with Larry Flynt.

Director Milos Forman: "When the Nazis and Communists first came to Czechoslovakia, they declared war on pornographers and perverts. Everyone applauded: who wants perverts running through the streets? But then, suddenly, Jesus Christ was a pervert, Shakespeare was a pervert, Hemingway was a pervert. It always starts with pornographers to open the door a little, but then the door is opened wide for all kinds of persecution."

Cover your own ass.

Cover yourself. Before each sex scene write, "It is dark; you can't see clearly"—just in case the director wants to shoot your script as an NC-17 or "a deep R" . . . and blames you for pornography if the movie fails.

You're asking for trouble if you write a scene with male frontal nudity.

Director Jean-Jacques Annaud: "The penis is a terrible, terrible actor. It is an actor who overacts."

And stay away from that backdoor hanky-panky.

Louis B. Mayer: "A woman's ass is for her husband, not theater-goers."

You can be your own test market.

If you're writing a script with a sexual content and find yourself getting a hard-on or a wet-on, it's okay. If you're getting turned on, it's not unreasonable to suppose that the viewer of the film might be turned on, too.

If, however, this happens to you while you're writing something without *any* sexual contact, seek company . . . or the company of a shrink.

Don't write a script with a lot of sex.

You won't get it made. They don't make movies like *Midnight Cowboy* and *Clockwork Orange* anymore. *Eyes Wide Shut* and

Crash and *Henry and June* and *Tie Me Up! Tie Me Down!* and *Show-girls* all failed at the box office.

Showgirls (my film) was the greatest commercial and cinematic disaster since *Heaven's Gate* and *Ishtar*. It failed because of liberal political correctness and conservative fundamentalism and because it was a bad movie.

I deserve the credit for it: I almost single-handedly killed off the sexual-content movie in America.

Violence is still fine, though—the bloodier and the more sexless (witness Tarantino) the better.

But you can go absolutely apeshit on the violence.

Director Phillip Noyce, discussing *Sliver*: "The MPAA have a phobia about seeing people joined together in lovemaking. So they wanted us to cut down on the amount of material where Sharon and Billy seemed to be truly coupling. I would cut it and they would say, 'No, no, no still too much.' I would try cutting it again. 'No, no, no still too much'—and this went on endlessly. Yet in any film that I have made in the U.S., there has never been any discussion with censors about violence."

Try to write a French movie.

Ron Shelton: "The French can make comedies about someone sleeping with their cousin. If that happens in an American movie, somebody gets their heads blown off."

If you write a violent movie . . .

You'll need some very good reviews to give it some respectability. That way, audiences can feel they're buying a ticket not because they want to see bloody, gruesome violence but because they want to see artistic accomplishment.

This doesn't mean that even without good reviews your violent movie won't be a hit—witness *Jagged Edge* and *Basic Instinct*.

Don't write another Dirty Harry.

Novelist/screenwriter George Pelecanos (*King Suckerman, A Firing Offense*): "You could never make a picture like *Dirty Harry* today because it's about a cop who, you know, shoots unarmed people and steps on 'em when they're wounded and beats 'em up and so on. And on the page [the studio executives' notes] say: *'Well, I don't really like this guy'*—like everybody has to like the protagonist of these movies. I don't understand that. Is that person interesting or not? That's what matters."

Crash-and-Bash Pictures

You know what they are. Please don't write them. Please don't want to write them. Everybody is writing them. Be the exception.

Whiz-Bang

As in, "We need a little bit more whiz-bang in the opening sequence," meaning action, visual pyrotechnics, more smoke and wacko camera angles.

The Whammo Chart, aka the Eleven-Minute Commandment

A formula invented by producer Larry Gordon for action films. The chart calls for an action sequence every eleven minutes. Time Joel Silver films like *Die Hard, Lethal Weapon,* and *Predator* and you'll see how religiously Joel believes in Larry Gordon's eleven-minute commandment.

If you're bored with your mate, do lots of research.

Studio executives are suckers for authenticity. Interviewing people, they can understand; creative genius, they can't.

In the course of my unhappy first marriage, I did studio-expensed research in the following locations: the south of France, Israel, Zurich, London (four times), Paris (three times), Hawaii (five times), and Los Vegas, of course (which I researched *in depth* innumerable times, and ways, for *Showgirls*).

About sitting down and writing—it's okay to be scared.

Screenwriter and director Billy Wilder: "I was only nervous when confronted with an empty page. One with nothing on it."

Don't do an outline for yourself.

It will lock the characters in step too much and not give them enough room to plot the course of their own actions in the script.

Give them the freedom to tell you what it is they want to do or say.

Do a character sketch for yourself instead.

Spend a page on each character. His/her back story, background, physical descriptions, interests, relationships, dreams, failings.

Do it for all the major characters.

Study it for a week, reread it and think about it as much as you can, and revise it as the week goes along.

At the end of the week, do a final version of it, and start writing your script.

Keep your character sketches handy and reread them as you continue to write your script.

Before you write anything, think about designing a jacket for your script.

Lloyd Levin, who worked for studio head Larry Gordon at Fox, took him a novel called *Nothing Lasts Forever,* by Roderick Thorp.

Gordon took one look at the book's jacket and said to Levin, "I don't need to read it. Buy it."

Old Hungarian saying . . .

The moment you begin writing is the moment "the monkey jumps into the water."

Go jump already!

Don't play it safe.

Screenwriter Larry Gelbart (*Tootsie*): "In half a century, we've gone from *Citizen Kane* to candy cane. That's what comes from playing it safe."

Shut up, don't worry so damn much about it, sit down, and write.

Raymond Chandler: "Ideas are poison. The more you reason, the less you create."

This is the most fun you're going to have.

Ron Shelton: "The best part of screenwriting—you do it alone. The stuff that scares most people is why I love it: the blank page, and you're alone. There's no committee, there's no bureaucracy, you're the boss, you're the czar, you're "*everything*.""

Go for it—get some boos.

Bob Dylan said, "If you haven't done anything, you've never been booed."

This is what you should do.

Screenwriter Dan Harris (*Imaginary Heroes*): "My script is my head vomited up on paper."

PART FOUR

WRITING THE SCRIPT

LESSON 9

Slit a Vein and Drip It on the Page!

Follow your bliss . . . or your body part.

I know it sounds like the worst New Age line you've ever heard (Joseph Campbell), but it's true. Write the story that's in your heart and gut and whatever other body parts you write from.

I've always been accused of writing from—Oh well, never mind. My wife, who loves me, says I'm a kinder and gentler Joe these days. *Ha!*

Buy yourself a good chair.

You can get them for sixty or seventy dollars at places like Office-Max. The less discomfort you have while you're writing, the more you can concentrate, and thus the better your script will be.

Don't sit there for hours.

Get up every hour or so and walk around for five or ten minutes. Otherwise, you'll ruin your back, your prostate, and possibly your relationship with your wife and kids. Say hi to them, give them a hug, drink some water, and go back to work.

You've got to forget about the money.

Writer/producer William Froug: "If you think about how much you can sell it for while you're writing it, you're lost."

Try to have fun writing your script.

Albert Einstein: "The highest level of creativity unfolds through play."

Keep some holy object near you as you write.

It has to have some relationship to what you're writing about: For my Otis Redding script, *Blaze of Glory,* it was a boyhood photo of Otis that his widow, Zelma, gave me; for *Basic Instinct,* it was a gleaming silver ice pick that I had found at a flea market; for *Music Box,* it was a photo of a group of Hungarian Jewish women being led by Hungarian gendarmes to a train.

Sometimes some unholy object will do, too.

For *Showgirls,* it was a pair of my wife's black lace panties.

Screenplays are a bitch to write.

One man wrote *War and Peace.* Thirty-five screenwriters wrote *The Flintstones.*

You don't have to love writing a script.

Screenwriter William Faulkner: "If I never do another one until I'm old and bent and grey, it will be too soon."

All you have to do is slit a vein and let it drip on the page.

Ron Shelton: "The hard part is getting from thinking about the script to the first page of writing. I might think about it for years. By the time I write page one, I like to have so much of it inside me it practically explodes onto the page."

Just write your first sentence.

Writing the first sentence," my writer friend Will Froug said, "is the toughest part of writing a script."

Don't be afraid to ask God to help you.

Ron Shelton: "For the first thirty-five years of your life you run from the Church, and somewhere in your thirties and forties you make peace with it and embrace it as a part of who you are, and thereby liberate yourself from it. I realized I could take from it those elements that comforted me and helped me to cope, and discard the rest."

Robert McKee says you have to defeat your fear.

McKee: "You have to think like an artist. If you know you're in over your head, and that doesn't intimidate you, you might just make it. The hard part is getting in the chair and writing. It takes tremendous willpower and discipline and the only way to defeat the fear is to gain the self-confidence that comes from knowing you've mastered the art form."

To Robert McKee: It's okay, Bob, I get scared, too.

Ian Parker in *The New Yorker:* "McKee motivates writers for a living, but he has not been able to get this book done. When I asked him why, he said, 'It's a good question. Why haven't I? Fear is part of it.'"

If you've written the first page, the rest is easy.

Now you know you can do it, because you've already done it once. All you have to do is do it about 110 more times. *But you've done it.* So what's the big deal?

Don't keep messing with the first scene.

Screenwriter Anna Hamilton Phelan (*Gorillas in the Mist*): "Don't go back and fix that first scene. Don't go back and fix that dialogue. Write yourself a little note saying 'Put in first scene such and such,' if you happen to think of something, then get a little stickum and stick that somewhere on the wall. But don't go back, because going back is a trap. It keeps you from going forward. It keeps you from going ahead. Your first enemy, of course, is yourself. Yourself is also that little critic that sits on your shoulder and says, *"This is terrible."*

Don't rush to finish your script.

Ben Hecht wrote *The Unholy Garden* in two days, dictating it to two secretaries. Sam Goldwyn congratulated Ben on his brilliant work. The script was shot without a word changed.

"It was one of the worst flops ever turned out by a studio," Ben said later.

Take your time writing your script.

I wrote *Basic Instinct* in a blind frenzy while listening almost non-stop to the Rolling Stones.

I didn't outline the script and I didn't know my ending until I was almost two-thirds finished.

It exploded out of my head—I kept hearing lines of dialogue and had to hurry to keep up with the voices I was hearing. I woke up at four in the morning and wrote lines of dialogue down.

I wrote it in two shifts each day—from nine in the morning till one in the afternoon and from three in the afternoon to eight o'clock at night.

From the time I began writing till the day my agent sold it at auction: thirteen days.

No Attachment to Outcome

This is *Gorillas in the Mist* screenwriter Anna Hamilton Phelan's phrase: "When I get bogged down I say 'No attachment to outcome.' Don't worry about what's going to happen to this. Just write the next word."

Shut the world down.

I have found that for me, the best time to write is from seven in the morning till one o'clock in the afternoon. I get up at six, shower, drink some carrot juice and tea, and am at my writing desk by seven. I don't take calls when I'm writing; my wife disturbs me only for emergencies.

I quit writing at one and have lunch with my wife. Sometimes I take a nap after lunch, but I'm back at my desk at three. Then I edit what I've written, sometimes rewrite it extensively, and make a note about scenes I'm going to write the next day.

I'm usually finished with that by five o'clock. I walk five miles then and spend the rest of the night with my family.

Put your laptop away.

I write my first drafts longhand. That's right—*longhand*, with a *pencil*. I feel it puts me more in touch with my characters.

I go to my laptop on my subsequent drafts.

That's a lie. I don't know how to *use* a laptop—I go to my manual Olivetti Lettera typewriter—but you can use *your* laptop while sipping a double latte at Starbucks. In my drinking days, *I* used to suck on a bottle of Jack Daniel's as I wrote—the only danger was that I sometimes couldn't read my own handwriting the next day.

Go sit in the tub.

Screenwriter Dalton Trumbo, revered as one of the legendary screenwriters of Old Hollywood, wrote most of his screenplays in the bathtub.

I've written a lot of scripts in the tub, too, but I'm Hungarian-born, and Hungary (a landlocked country) has more public baths than any other country in the world.

It also has the highest suicide rate in the world. That means that if your script is not going well, you can just slide down in the tub and . . .

If you're masturbating and writing a script, stop masturbating (but keep writing).

Screenwriter Dalton Trumbo: "It is then, while panic tightens my sagging throat, that I whisper to myself: It's true, after all. It *does* make you crazy. It *does* cause the brain to soften. Why, oh why did I like it so much? Why didn't I stop while I was still ahead of the game? Was it only one time too many that caused this rush of premature senility? Or a dozen times? Or a thousand? Ah, well— little good to know it now: the harm's done, the jig's up, you're thoroughly addled, better you'd been born with handless stumps."

Write six pages of script a day.

Stick to this schedule no matter what. You'll have a finished first draft in roughly twenty days.

Then go back and edit what you've written. Spend no more than five days on this edit.

Then rewrite your script from page one—with your edits. Spend no more than one week on this rewrite—that means twenty pages a day.

Put the script away for a week; don't even look at it.

Then edit it once again. Spend no more than four days on the edit this time.

Then rewrite it again from scratch with your edits—taking another week. This will be *your third draft.*

Now begin the process of trying to sell it—this, your official *first draft.*

At least write something every day.

John Lennon once said, "I haven't picked up a guitar in six years. I forget how heavy they are."

If you don't feel like writing today . . .

Comedian Rita Rudner: "People don't want to get up and drive a truck every day either, but they do—that's their job and this is my job."

Don't watch TV if you're writing.

Hunter S. Thompson: "No music and bad TV equals bad mood and no pages."

Don't watch any movies while you're writing.

You don't want to wind up "borrowing" from or paying "homage" to whatever it is you're seeing. There is a tendency while you're writing your script to feel lost and desperate, as in, Oh, Jesus God, I know this isn't "working." All you need is to watch some stupid movie that will give you a bad idea.

Keep your brain as inviolate and isolated as possible from *everything* while you're writing.

Music can help you.

As I said, when I wrote *Basic Instinct*, I played the Stones all the time, especially "Sympathy for the Devil," over and over again.

All the music in the film was supposed to be Stones music and "Sympathy for the Devil" was to play over the final credits.

The studio even bought the rights to "Sympathy" from the Stones for $750,000, but the director, Paul Verhoeven, changed his mind about using the song in the film, and the Stones were $750,000 richer.

Don't smoke while you write; if you smoke, stop!

Screenwriter Albert Maltz about his friend, screenwriter Dalton Trumbo: "He's a very feisty man, you know, a regular fighting cock. It's that damned cigarette smoking of his that put him in the shape he's in today. He just couldn't stop. He used to smoke the things one after another."

So did I. I smoked four packs a day and *always* chain-smoked when I was writing. I started smoking when I was twelve years old.

In 2001, when I was fifty-seven, I was diagnosed with cancer of the throat and 80 percent of my larynx was surgically removed.

I had a trache tube for months afterward and had difficulty breathing and swallowing.

I finally stopped smoking and have been smoke-free now for five years.

After I stopped smoking, I couldn't write for a year and a half. I can write now, finally, without missing the cigarettes.

Don't do what Dalton Trumbo and I did to ourselves; stop before it's too late.

Pay attention to every word.

Comedian Joe Bolster: "The difference between a laugh and no laugh is often a single syllable. You remember the 'Where's the beef' campaign? Initially, it was 'Where's *all* the beef?' But the director took out 'all' and without [him doing] that, it probably wouldn't have been as effective."

Keep a night-light, pen, and paper on your nightstand.

You never know when you'll wake up with a script thought in your head. That's how I came up with the ending of *Basic Instinct*.

I literally dreamed the final scene, with the ice pick under the bed. I woke up and jotted it down and used it when I wrote the ending.

Treat yourself well after a good day.

The novelist H. G. Wells told interviewers that after a good day's writing, he always celebrated by having sex.

Don't think you're better than your audience.

Ben Hecht did: "But among all my fantasies is none of writing and directing a movie that becomes the most famous movie of the week or even the month. I know why I don't have this fantasy. It is because my mind balks at the partner in this daydream—the audience. I have never fancied the pleasures that come from its applause and approval."

Write cinematically.

Raymond Chandler said to a friend, "I suppose you know the famous story of the writer who racked his brains [about] how to show, very shortly, that a middle-aged man and his wife were no longer in love with each other. Finally he licked it. The man and his wife got into an elevator and he kept his hat on. At the next stop a lady got into the elevator and he immediately removed his hat. That is proper film writing. Me, I'd have done a four-page scene about it."

Don't Mist the Orchids

Don't lay on the sentimentality too thickly.

"What's wrong with sentimentality?" a reporter once asked William Faulkner.

"People are afraid of it," he said.

Don't use voice-over unless you absolutely have to.

Most studio executives and directors view a voice-over as the kiss of death, to be used only if a movie's structure doesn't hang together.

If you hear a voice-over in a movie, it's a possible sign that the movie was, and/or still is, in great creative trouble.

How to deal with writer's block . . . the hotel room solution.

Screenwriter Jordan Roberts (Around the Bend): "I can only write in hotel surroundings. I like isolation, I like loneliness, and there's nothing lonelier than a hotel. When I'm lonely, I write more intimately. I need to be away from everything, including family and friends, so that I'm so desperate I will actually bother to write."

Each morning, reread what you wrote the day before.

Do this first thing in the morning, before you start writing for the day. Don't edit any of what you wrote the day before; just read it a couple of times to put yourself back into it.

As you approach the ending, reread the entire script each morning before you start writing. I find that doing this inevitably leads me to my ending.

Don't worry about writing too much in one day.

Ben Hecht sometimes wrote entire scripts in three or four days.

I am not advocating that, but I have found that on occasion I've had banner writing days, where I've written twenty to thirty pages in a single day, barely able to keep up with my characters' voices.

Just go with it, keep going, and when you are finished—*only then*—see how much of it works.

But, whatever you do, keep to your minimum—*six pages every day.*

If you feel you're roaring along . . .

Don't take the weekends off. Just keep writing. Try to explain to your loved ones what is going on. But even if they don't understand—even if they're pissed off at you, ignore them: Keep writing.

If, on the other hand, you don't feel like you're roaring along, take the weekends off, spend time with your loved ones, and air your mind.

Don't write on speed or cocaine.

It will affect the rhythm of your scenes. You're too wired or too zippy on either drug to get your rhythms right. I know; I've been there.

Don't write on booze and cigarettes, either. I've been there, too. I used to love writing on black coffee, cognac, and endless cigarettes.

Since I like writing and always wrote a lot, I smoked lots and lots of cigarettes and drank lot and lots of cognac.

That's one big reason 80 percent of my larynx is gone and I hack for an hour each morning until I get the phlegm off of what's left of my throat.

Don't think about the budget.

In my experience, if you write something really good, they will somehow come up with the money to film it.

In other words, the budget shouldn't shape your script; your script should shape the budget.

Let only your imagination limit you.

Don't worry about how they will actually film something. With technical advances and computerization, *anything* can be filmed.

Don't write camera angles into your script.

And don't mention POV (point of view), either. Don't do *all* of the director's work for him. Let him earn his wage by doing *something*.

You don't have to be rooting for anyone in your script.

As much as some studio executives feel that it is, a script is not a football, baseball, or basketball game.

If the story is fascinating enough, if the world it depicts is seductive enough, if your characters are interesting and complex enough, you don't need someone to wave the pom-poms every time he or she speaks.

I point to *Basic Instinct* as my best example. Its two central characters were both flawed and gray. The movie was the number-one movie of its year and made nearly half a billion dollars.

If you tell me that the reason it made so much money was because of that split-second beaver, I will tell you that even Sharon, who puts a very high price indeed on her beaver, would argue with you.

Structure your individual scenes the way you structure your script.

Ascene should have a beginning, a middle, and an end. The end of the scene should have the same kind of impact that the end of the script must have. So build your *scenes* to a climax.

How to deal with writer's block . . . the Robert Towne solution

If you can't write it, and if nothing works, do what Robert Towne does. He goes out to lunch with agents and producers and tells them the details of the story that he is blocked on. They beg him to write the story instead of telling it, and Bob goes home and doesn't write it; he abandons it. But at least he's impressed agents and producers, sellers and buyers, about how creative he is.

Each page of your script is a minute on screen.

But don't worry about this in your first draft. My first draft of *F.I.S.T.* was almost three hundred pages and I had a monologue that went on for seven pages—seven minutes.

Old rule: If it's there, you can always trim it. But if it's not there, you're in trouble.

Don't show the script to anyone as you write it.

Don't even tell anyone what you write each day. It is between you and your muse. Don't confuse your muse with anyone else at this point—your director, producer, agent, or significant other.

Only when you are finished with your script should you show it to anyone.

The easier your script reads, the better.

Most studio executives I've met think that if it takes them longer than forty-five minutes to read a script, then that script isn't very good.

Considering that most studio executives I've met are, charitably, slow readers—they don't *all* necessarily move their lips when they read—keep it simple, stupid . . . and readable.

A Good Set of Bones

A well-structured script with a strong "spine."

Don't lock yourself into your ending.

As you write, your ending will gradually become apparent to you . . . almost as though it were a ship coming out of the fog.

Keep it in mind, but don't let it block you from considering other endings—the ship coming out of the fog may be the wrong ship.

William Wyler agrees with me.

The director said, "A lot of people come to me with great openings. I don't want a great opening. I want a great ending, because with most stories you can't find a good ending."

Take George Foreman's literary advice.

The former heavyweight champ said, "So many people, especially young people, think that everything now is about digital and television, but nothing will ever surpass the written word. Character has to be written about. Writers used to give us character but now too many writers have abandoned character."

Take Mike Tyson's literary advice, too.

The people want to be lied to on a grand scale," said former heavyweight champ Tyson. "They want heroic characters. The people don't want to believe their idol is a freak; that he likes to get fellatio. They don't want to believe that he might want somebody to stick their finger up his butt."

Begin with your characters, not the plot.

Novelist Flannery O'Connor: "In most good stories, it is the character's personality that creates the action of the story. If you start with a real personality, a real character, then something is bound to happen."

The Core of the Character

What is it that makes your character tick?

You can't, of course, put it that simply when you are asked this question—What is the core of the character—by the producer, director, studio execs, and actors.

Be prepared to make up a whole bunch of fancy-sounding Freudian, Jungian, Shakespearean, Homeric *bullshit* about what makes your character tick.

If you have problems with your plot, you're not alone.

Oscar winner Alvin Sargent (*The Way We Were*): "When I die, I'm going to have written on my tombstone, 'Finally, a plot.'"

HOW TO DEAL WITH WRITER'S BLOCK . . . THE PAIN IN THE ASS SOLUTION.

This has always worked for me: Let's say I'm on page fifty-seven when I'm blocked. I go back to page one and retype the whole thing.

Through the process of retyping all the scenes, I have always found where I went wrong—and why, feeling that I went wrong, I shut down.

I have found that actual scene or sequence and, by rewriting it as I retype it, I have unblocked myself.

I know it's a terrific pain in the ass to go back to page one and retype the whole damn thing, but it's always worth it.

Character is everything.

Novelist/screenwriter Larry McMurtry: "Movies have largely lost interest in character. It is not without significance that two of the most publicized characters in the cinema have been a shark and a mechanical ape."

Listen to the voices of your characters.

Screenwriter William Faulkner: "I listen to the voices, and when I put down what the voices say, it's right. Sometimes I don't like what they say, but I don't change it."

Let your characters live.

Have a rough idea of where you're going with your story but not too clear an idea. Let your characters talk to you and determine their own way—within boundaries that are not clearly marked.

You'll know you're doing well when your characters start taking over and are nearly giving you dictation, which sometimes comes so quickly that it's tough to keep up with; when your characters are literally talking to you; when words and images are coursing through your brain (without drugs) at a meth-fueled pace.

Deliver the Moment

Realize your story; empower your characters to live up there on-screen.

Write human beings, not scenes.

Novelist Eudora Welty: "The frame through which I viewed the world changed, too, with time. Greater than scene, I came to see, is situation. Greater than situation is implication. Greater than all of these is a single, entire human being, who will never be confined in any frame."

Don't "nice" your script up.

Don't purposely set out to make your characters more likable and sympathetic so your box office will be bigger. Audiences aren't stupid and will smell the bullshit as it's being heaped on them from the screen.

Let your characters be themselves; don't make them share your opinions and convictions.

Screenwriter William Faulkner kept using the phrase "A character of mine once said" throughout his life.

Don't burden your lead character with too much back story.

The only time you need any back story at all is if the back story is relevant to the plot. This usually happens only in a thriller.

Otherwise, the personae of your lead actors is, in a sense, all the back story you'll need. It is part of what actors are paid for: They superimpose the public's perception of their personalities onto that of your characters.

The word *perception* is key here. For example, it doesn't matter if your male romantic lead is gay in real life and favors rough sex . . . as long as the public perception of him is that of a nice-guy heterosexual Romeo. It is also true that in Hollywood some of the gay romantic leading men who like rough sex are married and have kids (to make sure that the public perception of their images is a positive one).

Take your time revealing your main character.

Mystery goes a long way—don't tell me everything I need to know about him/her in the first ten minutes unless you're writing some real simpleminded television script.

Keep surprising me with little character twists all the way to the third act; unless you're going for a great big cathartic twist at the end of the movie, your main character should be completely defined by the beginning of the third act.

A Built-in Sphincter

A character who brings comic relief to a drama. My character Sam Ransom (Robert Loggia) in *Jagged Edge* was a built-in sphincter; he played it well.

A Black Shirt

A major character that you know will die.

Don't write a "leggy" script.

Even though character-driven scenes will be the first ones to be edited for time and budget reasons, these are the scenes that will give depth to your script. Give it some heart; otherwise, as they say, your script will be "all legs"—all plot, racing from one point to another.

The Meat of the Thing

The climactic moments that lead up to the moment of catharsis.

Don't show your characters smoking in your script.

For many years, because I smoked four packs of cigarettes a day, because I thought smoking was cool, and because I resented what I deemed to be politically correct assaults on my smoking, I showed my characters smoking in my scripts.

I didn't care if I was glamorizing smoking or causing young people to start smoking.

Then I got throat cancer. I consider my cancer my personal punishment for glamorizing smoking on-screen.

Don't bring the same karma upon yourself that I brought upon myself.

Let's repeat that.

Kirk Douglas: "Hollywood started me smoking, literally putting a cigarette in my hand. Who knows how many moviegoers have started smoking because of what they have seen on the screen? Too many movies glorify young people smoking. It doesn't have to be this way."

Conflict means spinal fusion.

The most important component of the spine of your script is conflict, and the dramatic tension that flows from it.

Without the introduction of conflict, you can't hold your audience; they'll get restless and leave what you've put your heart and soul into, going for the urinal or the candy counter instead.

Conflict doesn't have to be physical, of course; it can be cerebral, understated, and subtle. But it has to be there.

You can combine conflict with attraction and create a spicy and often sexy stew that will both hold and amuse your audience. I did that in *Betrayed, Jagged Edge,* and *Basic Instinct.* There was conflict between Tom Berenger and Debra Winger, between Jeff Bridges and Glenn Close and between Michael Douglas and Sharon Stone. But, as in real life, the conflict led to attraction, or attraction was part of the conflict.

The most hard-hitting of all conflicts is when the heart is in conflict with itself, when the heart is torn. In *Betrayed,* Debra falls in love with Tom even as she knows that he is a neo-Nazi murderer. When she kills him, she blasts away a part of her own heart. In *Jagged Edge,* Glenn falls in love with Jeff, saves him through her own skills and strength gained in prison, and then discovers that he is a murderer and that he's been using her all along. And in *Music Box*, we see the deadliest conflict of the heart: A woman who adores her immigrant father winds up protecting her son from being poisoned by her father's cruelty and racism.

When my friend Richard Marquand was shooting *Hearts of Fire,* he called me from the set one day to tell me that Bob Dylan and Rupert Everett, who played rockers vying for the same young woman, were getting along so well as actors that it was impossible to bring out the underlying conflict their characters were supposed to have between them on-screen.

Richard said, "I've decided just to let their characters be friends."

I said, "You can't do that. If there's no conflict between them, there's no triangle. If there's no triangle, the movie isn't about anything."

"I'm not disagreeing with you," Richard said. "But there's nothing I can do about it. Bob and Rupert like hanging out, and every time Rupert looks at Bob, Rupert says, Bob makes him laugh. And neither of them really want Fiona. Rupert, as you know, is gay, and Bob says he doesn't want to kiss Fiona."

I said, "He won't kiss Fiona? Why the hell not?" I'd had a long afternoon in New York getting to know Fiona—we'd begun with two bottles of Cristal at Tavern on the Green—and I thought her eminently kissable.

"I'm not certain," Richard said. "I think it has something to do with his newfound Christianity. He says he doesn't want to be seen kissing anyone on the big screen."

I realized we had a love triangle where the two guys didn't want the girl for different reasons and liked each other more than they liked the girl.

I feared the movie was dead. And it was. When it was released after Richard's death, there was no underlying tension to it, no conflict—just an actor and two tired rockers making tired, friendly, "Have a nice day" faces at everybody.

Categorical Imperative

**The underlying thrust of your script—the motivation that gives it
power, that makes your hero go the extra mile to achieve what he wants.**

Tone is everything.

The tone of your script is even more important than the structure of it. It is the key to your script's success. If your tone is
off, the movie will not work.

No matter how good the structure is and no matter how sharp the dialogue,
your script is hostage to its tone.

In my experience, hitting exactly the right tone comes with rewriting and
polishing. It is like selecting the right volume on a stereo or like the volume of
an actor's performance: If it's even slightly off, it's all over.

A Built-in Spine

What the movie is about—the drama at its core.

Slug it out with your second act.

The second act is the most difficult to write because the first and
third acts have built-in, surefire dramatic potential.

But in the second, you have to move your story and your characters along as
speedily as possible.

The director of *Jagged Edge* (Richard Marquand) and I kept taking the film
out to preview audiences and getting dismal responses. But when we cut eight
minutes from the film's second act, audiences erupted at the end of the movie
with applause.

Adrenalizer Scene

If things are slowing down, you inject one of these into the spine of the script.

Don't worry about first- or second-act curtains.

You don't need them. Just follow a general three-act format, but you don't have to pay off each act by giving it an ending. Your need is for one ending and one ending only—at the end of the film (the end of the third act).

Does Your Story Hang?

Does your story climax? Is it well-structured?

Don't be afraid of ambiguity.

The ambiguous ending of *Bridge on the River Kwai* was thanks to producer Sam Spiegel, who believed "that the audience should make their own choice."

Producer David Selznick believed in ambiguous endings, too: "Let the audience write their own ending."

Ambiguity can make you a lot of money, too.

Surveys after the success of *Basic Instinct* showed that many people were going back to see the movie twice, or even three times, because they were involved in arguments with others about who the killer was.

I was asked over and over again about the ending of the movie by people who recognized me.

"Catherine did it, right?"

Or: "She didn't really kill anybody, did she?"

My answer to every one was this: "Go back and see the movie again. Pay close attention; there's a clue near the end that will answer everything for you. If you still don't get it, see it again."

Needless to say, I had significant "points" in the movie. And made more money every time someone bought a ticket.

But if you want to sell your script, an ambiguous ending can be risky.
Michael Douglas had a full-rupture hissy fit over the ending of *Basic Instinct*. He wanted to blow Sharon Stone away at the end. He said the film "lacked redemption" and would fail at the box office.

The studio didn't like the script's ambiguous ending, either, and the only reason it stood is because the director, Paul Verhoeven, wouldn't allow the film to be focus-grouped. The focus group would certainly have voted down the ambiguous ending.

If you're writing a mystery, let it be a mystery to you, too.
I think the true test of a successful mystery, one that will fool audiences, is to be able to switch the last scene and still have the movie make complete sense.

Take the last scene of *Basic Instinct*. It would have made sense if Nick had killed Catherine, and it would have made sense if Catherine had killed Nick. But the ambiguous ending—the ice pick under the bed—was the most surprising.

The same thing is true with *Jagged Edge*. It would have made sense if the tennis pro had been revealed as the killer at the end instead of Jeff Bridges, but it wouldn't have been as daring. Partly because Jeff Bridges was the perfect casting for a killer—until *Jagged Edge*, he had always played some variation of the homespun, down-to-earth good ole boy.

It's okay to leave audiences confused at the end of your movie if you're writing a mystery.
If they're somewhat confused, they'll talk about your movie with others—and they'll argue about what happened at the end.

In the case of *Basic Instinct*, they argued about what the ice pick under that bed meant. Did it mean that she'd kill Michael? Or did it mean that she wouldn't use that ice pick on him because she loved him.

With *Jagged Edge*, as Siskel and Ebert discovered, people weren't sure *who* that was on the floor when the mask came off. Was it the tennis pro (played by actor Marshall Colt), or was it Jeff Bridges? So a lot of people went back to see it again—and the movie made a lot of money.

If you leave them confused, though, make sure they *like* the movie. Because if they don't like it, they'll never go back to see it again and they'll trash it to their friends.

My feeling is that people like to be fooled by a mystery's ending—to be taken in some direction they never expected—but a lot of studio executives would disagree with me. Their feeling is that a movie (even a tough mystery) needs a soothing last scene, one that will make people leave the theater happy— the classic television ending.

I point to box office. *Jagged Edge* and *Basic Instinct* both had surprise endings that faked audiences out. Both were huge hits.

Spell it all out in your script.

Leave as little as possible for the director to screw up. View what you're writing not as a blueprint for a film, but as literature. Lie to yourself—tell yourself that not only may millions of people see your movie but millions may read this script that you're writing.

So it has to be . . . perfect!

You can subvert your future director with beats and adverbs.

When you write a scene, control how the scene is paced by indicating "beats"—screen moments. If you indicate in the script when a character is to deliver a line of dialogue (after two beats, say) and then the actor is exposed to your description in the script, he will be influenced by your vision (no matter what the director tells him).

And if you describe how your character is to say a line (sweetly, with an edge, with a grin, etc.) and the actor reads your description, it will affect his performance.

Through the course of fifteen films, I had only one director who caught on to my game and stripped the script of beats and adverbs before he gave it to actors: Costa-Gavras.

"Why?" Costa said. A long beat . . . and then (sweetly): "Because I am the director and not you, okay?"

Use your iron.

Screenwriter/director Paul Thomas Anderson (*Boogie Nights*): "Screenwriting is like ironing. You move forward a little bit and go back and smooth things out."

Try not to masturbate too much while you're writing your script.

In a survey done a decade ago, it was determined that writers masturbate more than people in any other profession.

If you do, you'll go blind and grow hair on your palms and . . .

You will take that creative edge that should be going into your script and put it into your hand, so to speak.

How to deal with writer's block . . . the Lamborghini solution

If you live in L.A.—which I told you not to—go over to Budget in Beverly Hills and rent a Lamborghini for the weekend. Drive it out to Joshua Tree National Monument and then back. Tell yourself that if you finish your script and it's a hit movie, you'll be able to buy yourself one of these babies.

You'll finish the script (I promise).

More is more.

On the first draft of an original screenplay, don't make it too tight and lean. Don't worry if it's around 140 pages; producers and studio people have a theory that anything can be cut down. But if it comes in at around one hundred pages, many of them will ask, "Where's the beef?"

Screenwriter Michael Tolkin (*The Player*): "The director is someone who can take all the intentions and make sense of them for the reality of a production. All scripts are too long, all written scenes are too long, all dialogue is too wordy; this is the inevitable dividend of being written in a room, usually alone."

If you write a script that's too long.

Cheat on the margins. Extend and lengthen the margins on your page. Chances are good that the person timing your script (a minute a page is the rule) won't notice what you've done.

The downside is what happened to me on *Betrayed*. My script was about thirteen pages too long, but it read great. I didn't want to ruin how it read by cutting it down. So I extended the margins on both sides and at the bottom, too.

Halfway through the shoot, I got a call from the producer, Irwin Winkler, telling me that half the script had been shot and that at this rate it would be a three-hour movie.

I had to fly to the *Betrayed* set in Canada and cut my script—cut from the parts that *had not yet been shot.*

Cutting that way, I'm sure, threw the whole movie out of whack. It's not impossible that extending my margins ruined the fundamental structure of the movie.

But, as I said, the script read beautifully. It was passed around town and admired, and when the movie failed, there were those who said they're read the script and it was brilliant and that obviously Costa-Gavras, the director, had ruined it.

Tighten your script as much as you can.

Poor you. As studio head Arthur Krim said, "There's always going to be another turn of the screwdriver."

If your script reads beautifully, rewrite it.

A good script is about character and action, not language. If the language is literary and gets in the way of dialogue and action, it should be a short story or a novella, not a screenplay. In a script, the simpler the better.

It's okay to repeat yourself in a script.

An old studio rule: Never use anything once that you can use twice.

Pick your characters' names for how they sound.

For *Basic Instinct,* I named my burned-out, streetwise homicide detective Nick Curran because I thought the name made the character sound cool and tough. Catherine Tramell, I thought, sounded classy and vaguely threatening.

Sharon Shone thought I'd named her after a tramell, "a death shroud in Scottish mythology," and complimented me for my subtlety. I shouldn't have corrected her, but, being Hungarian, I couldn't help myself. She didn't believe that I'd named her after Alan Tramell of the Detroit Tigers, one of my favorite baseball players.

The truth is that I've named a lot of my characters after ballplayers; I keep the *Baseball Encyclopedia* near my desk.

I also tend to use first names that are classic and old-timey; I think there are way too many Brets and Austins and Dylans (even Jaggers) on the big screen. A Jack, I think, is ageless; a Dylan, I fear, might be out of style in a few years, replaced by an Eminem or an Usher.

Don't name your characters for personal reasons; it never works out well.

I gave a villain in *F.I.S.T.* the first and last names of an editor I had clashed with at the Cleveland *Plain Dealer* in my reporting days: Tom Vail.

I gloried in the notion that this person who had fired me from the paper would recognize himself on the big screen as a bad guy.

At the time, I didn't know that studios vet with a research firm all the names in scripts they are filming.

In this case, the firm's report came back with this notation: "Tom Vail was once Mr. Eszterhas's editor at the Cleveland *Plain Dealer* and fired him."

Don't ever name a character after the man or woman you love.

I learned the lesson painfully: Nomi Malone of *Showgirls* was named after my beloved wife's childhood nickname, Nomi—the name I called her in intimate moments.

Not anymore. Not after a stark-naked Elizabeth Berkley came up to her on the set and said, "Hi Nomi, I'm Nomi." Not after *Showgirls* turned into one of the great bombs of film history.

Some names can get you big laughs.

Every time this TV newsman introduced himself in *Jagged Edge,* we got big laughs from preview audiences. We couldn't figure it out until I changed the guy's name.

His new name was Tom—no laughs. His old name was Dick—big laughs. A producer friend told me that the name Peter on-screen always gets the same reaction.

Sometimes you can have a little fun with your names.

New York Times film critic Janet Maslin was always more than a little hard on my movies, once even calling me "the Andrew Dice Clay of screenwriters."

When I wrote *An Alan Smithee Film: Burn Hollywood Burn,* I created a fictional character named Janet Maslin, a critic and desperate wannabe screenwriter who hated the work of the fictional character Joe Eszterhas.

The studio's lawyers made me change the name of the fictional character Janet Maslin, first to Sheila Maslin and then to Sheila Kaslin.

I made sure, though, that the director, Arthur Hiller, cast an aesthetically challenged woman as the fictional Sheila Kaslin.

You can get a LITTLE cute naming your characters.

In the movie *Sliver,* one of the characters is talking on the phone to her agent. She says, "You're a sleazeball, Michael. You're a bully. You're two-faced, Michael. You're a sad excuse, Michael, for a human being."

You'll notice the constant reiteration of the name Michael.

I had very publicly fired my agent, Michael Ovitz, four years earlier.

HOW TO DEAL WITH WRITER'S BLOCK . . . THE VIAGRA SOLUTION

A screenwriter I absolutely, categorically won't name told me this story. He was blocked writing a script and he took Viagra. He figured if Viagra helped one thing, it might help another. He was still blocked, though, after he took the Viagra.

But now he was blocked and had a big hard-on. He called his girlfriend and said he was on his way over to see her. They got into an argument when he got there and he stormed out and went home, where he sat down and tried to write. He was still blocked.

But now, his hard-on was making him so uncomfortable that he couldn't even sit at his desk anymore. He lay down in bed and tried to figure out how to get himself unblocked. After awhile, he found himself unblocked with one thing but not with the other.

Don't try to write classic lines of dialogue.
If you write them, you'll write them accidentally, not purposely. They'll pop out of the material.

I've written two famous, or infamous, lines through the course of fifteen scripts.

Flashdance: "When you give up your dream, you die."

Showgirls: "How does it feel not to have anyone comin' on you anymore?"

Twenty years after I wrote that line (the former, not the latter), my parish priest told me it had been the inspiration of his life.

Take it from zsa zsa

At all costs, don't write lines like this.

Actress and famed Hungarian femme fatale Zsa Zsa Gabor: "I adore George [Sanders] in that movie because he was so rude with women, saying the words of Somerset Maugham, like: 'All women are like little beasts. You have to beat them and that's when they love you.'"

No one can predict what will become a classic line of dialogue.

The studio felt strongly that the last line of *Jagged Edge* would be an oft-repeated one.

After a bloody, nerve-racking battle between a masked Jeff Bridges and Glenn Close, private eye Robert Loggia looks at Jeff's body on the floor and says, "Fuck him. He was trash."

Nobody remembered or repeated the line. Some people, focus groups showed, didn't even hear it.

A Three Beat

Three lines of dialogue—the last line (the three beat) pays the first line off.

Read your dialogue aloud to yourself.

When you think you are finished writing your script, organize a reading with your significant other and your friends. The more you *hear* the words you've written, the more you'll want to polish the words to get them just right.

Play your dialogue back to yourself on tape.

I'm convinced that the really smart wannabe screenwriters driving aimlessly around the 405 or the 10 in L.A. aren't doing it because they read *Play It As It Lays*.

They're doing it because they're listening to tapes of themselves reading their screenplays.

You're better than a tape recorder.

Paddy Chayefsky: "I'd like to find a tape recorder as clever as I am in dialogue. The whole labor of writing is to make it look like it just came off the top of your head."

If you can come up with a good title, you're halfway there.

To boffo box-office heaven, that is, although the road to a good title, even a bad title, can be a circuitous, even byzantine one. Consider the following.

While everyone involved with the production agreed that *F.I.S.T.* was a great title, it didn't matter. The movie itself didn't work and *F.I.S.T.* tanked.

Flashdance was a great title. Indeed, while most of his script was gone in my rewrite, Tom Hedley, the original screenwriter, had come up with that great title.

Jagged Edge was a great title, but it wasn't mine. My title for the movie was *Hearts of Fire*—a crazily misfired title for this tough courtroom drama. The title *Jagged Edge* was the brainchild of a studio assistant who pored through every word of my script and found the description "knife with a jagged edge" for the murder weapon.

I used *Hearts of Fire* again years later for a rock-and-roll movie with Bob Dylan and Rupert Everett. It didn't work for *that* movie, either. Nobody saw it. The movie was so bad that it literally *killed* the director, my friend Richard Marquand.

My favorite title was *Telling Lies in America*, an offbeat piece about a young Hungarian man who wants to be a writer. The original title was *Magic Man,* and I changed the title so that studio execs reading *Telling Lies in America* wouldn't know it was the same script they'd read ten years ago.

The only way to outwit their computers and avoid old readers' reports was to change the title. I was pulling a scam, and the scam gave me the best title I'd ever come up with.

What do you expect from a young man who wound up making millions for the made-up stories—the *lies*—that he told to the world?

My worst title was probably *An Alan Smithee Film: Burn Hollywood Burn.* Too clumsy, too gawky, too geeky. I like the movie (I'm one of the few), but I hate the title.

That was God speaking to me.

My script entitled *Love Hurts* was in its brown envelope and I was almost out of the house on my way to Federal Express to send it to my agent, when I suddenly thought of another title for it: *Basic Instinct.*

I ran back inside the house, unsealed the envelope, and typed up a new cover page.

Did you see Anhedonia?

W oody Allen wanted the title of *Annie Hall* to be *Anhedonia* ("the inability to feel pleasure"). His cowriter, Marshall Brickman, wanted the title to be *It Had to Be a Jew.*

Save your titles.

I wrote a script about two little boys who go off on an adventure together. I called it *Pals.* I sold the script with that title to Lorimar Pictures. The studio didn't like the title and came up with a new one: *Big Shots.*

Years later, when Richard Marquand and I were talking about making a movie about a hardhearted man and his relationship with two little kids, I called it *Pals.* The title was again changed by the studio, this time to *Nowhere to Run,* although the studio had previously called it *Lion on the Lam* (yup, you read it right).

Since all these years have passed, and since I have four little boys now, I am planning to write a new script about a hardhearted man and his relationship with four little kids and calling it *Pals* (just kidding).

You can recycle your titles.

M y movie *Betrayed* was first called *Sins of the Fathers,* then *Father of Lies,* then *Heartland,* and then *Eighty-Eight.*

My movie *Music Box* was at first called *Sins of the Fathers* and then *Father of Lies.*

You can't copyright a title.

I n 1927, Ben Hecht wrote an original screenplay called *American Beauty.*

In 2000, another *American Beauty* (1999) won the Academy Award for Best Picture.

They can steal your title.

T he producers were working on a script with playwright Bernard Slade, who also had a play running in London that was called *Fatal Attraction.*

The producers decided not to make the script Slade was working on, then went on to work with a young writer named James Dearden on a thriller. The thriller became a hit movie.

It was called *Fatal Attraction*—nothing but a coincidence, of course, nothing at all to do with Bernard Slade's play.

How to deal with writer's block . . . the broken toe solution.

My wife bought me a heavy rock at an art fair. On it were written the words Writer's Block.

I kept it on my writing desk.

One day, blocked on a script, I smashed my desk with my fist and the Writer's Block fell on my big toe.

It hurt like hell. I put ice on it, but it still hurt like hell.

I went to the doctor and he said the toe was broken. There was nothing he could do, though, except put a bandage on it and tape that toe to another one.

I hobbled back home, sat back down at my desk, and found myself, miraculously, unblocked!

I moved my Writer's Block from my writing desk to my bedroom nightstand as a possible talismanic weapon in other creative situations.

My big toe still hurts, six years later, when cold weather sets in. The doctor says I've got arthritis in it.

There are obviously pluses and minuses, ups and downs, to a Writer's Block.

You're finished writing your script—this is your greatest moment as a screenwriter.

Playwright Robert Anderson: "I feel best about a play when I finish writing it, just before I send it off to anybody. I've written it, but no one has seen it, no one can say anything about it, no one can piss in it."

Hold on to the first draft of your script as well as all notes you may have taken in longhand.

You never know. Most scripts will rot away in storage somewhere, but . . .

I still have my rough draft of *Basic Instinct,* written on my manual typewriter and entitled *Love Hurts,* with notes to myself (in the second draft) in the margins.

Last year, a French movie memorabilia freak who loved the film offered me $500,000 for it. I turned him down. I figure that by the time my grandchildren sell it, it well be worth more than the $3 million I got for writing it.

I know that sometime in the future, the director of *Basic Instinct,* Paul Verhoeven, will be able to finance a movie with what *he'll* get for my first-draft script of *Showgirls.* Not because of the value of my script, but because each scene of his script is scrawled over with his pencil drawings of the way he saw the scene on-screen. Paul's script is an erotic comic book of breasts, butts, and vaginas, accompanied by my words translated into Paul's Dutch.

I know Paul also has, but probably won't sell, the scented pair of panties Sharon took off and handed him the morning he shot the beaver in *Basic Instinct.*

Once you finish your script, you don't have much control.

Novelist/screenwriter George Pelecanos: "There are so many things that are out of your control as a screenwriter. It's not just the 'evil producers.' It's also actors, directors, editors, cinematographers, the crew—anything that gets between you and your words, from when you're sitting in your room to the time it's up on the screen."

Make lots of copies of your script.

Thinking about posterity, send your script to friends and relatives and as many libraries as will accept it.

Screenwriter/novelist Raymond Chandler: "There is no available body of screenplay literature because it belongs to the studios, not to the writers, and they won't show it."

What can you do to prevent being ripped off?

It's not easy to do anything about it. You can do a few things to protect yourself, but not many. The day that you finish an outline or a script, send it to yourself in the mail. When you receive it, make sure *not* to open it and make sure you put it away in a safe place. That way, if you're ripped off somewhere along the line, your lawyer can dramatically open the envelope in a courtroom and prove (a) that you wrote it and (b) when you wrote it.

Just as important: You can send an idea, a script, or an outline to the Writers Guild of America and register it—even if you're not yet a member of the Guild. (You can even do it on-line. It will cost you twenty dollars if you're not a member.) If you're ripped off, you can then refer to the contents and the date in court.

If you are about to have a meeting with a studio executive, a development person, a producer, a director, an assistant to any of the above, or an agent to pitch a story, as soon as you get home from the meeting, write a memo describing the details of the meeting as well as the details of the story or stories that you pitched. Same drill as before: Put the memo in an envelope, send it to yourself in the mail, and don't open it when it comes back to you.

Besides these things, there's not much you can do if you're ripped off except sue. But suing is probably worth it. There are law firms that will take your case on a contingency basis. Studios and production entities usually don't want to go to court. So the chances are better than even that you'll make some bucks with a settlement.

Don't ever tell the press what you're writing.

I was ripped off with my very first movie, *F.I.S.T.*

Shortly after stories in the trade papers reported what *F.I.S.T.* was about, an Oscar-winning screenwriter—ironically, from my hometown—made a deal with a network to do the same story on television.

Because TV movies take a much shorter time to make, his film—*Power*—came out before *F.I.S.T.* did. So when *F.I.S.T.* came out, it appeared that I'd ripped off *Power*.

I was pissed, especially because I knew that this same Academy Award–winning screenwriter had been fired from my hometown newspaper—where I, too, had worked, albeit many years later—for stealing a watch from the scene of a jewelry store robbery that he was covering.

Interestingly, I, too, was fired from that same newspaper—not for stealing a watch, but for calling my editor some bad names in an article in a national publication.

A pox on both our houses, I say: He's a thief; I'm an ingrate.

The best way to avoid being plagiarized.

Jay Leno: "You have to write faster than they can steal."

Parallel Creativity

The phrase that will be used by someone who has plagiarized you.

PART FIVE

SELLING THE SCRIPT

How Do You Feel About Going to Bed with an Agent?

You've written your script. You need an agent or somebody in the business to read it. What can you do?

If you've read other screenwriting books, this is where everyone fudges. "Well," they say, "it's hard"—or they tell you to look up some agents' names in *Writer's Yearly* and send your script around.

This is what you do if you are a sexy, relatively good-looking man or woman willing to do *anything* to succeed.

You buy a plane ticket to L.A. You check yourself into a cheap motel in the Valley. You rent a car. You dress yourself up *good* to show your *assets.* Then you drive down to the bar of the Four Seasons or the Peninsula or the Mondrian in Beverly Hills or Hollywood and you pick out someone who looks like an agent or a development person (not that difficult to pick out: Prada or Armani black uniform, Cristophe haircut). And then you let yourself be picked up by him or her and you go home or upstairs in the hotel and you *fuck that person's brains out.* You fuck like you've never fucked before. You fuck like it's the bang of the century in *Basic Instinct.*

And before you leave, you give the person your script.

Let's go over that again.

Did you hear me right, though? Was I actually saying ... was I advocating *whoring* there?

No, no, no! Forget everything you've just read. That's truly diabolical advice and I'm not the devil, am I? *Am I?* I'm a former altar boy, a devout Catholic. I even carry the cross on some Sundays at the Church of the Holy Angels in Bainbridge Township, Ohio.

The kind of diabolic advice you've just read is given by the most jaded and corrupt Hollywood veterans, the kind of nontalents who tell you that it's not *what* you know but *who* you know that will make you successful.

So I was just kidding, okay? Playing a devilish joke on you. I was kidding the same way I was kidding when I told teenagers to bring their fake IDs to see *Showgirls*. I was kidding then, too, but America didn't get the joke. So I thought I'd put it into boldface type this time: **You do not—do not, do not—have to pop an agent to make it!**

What you have to do is much less demanding (both physically and morally). You have to sit in a comfortable chair and make up a story that hundreds of millions will want to see.

And while you don't have to sleep with an agent, nobody is saying your story can't include a bit of sex and violence. You can still carry the cross to the altar, even after writing *Basic Instinct* and *Showgirls*. You don't have to be cynical yourself to write about corruption and corrupt people (either in a script or in a book cynically entitled *The Devil's Guide to Hollywood*).

Don't follow Madonna's example.

She appeared in the office of Barbara Boyle, Orion's head of production.

She dropped to her knees and sexily said, "I'll do anything to get this part."

Boyle said, "I'm happily married and I'm straight."

Madonna said, "You should try everything once."

Madonna got the part in *Desperately Seeking Susan*.

Don't follow Warren's example, either.

When Warren wanted to convince studio head Jack Warner to make *Bonnie and Clyde,* he grabbed Warner by the knees, fell to the floor, and said, "I'll kiss your shoes here. I'll lick 'em."

Jack Warner was not convinced.

He said, "Yeah, yeah, get up, Warren."

If you need the home address and phone number of an agent who'd be perfect to help you, this is what you do.

Go to Variety.com and read stories about screenwriters selling scripts to the studios for big bucks. Make a list of five screenwriters.

Call the Writers Guild of America West and identify yourself as an assistant to producer Scott Rudin (or Joel Silver, Jerry Bruckheimer, or Edward

Pressman). Ask the Guild to tell you the names of the agents representing the five screenwriters you picked from the Variety.com site.

Armed with the names of the five agents, get in touch with a Los Angeles private eye and make a deal with him to get you the home addresses and phone numbers of the five agents. (There will be a fee involved here, but it will be well worth it.)

Send your script to the home addresses of the five agents and wait a week. After a week, call them at home and ask if they've read your script. If you get any kind of positive (or frightened) response, convince the agent to meet with you at his office.

If you get a rude refusal to read your script, take it in stride and keep sending your script to the agent's home once a week.

Always be very polite. Most agents are abject cowards. If you keep bugging them (nicely), sooner or later they'll read your script—or have it read by an assistant—and see you just to be rid of you.

A more traditional way to find an agent.

Screenwriter/director Ron Shelton (*Bull Durham*): "The best way to get an agent is to send the manuscript to every agent ten times. That's how I got an agent. I spent three years sending my script to everyone who would read it and knocking on doors. I sent it everywhere. Everyone in town is always looking for something they can sell. Get a list of the agencies that read unsolicited manuscripts."

Or you can do what Andrew Kevin Walker did.

He worked at Tower Records in L.A. for three years while writing the script he entitled *Seven.*

When he was finished, he called the Writers Guild with a list of writers who had written scripts about mass murderers. He asked for the names of their agents.

Then he called the agents, but, of course, he couldn't get through to them directly. However, he spoke to their assistants, who told him that they wouldn't accept unsolicited screenplays.

And then, brilliantly, he pitched his script to the assistants very simply: "It's about a serial killer who kills according to the seven deadly sins."

He went down the list, pitching to the assistants, until one of them said, "Okay, send it. I'll read it."

She did, loved it, and gave it to her boss.

Seven, a brilliantly written piece, became one of the biggest hits of 1995. And Andrew Kevin Walker quit his job at Tower Records.

Or you can join the Church of Scientology.

Many big-time Hollywood actors belong to the Church of Scientology, and you just might meet them if you join. If you meet them, you just might get a chance to slip them your script.

On the other hand, screenwriter Floyd Mutrux, a longtime member of the Church of Scientology, hasn't had very many movies made, making me think that the rumored rigorous discipline of Scientologists might not be worth the access to a star.

On the other hand, there's that machine called the E-meter that vets each screenplay its members are asked to star in.

If that's really true, though, I wonder how *Eyes Wide Shut* got past the E-meter for Tom Cruise.

If you don't want to become a Scientologist, this is what you can do to get your script read by someone important.

- You can skydive from a rented plane onto Steven Spielberg's Pacific Palisades estate and hope your daredevil exploit impresses the house manager enough so that she will give your script to Steven.

- You can streak naked through the shower room at the Riviera Country Club and hand your plastic-bagged script to Sylvester Stallone. (If he likes it, you'll probably have to share credit with him.)

- You can swim to shore off Brad Pitt's Santa Barbara estate and leave several copies of your script around the pool, then race back to the beach and swim back to your boat before security gets you.

- You can visit the Coppola Winery in the Napa Valley, shake Francis's hand, and slip him a couple of C-notes to get your script to Sofia.

- You can pretend to be an exterminator and show up at the door of David Geffen's estate in Malibu. Since Malibu always has a rat problem, chances are excellent that someone will let you in.

- You can go down to Maxfield's on Melrose or Chrome Hearts on Robertson and slip a clerk a couple of twenties for some Maxfield or Chrome Hearts boxes. You can then send the boxes (with your script inside) to the agents, producers, or directors of your choice.

  Maxfield's and Chrome Hearts boxes are almost always immediately opened by the addressees themselves, not assistants, because the addressees are afraid their assistants will steal whatever goodies are inside those boxes. Also, if the agents, producers, or directors are successful, chances are excellent that he or she shops at Maxfield's or Chrome Hearts.

- You can go down to the Coffee Bean on Sunset and slip your script to Jennifer Aniston.

  My brother-in-law, a sometimes-aspiring screenwriter, drinks double lattes there but so far has not had the cojones to slip any of the beautiful people there his masterpiece. He does, however, keep a chart on his wall of the stars he's sighted at the Bean, along with time and date of sighting and witnesses.

- You can go down to the office of Dr. Robert Koblin on Robertson or that of Dr. Edward Kantor off Wilshire Boulevard and wait around. Koblin is an internist who treats many of the most powerful people in the industry; Kantor is known as the "ENT man to the stars." These folks who walk into these offices may not exactly be happy to see you there waiting for them with your script, especially if they are in pain or stressed to the max, but you've got a living to make, don't you?

  And as my director friend Richard Marquand used to say, "Fuck 'em if they can't take a joke!"

You can follow them into the john.

Mike Medavoy: "I'll be using the men's room at the AMC Century 14 and some one will hand me a script. 'You should make this script,' the man will say; 'it's a lot better than the last film you made.' There hasn't been a woman in the men's room yet, but there will be."

A Script Stalker

A screenwriter capable of following you anywhere or doing anything to get you to read his/her script.

Even Steven Spielberg needs an agent.

Steven Spielberg hadn't had an agent in many years. He felt he didn't need one. Then he sent Tom Cruise a script he wanted Tom to do with him. More exactly, he sent Tom's agent at CAA— the Creative Artists Agency, run by Michael Ovitz—the script he wanted Cruise to do, an old F. Scott Fitzgerald short story.

Steven didn't get an answer—not a yes, nor a no—for six months.

At the end of six months, Steven Spielberg signed CAA up as his agents—so he would get an answer from Tom Cruise.

He got his answer: Tom Cruise said no. He didn't want to do that script with Steven, although he did hook up with Steven about a year later.

Steven Spielberg must have felt he needed an agent pretty badly.
It couldn't have been easy for Steven, the most powerful director in Hollywood, to sign up with CAA.

He knew that before he married Kate Capshaw, CAA head Michael Ovitz had chased her around his office.

Why Steven Spielberg has never been represented by Jeff Berg at ICM . . .
Jeff's brother, Tony, said, "A Steven Spielberg film is a classic example of a third-rate melodrama elevated way beyond its depth. I can't think of a filmmaker whose stuff I like less. His work is so manipulative."

Mike Medavoy isn't smart about everything.
When his client Steven Spielberg didn't walk out on his deal with Universal as he had recommended, agent Medavoy fired Spielberg. Medavoy: "I'm just glad that wasn't the defining point of my career."

An agent will help you to hold on to your aureole.
Writer/director Elia Kazan: "Let your agent tell the lies. Get a hireling to drop the axe so that you never fog your aureole of culture and gentility."

Your first agent won't be your last agent.
I had an agent who told me we'd spend decades together; six months later she stopped being an agent and became a very successful interior decorator in New York.

I had an agent who said, "My job isn't to give you advice. My job is to respond. When you say 'Jump,' I say 'How high?'" I fired him.

I had an agent who told me it would take him two weeks to read an original screenplay I'd written. I figured he was too busy to be my agent or that he moved his lips when he read. I fired him.

I had an agent who spoke with a thick English accent many years after she'd spent six months working in London. After awhile, the accent was driving me nuts. I fired her.

I had an agent who, in the middle of a negotiation with a studio, disappeared for ten days. Nobody knew where he was. He finally reappeared and whispered to me, man to man, that he'd gotten hold of a "big bag" of cocaine and had been in Puerto Vallarta with a well-known sexpot movie star. I fired him *after* he concluded the negotiation successfully. It's not impossible that I fired him because I was jealous.

I had an agent who was depressed and gloomy much of the time while he was representing me. A producer friend and I had a bet that one day he'd drive into the desert (he liked to go to Joshua Tree alone on weekends) and blow his brains out. But we were wrong. He went on Prozac, stopped being depressed, stopped driving out into the desert, married a beautiful, smart woman, and is now one of the most powerful men in Hollywood. I fired and rehired him *twice* in my career. I like him.

I had an agent who was one of the coldest people I've ever met and one of the smartest. We had nothing to talk to each other about besides business—our conversations usually lasted thirty seconds or less. I finally fired him because, although he was very good as an agent, I just couldn't tolerate his coldness anymore. He wrote me an affable postcard after I fired him, wishing me the best of luck. It was the warmest communication he'd ever had with me. He also said that sooner or later he knew I'd rehire him because I'd realize just how good he was as an agent. A couple years after he sent me the note, I rehired him. I was with him for a couple years, until his coldness got to me again and I fired him once more.

Don't let your agent give you creative advice.

Whatever he tells you will be stupid.

It's what George Bernard Shaw said to Sam Goldwyn: "Mr. Goldwyn, all you want to do is talk about art and all I want to do is talk about money."

I knew an agent who not only hired a reader to read all scripts for him but then hired another reader to read that reader's reports and compress them into one paragraph—or no more than thirty words.

A Rainmaker

An agent who makes a lot of money (with successful clients) for an agency.

Agents have their own agendas.

The morning that we began the *Basic Instinct* auction, I asked the head of my agency, Jeff Berg of ICM, who he thought was going to buy it and how much he thought it would sell for.

Jeff said he thought Mario Kassar at Carolco would wind up buying it for $3 million.

Jeff ran the auction himself. Everyone in town except Fox played and bid against one another. And at the end of that long day, Mario Kassar of Carolco bought it for $3 million.

How did Berg know? Was there a side deal between ICM and Carolco that I didn't know about? Was there a kickback to ICM? Not that I was ever able to uncover, but I was suspicious.

Of course it's also possible that Jeff Berg is more than just one of the smartest people in Hollywood. It's possible that Jeff is a genius and a seer.

The *Ubermenschen* of Hollywood

What CAA agents, led by Michael Ovitz, were known as in the 1990s.

How you can tell that your agent cares about you . . .

He calls you three times a week at least. He has nothing really to say to you, so he says, "I'm just checking in," thinking, maybe, that you've turned into a hotel.

He kisses you on both cheeks every time he sees you. He tells you he loves you every time he sees you.

How you can tell that your agent doesn't care about you . . .

He calls you three times a week at least. He has nothing to say to you, so he says "I'm just checking in," thinking, maybe, that you've turned into a hotel.

He kisses you on both cheeks every time he sees you. He tells you he loves you every time he sees you.

You're part of the ebb and flow.

There is an ebb and flow in the client business," agent Jeff Berg once told me. "You lose a client and you ask yourself, How can I get a new one?"

You don't want a sweet and adorable negotiator.

Legendary former agent Freddie Fields: "What excuse do you have, what defense against a proper negotiator, when you've been bettered? You call him a killer, a cold-blooded guy. They're all overused terms. There's no such thing as a sweet, warm, adorable good negotiator."

Try to find an agent who's seen it all.

Like my longtime agent Guy McElwaine—studio head at Warner Bros., Columbia, and Rastar; married seven or nine times; represented Frank Sinatra, Judy Garland, Peters Sellers, Yul Brynner, Burt Reynolds, Sharon Stone, Richard Pryor; married on three separate occasions to separate women at the Splendido Hotel in Portofino, Italy; once made love to Natalie Wood on top of a pool table in a bar where the jukebox was playing Sinatra; once won a white Lincoln Continental in a poker game from golfer Johnny Miller; once pulled producer David Geffen off a conference table when he was about to duke it out with Warner Bros. head Ted Ashley.

Be a pain in your agent's ass.

Screenwriter Anna Hamilton Phelan (*Gorillas in the Mist*): "My agent gave me the best advice an agent had ever given me. He said, 'I represent a lot of big people. I'm going to forget about you unless you bug me. You have to call me. You have to call me three, four times a week and you have to make me crazy. Make me hate you. If you don't, I'm going to forget about you, and this is not going to go anywhere.'"

Tumeling

Where agents want to be: at the center of the action.

If you've written a new script and want to give it to your new agent . . .

Wait until the next time he's flying to New York and give it to him the day before he leaves. He'll be captive for five hours, and that means:

1. **He'll probably be able to finish the script before he lands.**

2. **He won't stop reading it to take any phone calls.**

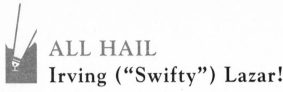

ALL HAIL
Irving ("Swifty") Lazar!

David O. Selznick, the most powerful producer in town at the time, said of him: "There is one man who is single-handedly ruining the motion picture industry as we know it. The ridiculous prices he demands for books and plays and writers will surely be the end of us all."

To Wirtschafter

To lose clients because of stupid things you said during an interview—like William Morris agent David Wirtschafter, who lost clients after an interview he did with *The New Yorker* magazine.

What was that about the black heart of an agent?

When agent Marty Baum retired from CMA, where he'd worked for many years, his fellow agents gave him a Cartier tank watch. He discovered that it was a Hong Kong knockoff.

I wouldn't hire this guy.

A CAA agent hustles new clients by saying, "I want to be your asshole," or "I want to be your bitch."

Try to get your agent to lie for you.

This won't be easy, because your agent will have better relationships with studio executives (whom he's known for a long time) than with you. But if you can somehow get your agent to do it, it will pay off big-time.

In 1980, I wrote a spec script called *City Hall* and sent it to my agent. He loved it and decided to auction it. He sent it out to Paramount, Universal, Warner Bros., and MGM at the same time. Within hours, Paramount, Universal, and MGM passed. Warner Bros. was thinking about it.

I asked my agent to tell Warner Bros. that one of the three who'd passed wanted to buy it. He said he couldn't lie to people he'd had a relationship with for a long time. I reminded him of my two little kids, the house we had just bought, the mortgage payments owed, the college educations I would one day have to pay for.

He interrupted me and said, "You really are a Hungarian, you know."

He called Warners and told them Paramount wanted to buy *City Hall* and he was only calling to inform them of this. Warners decided they wanted to buy it, too—but came in at a low figure. He told them Paramount was at a higher figure. Warners then came in so high that it set a new industry record for a spec script, beating the price for William Goldman's *Butch Cassidy and the Sundance Kid.*

Shortly afterward, the Warners executives who bought the script were fired. Almost twenty-five years later, *City Hall* is still up on the Warner Bros. shelf—unmade. The money they paid for it, though, has long been spent.

Don't be fooled by the paintings on the walls.

I had an agent who lived in a posh Beverly Hills house with spectacular art on the walls—sometimes.

Sometimes when I saw him, the art was there, but sometimes the walls were bare.

One of his colleagues explained it to me: The paintings were rented. Some months he was able to foot the bill and other months he wasn't.

As a matter of fact, I discovered, the house was rented, too, and both the Jaguar and the Mercedes were leased.

It's okay to be a pawn in their game.

If you write scripts that are made into movies, agencies will kiss your butt.

This isn't because they care about you—you are, after all, nothing but a schmuck writer—but because they can use you to convince superstar actors to let them represent them.

The superstar actor will think that if this agency represents him, he will get first crack at your script.

Michael Ovitz was a con artist.

When superagent Michael Ovitz graduated from Birmingham High School in Encino, California, he received an award of merit at the senior breakfast. It was for being "class con artist."

Michael Ovitz was a frat boy.

When superagent Michael Ovitz became president of his fraternity at UCLA, his fraternity brothers called him "King" Ovitz.

Michael Ovitz was a narc.

When the members of the rock band Sly and the Family Stone took a look at their new agent, Michael Ovitz, one of them yelled, "Narc!"

Michael Ovitz was a mensch.

This is how Mike Medavoy first met agent Michael Ovitz: "I'd never talked to him before, but I knew who he was and took his phone call. He said to me, 'My name is Mike Ovitz. I don't know you, but I intend to be your best friend. I want to come and see you.' I asked when. He said, 'Now.' Fifteen minutes later, he appeared at my door."

Michael Ovitz was a healer.

When superlawyer Bert Fields's wife was ill with cancer, agent Michael Ovitz arranged for the best specialists at UCLA to treat her. When screenwriter Robert Towne's Hungarian dog bit him severely, Michael Ovitz arranged for the best specialists at UCLA to treat him. When I hurt my back in Santa Fe, New Mexico, Michael Ovitz called me and offered to fly his acupuncturist to my home in Marin County.

Michael Ovitz was my fairy godmother.

The first thing Michael Ovitz asked me at our first meeting—this was about six years before he told me that his foot soldiers would put me into the ground—was this: "What's your biggest dream? I need to know so I can make it come true."

Michael Ovitz was Magic Johnson and Aristotle combined.

Superagent Michael Ovitz, explaining his success: "Read *The Art of War* and *Tao Teh Ching,* get it flavored by a little of Aristotle, and watch the Los Angeles Lakers do a fast break. It's like watching a Swiss watch work as they drive down the court, five guys; Magic Johnson would look, fake, and rarely take the shot. That was my philosophy."

Michael Ovitz used Robert Redford.

I'm not worried about the press," agent Michael Ovitz told me at a meeting in September of 1989. "All those guys want is to write screenplays for Robert Redford."

Michael Ovitz was Citizen Kane.

When he began representing Bill Carruthers, producer of game shows, Michael Ovitz asked him to give his wife, Judy, a spot as a model on the show *Give and Take*.

Michael Ovitz was a killer.

On rare occasions when he told something to his friends confidentially, Michael Ovitz said, "This is a private conversation. If you ever repeat it, I'm going to kill you."

Michael Ovitz was the Godfather.

After his first meeting with agent Michael Ovitz, comedian David Letterman told a friend, "I've been to see the Godfather! I had a meeting with the Godfather!"

Michael Ovitz was the Antichrist.

NBC president Don Ohlmeyer called superagent Michael Ovitz "The Antichrist." Producer David Geffen then commented, "Apparently Don Ohlmeyer thinks more highly of Michael Ovitz than I do."

Nobody punked Michael Ovitz!

When I read that Michael Ovitz blamed his demise on what he called "Hollywood's gay mafia," I remembered something he'd said to me in our famous meeting in 1989, during which he'd threatened to destroy my career if I left his agency.

"You think you're just going to leave this agency and I'm just going to take it?" he said. "Nobody makes a faggot out of me—nobody!"

How did Michael Ovitz get away with acting like the Antichrist?

Mike Medavoy: "Ovitz got away with it because people thought he had his hand on some kind of nuclear launch button. The moment fear of him disappeared, he became fair game for everyone who resented his methods."

I punked Michael Ovitz.

If you make me eat shit, I'm going to make you eat shit," superagent Michael Ovitz told me at a meeting in September 1989.

I even stole Michael Ovitz's best line.

Ten years after Michael Ovitz told me his foot soldiers who went up and down Wilshire Boulevard would "put me into the ground," and several years after Ovitz left CAA, his former agency asked me to appear in their annual video.

I improvised my line on the video: "My foot soldiers who go up and down Zuma Beach will put Mike Ovitz into the sand."

Michael Ovitz believed what they wrote about him.

In the 1990s, Michael Ovitz said to reporters, "I understand I am the single most powerful force in the entertainment industry." Ten years later, he was out of the business.

Now Michael Ovitz is a fucking bum.

Years before I had a public fight with him and fired him, Michael Ovitz tried to convince me to let him represent me.

I had a big meeting with him in a CAA conference room, where a bunch of other agents were present, and said no thank you to Ovitz's pitch and walked out of the room.

Ovitz called Don Simpson, the producer I was working with at the time, and said, "Who is this fucking bum to do this to me?"

Michael Ovitz had a role model.

When Tommy Dorsey wanted to leave MCA, his agent, Billy Goodhart, said this to him: "Tommy, if you continue this bullshit, making everybody miserable, you see these balls?" He bent over and grabbed his own balls. "I'm gonna cut yours off. Not only won't you be working for MCA, you won't be working for anybody else for maybe the rest of your life. You have something to say, put it in writing. Now get the fuck out of here—you irritate me."

A threesome: Michael Ovitz, Roseanne, and Zsa Zsa.

After Michael Ovitz threatened to destroy my career, Roseanne Barr, whom I'd never met, sent him a note with the words "Fuck you!" scrawled all over the page.

I was flattered . . . until I heard that after my fellow Hungarian Zsa Zsa Gabor was arrested for a scuffle with a Beverly Hills cop, Roseanne sent Zsa Zsa a note that said, "Fuck them all!"

The Writers Guild can be punked, too.

When I was in a public battle with agent Michael Ovitz—and he was denying the threats he had made to destroy my career—I asked the Writers Guild for support.

The Writers Guild issued a statement saying that "if Ovitz did the things Eszterhas alleges," he was wrong.

In other words, instead of supporting me, the Writers Guild was publicly questioning my integrity. And, of course, they launched no investigation of Ovitz or agency tactics.

The president of the Writers Guild at the time was George Kirgo, a television writer represented by the Creative Artists Agency, headed by Ovitz.

We'll Kill for You!

The sentence with which superagent Michael Ovitz concluded his pitches to prospective clients.

I tried that same phrase out on a literary agent who wanted to represent the books I wrote. "I want you," I said, "*to kill for me*!"

The agent, Ed Victor, urbane, sophisticated, and very *literary* (he lives in London) blanched, and looked like he was having cardiac arrhythmia.

This is the agent you need.

George Shapiro, a William Morris agent, had his assistant answer the phone by saying, "George Shapiro's office—kill for the love of killing."

Most agents don't read books.

When Julius Caesar Stein was running MCA, the superagency of its day, he decorated the building with antiques he bought in England.

The bookcases he bought needed books, so he bought roomfuls of leather-covered books he called "furniture books."

No one who worked at MCA ever read the leather-covered books, but Tennessee Williams, who was represented by MCA, told his friends, "If you're ever in the building, take five or six books. They'll never miss them."

Your agent can screw up.

Agent Swifty Lazar: "When I sold *Rich Man, Poor Man,* I made a great mistake—and, over time, it cost me my friendship with Irwin Shaw [the author]. The lowliest writer who sells his book to television gets, by union contract, at least a guaranteed minimum for repeat showings and spin-offs. In Irwin's contract, there was no such provision. I know what I was thinking—I'd had such a struggle selling it that I believed it would never get beyond the option stage—but I should have protected Irwin better. I had no excuse."

It's okay to fire your agent.

Sean Penn: "Changing agents is like changing lounge chairs on the deck of the *Titanic*."

If you make it big, you don't have to return your agent's call.

Sydney Pollack on not returning agent Michael Ovitz's calls: "Sometimes I didn't take his calls. And he would say, when I finally did, 'Did you get my message? You didn't return my call.' And I would tell him, 'I didn't return your call, Michael, because there's nothing to say. All you want to say to me is, 'I'm just checking in.'"

If you're angry at your agent.

Director Sam Peckinpah liked to get drunk and then hurl knives at a dartboard. He'd ask his agent over sometimes to hold the dartboard.

If you're successful enough, your agent will clean up the poo-poo.

Mae West told her agent, my fellow Hungarian Johnny Hyde, who would later make love to Marilyn Monroe, to clean up the poo-poo whenever her pet chimp had diarrhea.

I told that story to one of my agents, and she said, "That's what we do all right; we work with chimps and clean up their poo-poo."

But it might be smarter if you clean up the poo-poo.

Today's agent might be tomorrow's producer and next month's studio head.

Mike Medavoy: "In the entertainment industry, people change jobs faster than they change cars, girlfriends, clothes, sometimes even underwear."

Underwear?

If your agent dies, forget about him.

Agent mogul Julius Caesar Stein of MCA asked in his will that his clients Benny Goodman and Dinah Shore perform at his funeral.

When Stein died, both Goodman and Shore declined, citing previous commitments.

PART SIX

FILMING THE SCRIPT

LESSON 11

Steal As Much Memorabilia from the Set As You Can!

Your new agent has submitted your script to a studio. He tells you that a "studio reader" is reading it. Who is a studio reader?

The studio reader who first gets your script and either recommends it or not to the studio execs is your worst enemy.

This person is a wannabe screenwriter trying desperately to break into the business. He wants to shout out his own erudition and cinematic skills by impressing the studio execs—by deconstructing, castrating, disemboweling *your* script—and telling the execs how *he* could and would make it better.

Few readers ever *praise* a script, because they know that very few scripts ever become hit movies. They don't want to put their own pimply, pale skinnies on the line in support of a script that will probably never be made and would probably be a disaster even if it were made.

When I auctioned the script of *Basic Instinct,* a reader at Warner Bros. trashed the script and advised the studio not to bid on it. When the studio discovered a few hours later that everyone else in town was bidding on it, the Warner's executives decided to bid on it, too, although they hadn't read it and their reader had advised against it. The reason, of course, was that they figured if *everyone else* was bidding to buy it, the script *had to be good* and their loser reader/wannabe screenwriter *had to be wrong.*

The execs could have shut themselves off in their offices and read the script; it would have taken them an hour to two (even if they moved their lips while reading).

But since they all hated to read, they didn't read it; they just automatically *bid on it.* They ultimately bid $2.5 million; it sold for $3 million. And when the auction was over, they fired their reader/wannabe screenwriter for making an obviously bad call.

When *Basic Instinct* made $500 million, their woeful, misbegotten reader was captured by the studio's foot soldiers one night (at Starbucks), driven to the back lot (near the water tower) at Warner Bros., and beheaded.

Oh no, all those readers have been McKee'd.

Robert McKee's Web site bio says, "Several companies such as ABC, Disney, Miramax, PBS, Nickelodeon and Paramount regularly send their entire creative and writing staffs to his lectures."

If the first studio passes on your script . . .

Sugar Ray Robinson, former middleweight champion of the world: "You never know how tough you are till somebody knocks you down and you decide whether you wanna get yourself up or not."

A Calling-Card Script

A script that you don't sell but that studio execs read as an indication of your talent. Figure it his way: Even if you don't sell the script that you've put your heart and guts into, it still might get you a writing job—although this kind of figuring can get a bit overdrawn at times. I spoke to a wannabe screenwriter once, who said, "I haven't sold anything yet, but I've got six or seven really great calling-card scripts."

Cover the Waterfront

It once used to mean something very different, but now it means getting your script to as many potential buyers as possible if you're trying to sell it on a spec basis.

A Pussy Hair Away

According to producer Robert Evans, this is a deal that's almost but not quite done.

After several months of trying, your new agent has sold your script to a studio. They ask you how long it took you to write it. Lie.

After I had sold *Basic Instinct* for $3 million, many people asked me how long it had taken me to write it.

I had my answer down pat: "Well, I've probably been working on this script for most of my life. It's about homicidal impulse and thrill killing, and I was fascinated by those things even twenty-five years ago, when I was a journalist. I remember I interviewed a mass murderer named Edward Kemper when I was writing for *Rolling Stone* magazine, and before that, when I was a reporter in Cleveland, I interviewed two kids there who'd killed their parents, Freddie Esherick and Treva Crosthwaite. And I'd known and worked with cops from the time when I covered the police beat in Cleveland to the time I interviewed narcotics agents for *Rolling Stone.* I actually had my office in Cleveland in the basement at Central Police Station. I even covered a shooting where eight policemen were shot down in the streets a couple hundred feet in front of me. And I did a profile of a burned-out cop very much like the Nick Curran character in my script; he was involved in so many shootings, he was suspended from the force. And, from the point of view of the other central character, Catherine Tramell, well, I've already written three films where women were manipulated by men—*Betrayed, Jagged Edge,* and *Music Box*—and I wanted to write a story about a woman who is so smart and so sensual that she can manipulate even the smartest streetwise homicide cop. And, of course, I'm a writer and the central character of this piece is a writer. I wanted to get into the whole notion of becoming your characters, of getting too close to the fire and getting burned. So, as you see, this script comes from deep in my soul, and maybe the reason it was sold for so much money is because the buyers sensed the authenticity, the reality, of it."

This was all true, but it was also malarkey. Because while it was true that I had done all the things I referred to in my little speech, it had taken only thirteen days from the moment I had the idea to the moment my agents sold the finished script at auction.

Truth is, I had gotten $3 million for maybe ten days' writing.

I certainly wasn't about to tell anyone *that.*

Had I said that, many people in Hollywood would immediately have said, "Never mind that it sold for three mil, if all it took to write it was ten days, then it's a piece of shit." (Few in Hollywood knew or would have cared that it took William Faulkner *six weeks* to write *The Sound and the Fury,* one of the most complex *novels* of our time.)

Only after *Basic* was a smash did I tell the press that it had taken just thirteen days from inception to sale.

I told the truth, then, to flip a gigantic bird in the face of Hollywood.

Thirteen days and five hundred mil! I can do that and you can't!

But nowhere have I revealed my real motive for writing that script. In 1980, I had set a record for a spec script by selling *City Hall* for $500,000. I had broken my own record a couple of years later by selling *Big Shots* for $1,250,000. Then a writer named Shane Black had broken my record by selling *The Last Boy Scout* for $1,750,000.

I read about Shane's sale—and my record being broken—on the front page of the *Los Angeles Times* while I was vacationing at the Kahala Hilton in Hawaii. Shane's sale pissed me off. I wanted my record back. I wanted to see an article on the front page of the *Los Angeles Times* about me setting a *new* record.

I flew home from Hawaii and sat down immediately and started writing the most commercial script I could think of.

Twelve days later, I had my record back. I had the article on the front page of the *Los Angeles Times* about *my* new record. And I had my $3 million.

Arthur Miller lied, too.

He didn't tell anyone for many years that he wrote the first draft of *Death of a Salesman* in one day and part of a night.

Always lie about how many drafts you've done.

Tell the studio or the producer that it's your fifth or sixth draft but that it's just the first one you're turning in.

Gore Vidal tells this story: "After about three weeks, I turned in my first draft. The producer couldn't believe it, he wanted me to work forever and ever because he wanted his money's worth. I remember telling him, 'Yes, but what I do in the first draft is generally the best, and people usually end up going back to it.' He said, 'No, no, no, no, we must work harder.'"

ALL HAIL
William Saroyan!

Agent Swifty Lazar: "One day L. B. Mayer mentioned that he was looking for some new stories. By coincidence, Saroyan had just called me—he always rang when he was broke. I explained what Mayer was looking for and urged him to come up with something. I then told Mayer that I had a Pulitzer Prize–winning writer with a great story. A few days later, I brought Saroyan to Mayer's office. As Saroyan took him through the plot, L. B. Mayer began to tear up—he was a real crier. My heart was less moved: I knew Saroyan was making it up as he went along.

"'That's terrific,' Mayer said, when Saroyan finished weaving his tale. 'Now go wait outside and I'll talk to Irving about it.'

"Saroyan dutifully strolled out to the parking lot.

"'How much?' Mayer asked.

"'He wants one fifty,' I said.

"'He's got it.'

"I went to Business Affairs to work out the payment: fifty thousand up front, fifty thousand when he hands in half the story, then a final fifty thousand when he turns in the ending. Elated, I hurried out to the car to tell Saroyan I'd gotten him fifty grand to start.

"'What's the total?' he asked.

"'One hundred fifty.'

"'Get me the one fifty. I need all of it right now.'

"'You're crazy.'

"'Tell him I want the one fifty now or no deal.'

"I went back to Mayer's office and explained the situation—and he agreed to give Saroyan a check in full. I raced back to Saroyan and told him I'd deposit the check, take my commission, and give him the rest tomorrow.

"'No, I want the money in cash, now.'

"'You're crazy, can't you wait two days?'

"He apparently couldn't—his bookies had threatened him.

Back I went to Mayer, who called Business Affairs. And they arranged for the bank to bring the money over to the studio in hundred-dollar bills. I took the loot to the parking lot, and stood with Saroyan as we counted the money out on the hood. With every ten thousand he took, I'd take a thousand for myself, until I had my fifteen grand and he had the rest. Then he went off to pay his bookie."

Get a piece of the ice pick and white scarf sales.

My lawyer got me a healthy percentage of the merchandising from *Basic Instinct* after a long struggle with the studio's Business Affairs lawyers.

Of course, there *was* no merchandising for *Basic Instinct*.

If you sell your script, try to get a credit as executive producer, too.

There are so many producer credits these days that your agent shouldn't have much of a problem getting this in your contract.

If you get the credit, it means you'll get your name on-screen and on the poster (the "one sheet") twice—as writer and executive producer.

Seeing your name on-screen twice might help the audience think that this is *your* movie and not the director's.

What kind of power does being executive producer of your film give you?

None.
　　I know. I executive-produced many of my films. Anyone from the actor's manager to the producer's son to the director's mistress can get a producer credit today.

"Producer" and "executive producer" credits have become more or less meaningless except for people like Jerry Bruckheimer, Brian Grazer, or Scott Rudin, who truly are old-time Sam Spiegel–like producers.

What being the executive producer of your film might give you—if your agent insists—is your own *director's chair* with your name imprinted on it.

Naomi and I have several of these scattered around the house. Our cats love them, but because of their height, they're a potential death trap for toddlers.

So take care. If your *director's* chair breaks your child's neck, well, that would be the ultimate irony, wouldn't it?

Back-End Points

What Eddie Murphy referred to as "monkey points," a percentage of profits. They are called back-end points not just because the terms are defined in the back of a contract but because—since the points never pay off, due to the studio's accounting practices—they stick it up your back end.

ALL HAIL
Preston Sturges!

He was the first screenwriter to get a percentage of his film's profits. He sold *The Power and the Glory,* an original script, in 1930 for a small advance and big back-end points.

Now that you've sold your script, you're really in deep shit.

Mike Medavoy: "The average studio now has thirty people doing story notes, twenty people playing producer (and taking screen credit for it, too), and focus groups composed of disaffected Generation Xers causing entire films to be reedited into cookie-cutter models."

Google the studio execs you'll be meeting with.

The first time I met Brandon Tartikoff, I was armed with every detail about the life of Ryne Duren, a near-blind former New York Yankees relief pitcher who, I knew, was one of Tartikoff's heroes.

As soon as I walked in, I spotted a framed baseball card of Duren on a wall. I was off to the races, talking about Duren, telling Brandon things even *he* didn't know. The object of my meeting was to try to get Brandon to approve my friend Tom Berenger in the cast of *Sliver.* Thanks, I am convinced, to Ryne Duren, Brandon agreed to cast Tom "as a favor" to me.

Prepare for your creative meetings.

I realized a few hours before Jimi Hendrix's sister and brother-in-law were to come to my house in Malibu that I didn't have any paintings of Jimi on my walls, while I did have paintings of Dylan and the Stones on display.

I quickly called a friend who had a Ronnie Wood print of Jimi, and he took it off his wall and messengered it to my house. I put it up on my wall, replacing Dylan just as Jimi's sister and brother-in-law were pulling into my driveway.

They were impressed by the print of Jimi they saw on the wall, but ultimately they turned down my offer to do a script of Jimi's life.

If you're going to your first studio meeting and you're terrified, remembering this will terrify you.

Keep in mind what Mike Medavoy, former studio head, said about studio people: They don't change their underwear all that often.

If you have a meeting at the studio, don't park on the lot.

Screenwriter James Brown: "I meet with the producer at Warner Bros. At the main gate that afternoon is a long line of cars waiting for the guard to check them through. Ahead of me are a Mercedes, two BMWs, and a Porsche. I am driving an eleven-year old Nissan pickup with a broken muffler, and it's loud. People are staring at me and I'm suddenly self-conscious. On a whim I put it into reverse, and instead of parking on the studio lot as I was instructed to do, I leave my old truck at a meter down the street and walk back to the guard's booth."

Don't take any breakfast meetings.

Novelist/screenwriter Jay McInerney: "A breakfast meeting is the nastiest and most inelegant of Hollywood inventions."

Tell the people who want to meet with you for breakfast that you write at night and don't get to bed till five or six in the morning.

Try to avoid meetings with a whole roomful of studio executives.

John Gregory Dunne: "To attend one of those meetings is to understand the cold truth of the saying that a camel is a horse made by a committee."

Check your crotch before a meeting.

Comedian Alan King: "Never walk into a meeting with a creased crotch."

Don't wear shorts to a studio meeting.

There is a dress code you should follow—jeans, sneakers, vintage rock-and-roll T-shirt or new Tommy Bahama silk shirt (not oversized, but hanging out), and a baseball cap (not a MLB hat or a trucker's hat—they're for star actors—but the kind that sits snugly over your head and doesn't sit like a crown up there). Shades are okay, but they should be taken off as soon as you walk into the room.

If you go to a script meeting at a studio, hug everyone there.

Hugs are much better now than they were in the past," a retired agent in her seventies said to me. "People are in much better shape than they were in the old days, when a hug meant being bounced off of some fat belly."

If you're sitting in a story meeting . . .

Let them talk first, even if they want *you* to.

Dodge and say, "You know, I'm really interested in hearing your ideas. I've always been much more of a listener than a talker."

Someone in the room will invariably say, "That's why you're such a good writer."

Smile shyly then and, looking humble, say, "Thank you."

In a story meeting about a script they haven't yet bought . . .

Say as little as possible.

There are probably people in the room who will steal what you are saying and plug it into another project they are overseeing.

The surest way for a studio to get a bunch of fresh ideas on a doddering project is to do a series of meetings with auditioning screenwriters who want to be hired for the project.

Chances are good that the studio will steal your ideas and then hire a "pro" who doesn't do auditions.

The studio will then give the this so-called pro their "notes," incorporating all the ideas that the studio execs stole from all the screenwriters they auditioned.

In a story meeting after they've bought your script . . .

Understand that no matter how friendly these people are being to you, all they really want to do is to *impregnate* your script with their syphilitic story ideas.

You can do a little kissy face, and you can even do a little petting, but don't let them stick it in. Once they stick it in, they will not pull it out before the movie comes out.

When the movie comes out, it will minimally look like them and not like you.

If you let them stick it in often, the movie won't look like you at all. It will be all theirs.

Know, too, that if the movie is stillborn, the film doctors will blame *your* script for its demise. The name on the script will be yours, not that of the studio executives who stuck it into you.

Steal their cigars.

Screenwriter Calder Willingham felt producer Sam Spiegel was picking on him unfairly during their story meetings. So each time Spiegel went to the bathroom, Willingham stole one of his cigars.

Studio execs know they can't write.

That's why they need *you.*

So as you sit there in a meeting with them, don't take notes on the stupid ideas they are telling you, and don't tell them how smart they are, because underneath their BS, they know they can't write.

Don't be afraid to tell them they don't know what they're talking about; *they know they don't* and in their hearts (deep, deep in their plaqued-up hearts) they agree with you.

To put it in Hollywood terms:

They won't respect you if you swallow. So gag.

And spit it back up in their faces if you don't like the taste of it.

It's okay to throw up after a meeting.

Screenwriter/playwright Harold Pinter: "As soon as he read my script *Accident,* the producer Sam Spiegel summoned me to his office. He began his commentary by saying, 'You call this a screenplay?' He then said, 'You can't make a movie out of this. Who are these people? I don't know anything about them. I don't know anything about their background. I don't know what they're doing. I don't understand what they're up to. I don't understand one thing. I think you have to seriously rethink the whole script.'

"I said, 'No, I'm not rethinking it. That's it.' When I got out of there, I was sick on the pavement."

Your script is probably doomed.

Director Jean-Pierre Melville: "I'll tell you what makes a good film. Fifty percent is the choice of the story. Fifty percent is the screenplay. Fifty percent is the actors. Fifty percent is the director. Fifty percent is the cinematographer. Fifty percent is the editor. If any of these elements goes wrong, there goes fifty percent of your film."

If they can't find a director willing to direct your script . . .

Remember that Elia Kazan, John Ford, Howard Hawks, Nicholas Ray, Carol Reed, William Wyler, and Fred Zinnemann all passed on directing *The Bridge on the River Kwai*.

If they can't find a producer willing to produce your script . . .

Remember that producer Sam Spiegel passed on the first James Bond script, saying, "It's utter nonsense."

If they've been trying to cast your script for six months without success . . .

Remember that Albert Finney and Marlon Brando turned down playing the lead in *Lawrence of Arabia*.

If you want Spielberg to read your script and Tom Hanks to star in it . . .

Convince Lori Goddard, who highlights hair in Beverly Hills, to read it.

If she likes it, she can tell Kate Capshaw about it—Lori does Kate's highlights.

If Kate likes it, she'll tell her husband, Steven Spielberg, about it and Steven will read it.

If Steven likes it, he'll tell his friend Tom Hanks to read it, too.

Don't worry about getting a big star into your film; stars don't matter.

When we got Sylvester Stallone into *F.I.S.T.*, coming right off of *Rocky*, we were overjoyed. The movie tanked.

Jeff Bridges hadn't had a hit movie in many years when he did *Jagged Edge*; nevertheless, the movie became a hit.

Sharon Stone was perhaps the biggest star in the world when she did *Sliver*, coming right off of *Basic Instinct*. It didn't matter. The movie failed.

Nobody had ever heard of Jennifer Beals when she did *Flashdance*; despite that, the movie went on to make $500 million.

I got Sylvester Stallone, Jackie Chan, and Whoopi Goldberg into *An Alan Smithee Film: Burn Hollywood Burn*; the movie bombed.

Also think Harrison Ford in *Random Hearts,* Kevin Costner in *The Postman,* Sean Connery in *The Avengers,* John Travolta and Dustin Hoffman in *Mad City*.

How not to deal with the director of your film . . .

You don't have to bend over *this* low . . . or stick it up in the air *this* high.

Screenwriter Ron Bass (*Rain Man*): "I wasn't smart enough to get it right away, but Steven Spielberg was extremely patient with me. He talked with me until I started to realize this was not only something to get behind but was really a much better way than I'd been going. Then we started to meet with Dustin Hoffman and Tom Cruise. There were four-way meetings at Steven's house at the beach. Tom was in many of them and Dustin was in all of them. *They were cowriters.* It was just unbelievable. We invented scenes together; we invented the character together. . . . I can't tell you how much Dustin contributed and how much Steven contributed. Then I went away and wrote this long draft. Dustin really liked it and Tom really liked it. Steven liked it, but he felt it needed more work than the actors did. So we continued to meet and talk about what it needed. And then we reached a moment in time when Steven realized that he wasn't going to be able to do the movie . . . so [Dustin] went to Sydney Pollack, obviously one of the great directors who's ever directed. . . . And he's a very gracious guy. . . . These are like the nicest guys, these directors. They're not only great directors, they're also really great people to work with."

Don't be open to too many ideas about changing your script.

You're the writer; *they're* not. Plus this: Most of *their* ideas will be asinine. Believe me: I've heard *thirty years* of asinine ideas.

Gather around, class, here's point number one: A gaffer on the *Betrayed* set told me he had an idea about my script that he wanted to discuss with me. I grabbed him by his lapels, bounced him off the wall, and hit him in the liver with a beautiful left hook.

Point number two: I carry a hunting knife with me to studio meetings sometimes. I began one meeting by taking the knife and sticking it into the middle of a studio conference table, a stunt I had learned while I was a writer at *Rolling Stone.*

Point number three: I left a gigantic dent in a William Morris Agency's conference table by smashing it with my African Dogon walking stick.

Class dismissed, boys and girls.

If they mess with you, give them a little taste of the old ultraviolence.

Fight the morons if they want to change what you've written.

Paddy Chayefsky: "You spill your guts into the typewriter, which is why you can't stand to see what you write destroyed or degraded into a hunk of claptrap by picture butchers."

After a young director butchered one of my scripts behind my back, I sent him a twenty-page memo when I discovered what he had done. The memo questioned his brains, his lineage, and his masculinity. He had a heart attack after reading the memo and almost died. He was in his *thirties.*

Don't let 'em convince you to rewrite it.

A playwright completely rewrote his play when producers told him it was unproducible. They also told him to change the title to *Free and Clear*.

He threw his rewrite away and decided to go with his original title. Arthur Miller did very well, thank you, with *Death of a Salesman*.

ALL HAIL
Harlan Ellison!

When *Star Trek* producer Gene Roddenberry rewrote one of Ellison's scripts, the screenwriter/novelist publicly said this about him: "Gene Roddenberry has about as much writing ability as the lowest industry hack."

If your script gets butchered, Robert McKee may have done it.

McKee told a reporter in Melbourne, Australia, that he works for studios sometimes as a "story doctor."

This is a doctor whose patients (his own scripts) have all died (unproduced) except for the one patient who lived and became a television movie.

First he teaches you how to write and then he kills what you've written.

Don't worry about hurting their feelings.

I've said things like this to studio execs:

"You don't know what the fuck you're talking about."

"That's the stupidest thing I've ever heard in a meeting like this."

"I make more money than you do, so don't give me any suggestions."

One executive called me "temperamental."

Another executive said, "That's why you write so well. Because you believe in yourself so much."

Another thanked me for my "passion" and said, after I'd insulted her, "That's why you're so successful, because you're so passionate."

I grabbed her and kissed her hard, put her across her desk, knocking the silver-framed picture of her husband and kids down, and tore her black Prada. (Just kidding, and apologies to Mickey Spillane, Frank Miller, Michael Ovitz, and my friend Gloria Steinem.)

If the studio gives you script notes . . .

Tear them up.

That's what screenwriter/novelist Michael Crichton does when the studio gives him notes. When he finishes writing his first draft, he walks away and says, "Thank you very much and fuck you."

Most of the people who are writing these memos today have MBAs, don't read, are too busy writing script notes to see too many movies. Their references in the script notes are to other movies—none going back past 1985—few of which they've actually seen, and certainly none shot in black and white.

If you listen to the suggestions contained in these notes, it's possible that you'll get your script made, but it is also very possible that critics will eviscerate it (and you) and other studio execs won't hire you to do anything else or buy any of your other scripts.

Buy your own shredder and carry it with you.

Screenwriter Julian Fellowes (*Gosford Park*): "A screenplay is a collaborative business because making a movie is collaborative. You write synopsis after synopsis until you find one that's agreeable to the executives. Then you write your first draft and get sixty pages of notes from producers and 150 pages from the studio, then you write the second draft and the director comes in with 400 pages of notes, and then the star does their thing. I understand all of that, but there is a time when you get a little tired trying to accommodate a billion different interests, of the fact that your business is one of compromise where your voice is constantly being given direction."

You didn't have to do it, Ben; you elected to.

Ben Hecht wrote, "My chief memory of movieland is one of asking in the producer's office why must I change the script, eviscerate it, cripple and hamstring it? Why must I strip the hero of his few semi-intelligent remarks and why must I tack on a corny ending that makes the stomach shudder?"

The director tells you to rewrite your script in a way that you know will damage and possibly destroy it. What do you do?

William Goldman: "This is not an isolated incident. It happens to us all. And it happens a lot, usually because of star insecurity, but directors can fuck things up pretty good, too. I did what Michael Douglas wanted. The alternative, of course, was to leave the picture. Which would have been stupid, I think, because the instant I am out the door, someone else is hired to do what I wouldn't."

This is the moment when you separate the writers from the whores. I was confronted by the same dilemma—with the same star.

Michael Douglas (and the director, Paul Verhoeven) wanted me to make a bunch of changes to my first draft of *Basic Instinct*. Convinced that the changes would destroy the film, I refused.

I publicly walked off, which made me look like the greatest intransigent asshole in the world, because I had been paid $3 million for the script.

I kept arguing publicly that the script should not be changed, putting a lot of pressure on Verhoeven (and Gary Goldman, the writer he brought in to rewrite me).

And guess what happened? Because of how hard I fought, because I had publicly walked off, and because I refused to mutilate my own child, Verhoeven, after working with the new writer, changed his mind.

He went back to the first draft of my script and shot it. He fired the other writer. He made Michael Douglas accept the fact that my script could not be changed. And he publicly apologized, saying that he hadn't understood "the basement" of my script and was wrong.

I saved my script from being destroyed by my intransigence and my willingness to fight.

Our scripts are our babies; we create them. Bill Goldman mutilated his own baby and advises that you should mutilate yours—at the behest of a star or a director.

Please don't do that.

I don't know how you (and Bill Goldman) can look yourself in the mirror once you do that.

P.S. The script that I wouldn't change was the biggest hit movie of the year. The script that Bill Goldman changed was a disaster.

If you start rewriting, you can be rewriting for years.

From the time screenwriters John Gregory Dunne and Joan Didion began work on a script called *Golden Girl* until the time it was filmed as *Up Close and Personal,* they did *twenty-seven* drafts of the script over the course of *six* years.

What can they do to you if you refuse to make their changes?

Nothing.

They can fire you and bring another writer in to do their dirty work.

Chances are good that they'll even pay you fully. They can't blackball you, because the town runs on greed and tomorrow you might write something that would make some studio or producer $100 million.

Steven Bochco, probably the best writer working in television, once said, "What are they gonna do? Take me out on the back lot and shoot me? What are they gonna do? They can't take my typewriter; it's mine. They can kick me off the lot, but I'll just write another one."

The agent Michael Ovitz once wanted me to do something I didn't want to do, and I wrote him a letter that ended this way: "So do whatever you want to do, Mike, and fuck you. I have my family and I have my old manual imperfect typewriter and they have always been the things I've treasured the most."

Notice how Bochco and I love our *typewriters?*

Spell it out for 'em.

If they want you to rewrite your script in a way you disagree with, point out to them that *script* is the root of the word *scripture,* as in Holy Scripture.

They wanted Paddy to do some rewriting, too.

So don't get discouraged if you're asked to rewrite. But Chayefsky said, "Can you believe it? These *cruds* want rewrites."

Don't explain anything to anybody.

Screenwriter Dan Pyne (*Pacific Heights*): "When you go to make the movie, you've got to be able to explain to everybody on the movie, from the director on down, what that core idea [for the script] was so that they can see where you started. You have to strip it all back away."

No, you don't. Your deal is to *write* it, not to write and *explain* it. To begin with, have no discussions with anyone on the set except the director. Explain this by saying the director is in charge of the set and you don't want to put yourself in a situation where you're undercutting the son of a bitch.

Otherwise, you'll be having creative discussions with the stars, the gaffers, and the makeup people, who stand around doing nothing and want to express how creative they all are.

Don't strip it away for them. Tell them it's complex and works on different layers, so everyone is free to interpret it according to his or her *own* layer.

Try to do what I did when anyone I met who had seen *Basic Instinct* asked me to tell them if Catherine really did it. I said, "I'm not allowed by contract to tell you that. But go see it again and look for a clue that will definitely give you the answer."

Don't ignore it, fight it.

Screenwriter Jeffrey Boam (*Indiana Jones and the Last Crusade, Lethal Weapon 2*): "I get notes on a script from the lowest-ranking junior executive's assistant reader, who suggests rewrites for dialogue. And I have to endure this. I throw the notes away. I ignore them. I just pay no attention to them at all. You shouldn't fight it. You should just ignore it."

No, Jeffrey. You *should* fight it. You should write the person who sent you the notes a memo, pointing out how stupid, insipid, and benighted his or her ideas are. You should point this out at length and in great detail. And you should send a copy to all the other executives, the producer, and the director.

Your movie has been cast and shooting has begun. They want you to go to the set. What do you do?

Hell no, don't go.

Screenwriter John Gregory Dunne: "I think the writer's presence on the set is just another element in what is often a volatile mix. Tension is the given of a movie, and it has less to do with ego than with the intensity of short-term relationships, a lifetime lived in a seventy-day shoot; if there are location romances, there are also equally irrational location hatreds. If the writer is hanging around, actors ask for a script fix, or why a speech from draft eight can not be substituted for the one in the scene just setting up. I also never speak to a star actor on a set unless spoken to first; this is the actor's office and in his office he or she sets the rules."

In my own experience, everyone will come up to you and present some dumb-ass idea to incorporate into the next scene.

If an actor is having a problem with the director, he'll try to get even with the director by sucking up to you and trying to get you to take a position against the director.

If the director is having trouble with an actor, he'll recruit you to talk the actor into doing the scene his way, not the actor's.

The actor Peter Lawford saw that Dalton Trumbo was on the set of *Exodus,* the script of which Trumbo had written. He went over to Trumbo and asked if he could discuss his character with him.

Otto Preminger, the director, saw Lawford huddled with Trumbo and yelled to Lawford, "You are not to discuss the script with Mr. Trumbo. He is here as a guest and not as a writer."

Lawford said, "Yes, Mr. Preminger," and hurried away from Trumbo.

Don't get too excited watching your film's dailies.

Sam Goldwyn said, "If everyone likes the dailies, the picture's gonna stink."

Try to get videotaped copies of the dailies of your film.

Do this for posterity, of course, and also for eBay, if times get tough in the future.

I've got all the dailies of *Sliver,* including three full tapes of Sharon and Billy "rutting," as Robert Evans, the producer, termed it.

"They're like horses at each other" was the way Evans described it.

Anybody interested?

Steal as much memorabilia from the set as you can.

Everybody does it. If you don't do it, the director will.

Dick Donner has a house in Montana furnished mostly with props and sets from his movies. I visited Steven Spielberg's house in the Palisades years ago and it was filled with what he called "toys" from his sets.

A friend of mine stole the real ice pick from *Basic Instinct* (Planet Hollywood was displaying a phony one for a while), and someone stole my old Royal typewriter—the typewriter I'd actually used to write the script and which also had a cameo in the film—from the *Jagged Edge* set.

The Theory of Creative Conflict

As defined by producer Sam Spiegel: "Films that run smoothly are colorless—only those which are produced in strife have an outstanding merit."

A Production Fuck

An affair that lasts only as long as the shoot.

You can make sure your film will be distributed.

Afraid that Disney wouldn't release *An Alan Smithee Film: Burn Hollywood Burn,* I was ready to show it myself in church halls and school cafeterias.

So I had a copy of the negative illicitly duped, and then I *stole it* (a federal offense)!

I still have it in a closet in the baby's room, hidden underneath a big box of old toys.

Sit in the back row at a studio screening of the rough cut.

John Gregory Dunne: "Don DeLine, the head of production, was sitting directly behind us, and I wished we were sitting behind him so that we could measure his reaction, see where he took notes."

If the Writers Guild arbitrates your screen credit . . .

Remember that the Writers Guild committee that will decide whether to award you screen credit (and more money) is made up of people like you—writers who want credit (and more money) on their writing projects.

The people on this committee *want* to award you the credit, so make it easy for them. Give them a lengthy, scholarly, lawyerly document pointing to all your plot, character, and name changes—and be sure to use a lot of yellow Magic Markers.

I know a screenwriter who, in an effort to get screen credit, sent the Guild committee a document that was longer than his script.

You might have to stand in line to get your screen credit.

John Gregory Dunne: "Prevailing industry wisdom is that the more writers there are on a script, the better that script will be. On our version of *A Star Is Born*, eight of the thirteen writers who actually worked on the script filed for credit.

Scratch and claw for your credit.

Screenwriter Budd Schulberg: "The billing on *On the Waterfront* soured the sweet taste of all of it for me. There was Sam Spiegel's billing twice as big as life, while the name of the writer, and in this case the originator of the project as well, is either left out entirely or reduced to almost ridiculous minuteness."

Your director will try to screw you with your screen credit.

Two easy and common ways:

1. Your name as screenwriter stays up on-screen for three seconds; the director's name stays on-screen for eight seconds.

2. Your name on-screen—in black letters—is against a black background, so the audience can hardly make it out. The director's name—also in black letters—is against a crisp white background, so it is glaringly visible.

If the movie has little to do with the script that you wrote, take your name off of it.

Unless you want to paint the scarlet letter on yourself, don't let your name be on something that isn't yours.

I realize giving up the credit may cost you money, but I argue that you will damage yourself more by feeling like a hypocrite or a hooker.

When I saw the final cut of *Nowhere to Run* (starring Jean Claude Van Damme), which was based on my script *Pals,* I didn't recognize it as mine. I told the studio I wanted my name off of it.

The studio said no. They wanted to use my name in the trailers for the movie, running the line "from the writer of *Basic Instinct,* Joe Eszterhas."

I went to the Writers Guild and demanded that my name be taken off, but the Guild said I couldn't do it—I'd been paid too much money by the studio.

So I petitioned the Guild to give credit to the two guys who'd rewritten me, as well. I was told that it was the first time in Guild history that a writer had petitioned for credit for his "competing" cowriters.

The two guys who had rewritten me got credit behind me, and that way, at least, I was able to spread the blame for the mess that was on-screen.

If they ask you how you like the movie you wrote, tell 'em the truth.

Director Joseph von Sternberg: "When he saw the movie he wrote and I directed, Ben Hecht told the press that he was about to vomit, his exact words being—'I must rush home at once, I think it's mal de mer.' "

Try to find something positive to say about your film.

Sharon Stone, after the release of *Basic Instinct*: "At least it proves I'm a natural blonde."

You might have to drink whiskey from a vase.

If you're attending the first screening of the film and you wrote the script, that is.

Tennessee Williams, attending the first screening of his film *Suddenly Last Summer,* drank whiskey from a vase and muttered, "Who wrote this shit?"

Watching your movie might hurt.

Jim Harrison: "Sitting there in the dark before the projector starts you have the distinct feeling you might be raped by an elephant or, if your imagination is running to the sea, a whale."

Don't tell your friends when or where your movie will be screened.

Actor/producer Danny DeVito: "I've heard stories where people have actually paid other people to call newspapers and say they've seen screenings of movies that were bad—just because they wanted to sabotage the movie. That happens all the time."

Do whatever you can to stop the studio from market-researching your film.
Director Phillip Noyce: "Then we did the first screening for a recruited audience on the lot at Paramount, as was customary for a Paramount film. The guys from a company called National Research Group, run by Joseph Farrell, would go out to malls and cinemas and recruit an audience for these previews. In Los Angeles people are pretty used to being invited. It's a way of getting the lowdown on films many, many months before their release, and, in a town devoted to the entertainment industry, it's also become a way for the ordinary man and woman to have their say. *They can become not just a film critic but a film executive.* The tick of their pen, the cross of their pencil, can decide the fate of the movie they're judging. The preview audience's power has been further increased since the late 1990s by advance reviews appearing on Internet sites such as 'Ain't It Cool.' "

Don't go to any focus-group screenings.
L.A. is a city full of make-believe film critics who wanna be screenwriters. They turn out en masse at focus-group research screenings.

Every twit out there thinks he's a critic, and they all think they know better than guess who?

Not the director, because the director knows things about camera angles and cameras that they don't.

Not the actors, because, well, they're handsome or beautiful or, minimally, graduate students of the Method.

Okay, all together now, they think they know better than—*ta da*—the highly paid, millionaire screenwriter!

And here are all these twits, gathered together in this room, part of a focus group, with the screenwriter usually there, and they have a chance to tell him (with studio execs listening) how it *should have been* written.

And maybe, in the process, they'll be discovered by the director or producer—it's their big chance at the brass ring, at discovery, at stardom, if they can just sound smart enough about what the screenwriter did wrong.

I saw one guy in his late thirties in three of my focus groups at research screenings—*the same guy at three of them,* at *Jagged Edge* and *Betrayed* and *Music Box*—and in all three cases, the guy lectured me about how bad my ending was.

See your films in a theater with real people.
Most people in Hollywood see movies in a screening room or on their home screens. But it's important for a writer to see how a

film affects real people—especially the impact your own lines of dialogue and your story have on them.

This should be the final part of your creative experience of writing a screenplay. It begins in a little room, with you sitting there all alone, making it up, and it ends in a big room, with hundreds of people communicating to you their reactions to what you've written.

If you don't experience what you've written with an audience, then you're not bringing your communication process to a conclusion.

Avoid the industry premiere of your film.

Mike Medavoy: "Industry screenings might be the ultimate hypocrisy in a business that can be very hypocritical. The audience is usually composed mostly of the filmmaker's genuine friends, who applaud and laugh at all the right moments. They want the studio executives in the audience to hear what a great film it is so the studio will support their friend's film with marketing dollars. The studio executives tend to be a group of people who either inherited the film from a previous regime or don't want anything to do with what they think is a potential turkey, so they walk out and praise the film in Hollywood doublespeak. Typically, they can be heard telling the producer and director things like "You did it again" or "What a picture!" neither of which says what it really means. Those executives also know they might need that producer or director in the future. So in the end, everyone runs from a failure and tries to walk alongside a success."

Make sure you're part of the junket interviews.

Some directors like to exclude screenwriters from these interviews because the journalists who fly in from everywhere are bought and paid for—literally. The studio covers all their expenses. That means they're not going to write anything bad about your movie or, if you're there to be interviewed, *you*—not unless they want to lose their sunny weekends sitting by the pool at the Four Seasons, enjoying anything they want to order from room service.

Wash your hands of any blood.

If your script becomes a movie and on the first weekend of its release some sick freak in Omaha kills his girlfriend in the same manner in which you killed one of your characters, forget about it.

Remember that Mark Chapman had a copy of *Catcher in the Rye* in his pocket when he shot John Lennon. And keep in mind that more killers have carried the Bible in their pockets during the act of murder than any other book.

Your words can become toys and trading cards.

Traveling through Italy while *Flashdance* was being released there, I started collecting *Flashdance* trading cards. Each shot of the film I had cowritten had been turned into a trading card. I saw little Italian kids flipping the cards against the curb and trying to win them from one another.

Screenwriter Dan O'Bannon (*Alien*): "When *Alien* was made, I went into a Thrifty Drug and there was a little *Alien* doll in the toy stand. When your work begins to become somewhat influential like that, you do see pieces of yourself come floating back in the oddest places."

If your movie fails, they'll blame the marketing department.

When three straight MGM films with big budgets and big stars failed miserably—*Windtalkers, Hart's War, Rollerball*—the studio didn't fire its head of production and didn't hesitate to make new development deals with the screenwriters and directors of those three disasters. Instead, the studio got rid of two people in the marketing department.

Aw, stop whining already.

Screenwriter/director Larry Kasdan (*Body Heat*), talking about screenwriting: "The movie comes out and there's the pain that your movie never got made; there's this other movie instead. But everyone says *you* wrote it, and they blame *you* for it anyway. So you're getting it from both sides: from inside and outside."

Pissing on Your Leg

What audiences do when they don't like something they see on-screen—that, at least, is how Warren Beatty puts it.

If your movie fails, blame it on the director.

Tell everyone he trashed your script and/or let the actors improvise.

As my good friend Don Simpson used to say, "It's not how you play the game; it's how you place the blame."

Or blame it on the good old USA.

In an interview in Budapest, Hungary, director Oliver Stone blamed the failure of his film *Alexander* on American audiences. "Americans aren't interested in history," he said, "and can't concentrate enough for a three-hour film."

And talk about how huge it is in Croatia.

Oliver Stone, discussing the failure of *Alexander*: "Europe was spectacular. Not the major territories—that's in January. What's positive is that it opened in various regions very strongly— Russia, Sweden, it moved down to Croatia. And then you go down to Turkey, Taiwan, the Asian side. Then to Bangkok and the Philippines. That was very, very encouraging. I don't follow these things—I'm told it's like Number One."

Or use Shakespeare, Marlowe, and Goethe as your alibi.

Oliver Stone, discussing the failure of his film *Alexander*: "I mean—why didn't Shakespeare touch Alexander, or Marlowe or Goethe? Alexander was famous. Nobody touched him. Why? Because there's too much success. He's too much—too much for people."

In other words, while Shakespeare, Marlowe, and Goethe chickened out, at least Oliver tried!

But you won't be able to fool Robert J. Hurns of Mount Prospect, Illinois.

After reading Oliver Stone discussing the failure of *Alexander,* Mr. Hurns wrote a letter to *The New York Times* (January 2, 2005):

"The failure of his film wasn't due to a lack of interest in Alexander the Great, but rather to the unwillingness of moviegoers to invest their time and money in a product associated with Oliver the Opinionated.

"Mr. Stone states that Alexander was 'too much' for Shakespeare, Marlowe and Goethe. The true epic here is that of Mr. Stone's bloated ego."

Once you write some hit movies, you'll have much more power.

Screenwriter Jeffrey Boam (*Indiana Jones and the Last Crusade, Lethal Weapon*): "I get no more respect now than I did when I first started. Absolutely none . . . I feel that I've earned more respect than I'm getting. And that my ideas shouldn't be dismissed out of hand, which they often are. I'll throw out an idea at a meeting, and the director or producer or the studio executive will say, 'I hate it.'

They won't explain to me why; they feel like they don't have to. They're not curious to know how I would actually execute this idea. They stop me and say, 'That's terrible. We don't like it. Move on.' You know, just like I'm the errand boy."

If you let 'em treat you like an errand boy, Jeffrey, then you're an errand boy.

If somebody says "I hate it," one possible answer, with your record of hit movies, is, "Oh yeah, how many millions have your movies grossed, asshole?"

In my experience, I've found that most producers, directors, and studio execs don't know how to deal with that word—*asshole*—when it's directed at them, possibly because deep in their hearts they know that they're . . .

If your movie fails, there's a good chance that one day it will be remade. Samuel Goldwyn: "It's a mistake to remake a great picture, because you can never make it better. Better you should find a picture that was done badly and see what can be done to improve it."

PART SEVEN

WORKING WITH THE DIRECTOR

LESSON 12

He's a Passive-Aggressive Snake!

Defining the director . . .

Screenwriter William Faulkner describing his director friend Howard Hawks: "He's a cold-blooded man, but he will protect me if I write a script that will make money for him."

Another definition of the director . . .

The starlet offers the director a blow job for a bit part.
     The director says, "What's in it for me?"

It's all about the next job, isn't it, Ron?

Oscar-winning screenwriter Ron Bass (*Rain Main*) on the director: "He's a *fascinating* guy. He's a *brilliant* guy. He's really a *challenging* guy. . . . Everything he wanted to do, even when I didn't see the sense of it at the time or I didn't see where he was going, it all did make sense and it was all going toward *a vision that was his vision. . . .* This was my first lesson in trying to let go of my vision of the piece and understand that there comes a point when the director's the guy who's got to make the movie, and you really have to be *servicing his vision. . . .* I see the film and I say at the end of it, 'Boy, *he's a lot smarter than I was* and smart enough to realize it.' . . . *The director is the author of the film. . . .* The farther I go in my writing career, the more I enjoy what I'm doing, *the more sympathetic and admiring I am of directors.* I think directing is the lousiest job in the world. . . . *The directors are the victims.* They are controlled by the movie. They are the victims of the flaws in my script."

Directors can plagiarize anything they want.

If *they* steal, it's called an *homage.* The director Brian De Palma has done whole film-length homages to Hitchcock—*Sisters, Blow Out, Obsession.*

Directors are petty despots.

Director Ken Russell to screenwriter Paddy Chayefsky: "What's it to you whether you like the set or not? You're only the writer! . . . Take your turkey sandwiches and your script and your Sanka and stuff it up your ass and get on the next fucking plane back to New York and let me get on with the fucking film."

Avoid auteur directors.

The director's job is to put *your* vision up on the movie screen.

If you work with an auteur director, he will steal *your* vision and change it enough so he can call it his own.

Stanley Kubrick, perhaps the best director in the world, wanted to direct Paddy Chayefsky's *Network.* Paddy wouldn't work with him and stopped the studio from hiring him. *Network* won the Oscar for Best Screenplay and was a huge worldwide hit. It remained very much "a Paddy Chayefsky film," not "a film by Stanley Kubrick."

An Ambience Chaser

A director who uses smokepots in every scene.

Don't work with any director who's just won an Oscar.

That director will be so impressed with his accomplishment that he won't work again for many years.

Robert Redford didn't work again for eight years after he won for *Ordinary People;* Warren Beatty didn't direct again for nine years after *Reds;* Milos Forman didn't direct for five years after *Amadeus.*

What these guys all did, though, for all those years they didn't direct, was *develop* properties.

They worked with screenwriters like you, trying to get a script in good-enough shape to shoot. The fact that they found no scripts in all that time good enough to shoot may have had something to do with how petrified they were to direct after winning an Oscar.

To Do a Cimino

To direct a film that fails so badly that it kills the studio, like Michael's *Heaven's Gate.*

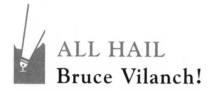

ALL HAIL
Bruce Vilanch!

Never mind all the producers and directors and hosts, Bruce Vilanch, screenwriter, has been writing the Academy Awards show for fifteen years and is its true voice.

Work with a director when he is "briefly, temporarily, human."
Producer Robert Evans: "The time I want to work with a director is when he's just had a gigantic failure. Think Cimino after *Heaven's Gate,* Spielberg after *1941,* Coppola after *One from the Heart,* Verhoeven after *Showgirls.* That's the time to work with them—when, briefly, temporarily, they're human."

Try to work with directors who began as producers.
Joe Mankiewicz, Alan Pakula, and Irwin Winkler all began as successful producers and then became successful directors. Knowing so much about film, there is less chance that they view themselves as omnipotent auteurs.

If you hook up with the wrong director, it can be hazardous to your health.
Raymond Chandler: "I went to Hollywood to work with Billy Wilder on *Double Indemnity.* This was an agonizing experience and has probably shortened my life."

Directors resent the money you're paid.

Director David Lean wrote a memo to the producer about Michael Wilson, the screenwriter they'd been working with on *Lawrence of Arabia*.

Lean wrote, "He's shot his bolt as far as this script's concerned and whether he's bitter with you and me or both of us we've got to lump it. I only note him because I hope you are not proposing to give him the two and a half percent profit because, softy as I am, I would resent it very much."

Some directors will try to take your credit away from you.

Screenwriter Walon Green (*The Wild Bunch*) on director Bob Rafelson: "If he wrote ten words, he'd say he wrote the whole thing."

A Credit-Card Filmmaker

A guy who's broke and can't pay for an option on your script but wants to direct it—though he's only directed a couple of TV ads in regional markets—and wants to sit down with you first to share some ideas he has about the script.

ALL HAIL
Director Philip Noyce!

My friend Phillip refuses to take the "film by" credit on any of his films.

He explained it to me this way: "I don't deserve it any more than you deserve it or the stars deserve it or the DP deserves it or the editor deserves it or et cetera, et cetera, et cetera."

Beware of world-famous, highly publicized auteur directors.

Film editor Lou Lombardo, who worked with both men, compared Sam Peckinpah and Robert Altman this way: "Peckinpah is a prick and Altman is a cunt."

Don't work with a busy director.

Director Jon Avnet and screenwriter John Gregory Dunne were having a script discussion on the phone, when Avnet got another call and told Dunne he'd call him right back. He called him back *eleven days later,* but explained that he'd been very busy.

A director can agree to direct your script for the wrong reasons.

Director Phillip Noyce, on directing *The Saint*: "It was an opportunity at the time to create a franchise. Although in the end, what I really found attractive about it was the opportunity to choose my own location to set the story. So, it became as much about the adventure of making the film as the adventure of the story of the film. It was as much about the adventure *off the screen* as the adventure *on the screen.* I satisfied my curiosity about post-Soviet Russia during the making of that movie."

In other words, Phillip just wanted to take an extended trip to Russia.

Some directors are only as good as their wives.

Bob Rafelson's and Peter Bogdanovich's best work was behind them the day Bob divorced Toby and Peter divorced Polly Platt.

Directors are incessantly looking for their next job.

The director Adrian Lyne and I were discussing *Flashdance* many years after we'd made the movie. A young supporting actress in the film had died tragically, as had studio executive Dawn Steel and our producer, Don Simpson.

"But that's nothing compared to *Superman,*" I said. "George Reeves, the guy who played him on TV, was murdered. Look what happened to Christopher Reeve, and then there was poor Margot Kidder, found wandering around that guy's backyard out near the airport."

"Bloody hell," Adrian said. And then he added, "Do you think there's a movie there? Our sequel? *The Curse of Flashdance?*"

If you wrote and directed it, then you're an auteur.

If you're the screenwriter, you are not the author of the film; you, the director, the producer, the actors, the editor, and the cinematographer are *collaborators.*

That's why it's immoral and absurd for directors to take a credit that reads "a film by Bill Hotshot."

Newspapers and magazines, staffed by reporters and critics who'd love to make screenwriter wages, rub this in. They refer to movies as simply "by" the director.

Don't ever refer to a movie as the director's possession; that's incorrect and morally wrong.

It is not George Roy Hill's *Butch Cassidy and the Sundance Kid*. It is not Steven Spielberg's *E.T.* It is not Sidney Lumet's *Network*. It is not Sam Mendes's *American Beauty*. It is not Clint Eastwood's *Million Dollar Baby*. It is not John Avildsen's *Rocky*. It is not Ridley Scott's *Thelma & Louise*. It is not Richard Marquand's *Jagged Edge*. It is not Paul Verhoeven's *Basic Instinct*. It is not Billy Friedkin's *Jade*.

It is just as wrong to refer to a movie as the screenwriter's possession, but it's a helluva lot of fun.

It is William Goldman's *Butch Cassidy and the Sundance Kid*. It is Melissa Mathison's *E.T.* It is Paddy Chayefsky's *Network*. It is Alan Ball's *American Beauty*. It is F. X. Toole's and Paul Haggis's *Million Dollar Baby*. It is Sylvester Stallone's *Rocky*. It is Callie Khouri's *Thelma & Louise*. It is Joe Eszterhas's *Jagged Edge*. It is Joe Eszterhas's *Basic Instinct*. It is Joe Eszterhas's *Jade*.

When working with the director, always say "my movie" while talking to him.

This is, of course, your revenge for what you will see on-screen and in ads: a film *by* the director.

Just because the Writers Guild doesn't even care about this usage doesn't mean you can't get your sweet little pound (okay, ounce) of flesh.

Orson Welles told the truth.

Welles told French critic André Bazin, the father of the auteur theory, this: "Directing is an invention of people like you. It's not an art, it's at most an art for one minute per day."

Yours is a creative art; the director's is interpretive.

Screenwriter/novelist Donald Westlake: "I am not a proponent of the director's auteur theory. I think it comes out of a basic misunderstanding of the functions of the creative versus interpretive arts."

You've got the power.

A screenwriter and a director were on a trip, scouting locations. The script called for "white houses dotting the hillsides." The hills they were looking at were perfect except for the fact that blue houses were dotting the hillside, not white ones.

The director, a freak for authenticity, turned the location down because of the blue houses.

The screenwriter took the script out of the director's hands, then crossed the word *white* out and replaced it with the word *blue.*

The director approved the hillside.

The vision is yours, not the director's.

I had an agent named Rosalie Swedlin, who, after a research screening of my film *Betrayed,* turned to the director (Costa-Gavras), who was standing next to me, and congratulated him for his "vision."

I fired her the next day.

Anybody can direct.

Producer David O. Selznick: "There is no mystery to directing. I don't have time. Frankly it's easier to criticize another man's work than to direct myself. As a producer, I can maintain an editorial perspective that I wouldn't have as a director. I consider myself first a creative person, then a showman, and then a businessman."

You, too, can give your director directing lessons.

Director David Lean not only asked screenwriter Robert Bolt to read his script of *Lawrence of Arabia* but also taped Bolt reading it. When shooting began each day, Lean listened to Bolt's recording of that day's scenes before he started shooting.

Directors can't write.

Vincent Canby of *The New York Times* wrote, "Mr. Cimino has written his own screenplay whose awfulness has been considerably inflated by the director's [Mr. Cimino's] wholly unwarranted respect for it."

When will they ever learn?

Martin Brest directed the hit movie *Beverly Hills Cop,* written by Danilo Bach and Daniel Petrie, Jr. He then directed the hit movies *Midnight Run,* written by George Gallo, and *Scent of a Woman,* written by Bo Goldman.

And then he directed *Gigli,* which he also wrote. It was one of the biggest cinematic disasters in years.

Stay away from Michael Cimino.

Michael Cimino directed *The Deer Hunter* brilliantly. He didn't write it. He won the Oscar for Best Director; the movie won for Best Picture.

Then he directed *Heaven's Gate.* He wrote it. It became the greatest financial and critical disaster in film history.

Michael Cimino has directed many films since then. He has cowritten or written all of them. All of them have failed.

He is rewriting himself now. He is sometimes seen around Hollywood wearing dresses and a wig.

Renny Harlin's writing advice . . .

Harlin (*Cliffhanger, Exorcist: The Beginning*): "I don't want accidents, I want disasters. I don't want dirt, I want filth. I don't want a storm, I want a hurricane. I don't want fear, I want panic. I don't want suspense, I want terror. I don't want humor, I want hysteria."

Directors confuse psychodrama with drama.

Adrian Lyne, the director of *Flashdance,* tried to talk me into having Alex, the central character, be raped by her father at the age of eight.

Larry Peerce, the original director of *Love Story,* wanted Ryan O'Neal to be a returning Vietnam veteran suffering combat flashbacks.

No wonder he screwed up my script of Jade.

Billy Friedkin, to an interviewer in 1967: "The plotted film is on the way out and is no longer of interest to the serious director."

Your director will hate you because you can write.

On July 18, 2003, Alessandra Stanley wrote this in *The New York Times*: "Mr. Affleck and Mr. Damon, who were themselves awkward newcomers when they won an Oscar for best screenplay for their first film, *Good Will Hunting,* sponsored a competition for thousands of unknown, inexperienced writers and directors, summoning the semifinalists to the 2003 Sundance Film Festival. Erica Beeney, 28, whose screenplay about a troubled teenager in Shaker Heights won first place, was teamed with Efram Potelle and Kyle Rankin, both 30, long-time friends and directing partners. . . . The two directors' desire to exclude the reticent Ms. Beeney becomes increasingly obvious in each episode. By this Sunday, she had finally moved from wounded perplexity to sarcastic rage. 'Do phones work?' she finally barks at Mr. Potelle when she realizes that they have once again made last-minute changes behind her back. She bonds with the slick producers who report to Miramax and try to keep the directors' inexperience and egotism in check."

Writing is more difficult than directing.

Writer/director Elia Kazan: "Writing, in case you don't know it, is much harder than directing films. It may be the reason why I, perverse I, do it."

A director isn't a writer or an artist; he's a general.

Director Orson Welles: "A poet needs a pen, a painter a brush, and a director an army."

Directors are artists.

Director Herbert Brenon delayed shooting a scene while an assistant searched Hollywood for a fifty-pound note.

When the note was brought to him, Brenon sealed it in an envelope and handed the envelope to the actor, who, the script said, was carrying a brown envelope with a fifty-pound note in it.

It's the scenery that makes a great movie, not your script.

Director David Lean in a memo to his *Lawrence of Arabia* producer: "Listen to me. The thing that's going to make this a very exceptional picture in the world-beater class are the backgrounds, the camels, horses, and uniqueness of the strange atmosphere we are putting around our intimate story.... This is our great spectacle which will pull the crowd from university professor to newsboy."

What to do when a director calls you to tell you he likes your script.

When Barbet Schroeder called screenwriter/novelist Charles Bukowski to tell him he liked *Barfly*, Bukowski said, "Fuck off, you French frog!"

Directors certainly haven't changed much.

Ben Hecht, discussing a first meeting with a director in 1937: "I've never met anyone so eager to flaunt his stupidity, low-grade human values and jackass vanities in the world."

Directors hate what they do.

Director Stephen Frears (*My Beautiful Launderette*): "There's nothing more loathsome than actually making a film."

Directors use people.

They don't say, "He's perfect—we'll cast him." They say, "He's perfect—we'll use him."

Don't give any ideas away.

The director Ivan Reitman was the producer of *Big Shots,* a comic adventure about two little kids.

As Ivan and I talked for days about the script, I suggested putting adult stars Arnold Schwarzenegger and Danny DeVito into the kids' parts.

A couple of years after *Big Shots,* Ivan made a comic adventure about two adult kids. It was called *Twins* and starred Schwarzenegger and Danny DeVito.

Big Shots failed, but *Twins* was a huge hit.

Most directors are passive-aggressive snakes.

This will seriously complicate your life.

It means they won't tell you if they dislike your script or something in your script. They'll rewrite it themselves behind your back or try to get a screenwriter friend to do it. Or they'll tell you they love your script but that the studio wants another writer to come in and do some "very minor rewriting . . . nothing more than some touching up, really."

They hate confrontations and will agree with you about most things and then do exactly what they want to do when you aren't on the set. And if you see the finished film and then confront them and say, "What the fuck did you do to my script?" they'll say, "What do you mean? I didn't change a comma."

Or: "I didn't have a choice. The studio ordered me to make those changes. I didn't want to tell you because I knew how bloody upset you'd get."

Or: "I was just trying to prevent you from getting hurt."

Or: "The star just didn't want to do the scene. I tried to insist on doing it the way you wrote it, but you know how arrogant he is. Defending your script almost cost me my job."

Martin Scorsese is paranoid.

Martin Scorsese puts a mirror on top of the monitor while he's filming, so he can see who's standing behind him, watching.

When he was shooting *Gangs of New York,* producer Harvey Weinstein put a giant truck mirror on Scorsese's monitor. Written on it were these words: "Caution, objects in the mirror are larger than they appear."

In the middle of the jumbo mirror was Weinstein's huge face.

The director always thinks he is the star.

According to Hal Ashby's producing partner, Charles Mulvehill: "Hal felt the picture should be the star, not the actor. But what that meant is that the star was the director, Hal Ashby."

ALL HAIL
Barbet Schroeder!

He's a director, I know, but still . . .

Learning that the studio had just pulled the plug on his film, he bought a Black & Decker circular saw, took it into the office of the studio head, plugged it in, turned it on, and held the blade over the studio head's hand, threatening to slice his finger off.

At that moment, the studio head changed his mind and decided to make Barbet's film.

Directors have always been full of it.

Screenwriter Ben Hecht: "My movie, *Underworld*, was the first gangster film to bedazzle the movie fans; there were no lies in it—except for a half dozen sentimental touches introduced by its director, Joe von Sternberg. I still shudder remembering one of them. My head villain, after robbing a bank, emerged with a suitcase full of money and paused in the crowded street to notice a blind beggar and give him a coin—before making his getaway."

You don't want to get this close.

According to the producer Gerald Ayres, who worked with them, screenwriter Robert Towne and director/star Warren Beatty liked having sex with different women at the same time in the same room.

Hanging out with your director can be deadly.

Screenwriter/film critic James Agee went off to write at the San Ysidro Ranch, near Santa Barbara, with director John Huston. They drank and played tennis, and Agee had a heart attack and almost died.

ALL HAIL
Carole Eastman!

Screenwriter Eastman (*Five Easy Pieces*) "felt she would become polluted if she had to talk to the director," said her friend Richard Wechsler.

You don't want a director as your best friend.

When director Bob Fosse was dying, he asked his best and oldest friend, Paddy Chayefsky, to look over his will.

"Hey," Paddy said to Fosse, "why am I not in your will?"

"I'm taking care of my wife and my kids," Fosse replied.

"Fuck you, then," Paddy said. "*Live!*"

Don't be anybody's "pocket writer."

This can happen when you get to be pals with a director. In most cases, a director will be pals with you if you do exactly what he tells you to do, *if you write what he tells you to write.*

If you do that, he will then bring you into his future projects (written by others) and get you a lot of money to rewrite those scripts.

Kurt Luedtke (*Absence of Malice*) and David Rayfiel (*The Firm*) made a lot of money being director Sidney Pollack's "pocket writers." As a result, though, they were mistrusted by other directors, who feared that if they worked with them, these writers would pass their ideas on to their pal Pollack.

If you're working with a director, don't just "come up with the details."

Screenwriter José Rivera, talking about working with director Walter Salles on *The Motorcycle Diaries*: "Some of the best collaborative work I have ever done with a director was with Walter because he doesn't rewrite you. He makes very precise and interesting comments on everything you've written, and some of them yield new things . . . He would have an idea and I would come up with the details."

Directors like being deified.

Billy Friedkin about Alfred Hitchcock: "I don't give a flying fuck about him, and I'm not a worshipper of his, nor have I ever set out to emulate him. But I'm glad that people deify directors because I make more money that way."

But you don't really have to deify your director.

Screenwriter Brian Helgeland on director Dick Donner: "With his leonine head and booming voice, he seems more like a movie star than the stars he's directing. When Donner shouts action on a set, it's the voice of God coming down from on high."

Oh gag me!

Screenwriter Darryl Ponicsan on director Martha Coolidge: "She values words, but she knows the silences are worth more. A rambling rose rambling down a Texas street says more than words can convey. Come to think of it, so does this photograph of Martha."

Please pass me that barf bag.

Screenwriter Jeff Davis, asked to adapt a novel for director William Friedkin, whose wife, Sherry Lansing, headed Paramount at the time and who hadn't had a hit movie in thirty years, said, "To be writing a psychological horror film for William Friedkin, the man who set the standard in the genre by directing what is considered to be the scariest and most viscerally disturbing movie of all time, is more than a writer could hope for."

You can get up now, sweetie.

Ronald Harwood won Best Adapted Screenplay for *The Pianist* and said in his acceptance speech, "Roman Polanski [the director] deserves this."

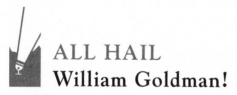

ALL HAIL
William Goldman!

He wrote an article in *Daily Variety* saying that Martin Scorsese did not deserve to win an Oscar for *Gangs of New York*: "*Gangs of New York* is a mess."

He also wrote that he would never forgive Miramax for "hyping the Oscar to Robert Benigni, the scummiest award in the Academy's history."

Don't ever trust your director.

Jean Renoir, the king of auteur directors, said, "Is it possible to succeed without any act of betrayal?"

You can't ever overestimate a director's ego.

Billy Friedkin told screenwriter William Peter Blatty that he refused to cast Marlon Brando in *The Exorcist*. Blatty: "His reason was that if he cast Brando, it would be Brando's picture, not his."

Where do their brains go? Be prepared for the director of your film to have an affair on the set with the lead actress.

It happened to me twice—with Costa-Gavras and Debra Winger on *Betrayed* and, more famously, with Paul Verhoeven and Elizabeth Berkley on *Showgirls*.

Costa's affair didn't hurt *Betrayed,* but Paul's destroyed *Showgirls*.

After the film bombed, I said to Paul, "When a man gets a hard-on, his brains slide into his ass."

Paul laughed; he didn't argue with me.

But they can't walk the walk.

Directors know they can't write, but they try to make up for this by *talking* about writing.

They are similar to the screenwriting teachers in this regard—the teachers who can't write scripts but tell you how you should write them.

Directors will talk to you about the "through line" and "the arc," ask "Where is the redemption?" . . . and refer to "deep in the subtext" and "the door to the character's motivation."

Some directors, interestingly, have taken screenwriting courses from the likes of Robert McKee, but even those who haven't have learned how to speak this cinema-lit psychobabble.

They can't write, but while *you're* writing, they have to do *something* creative—they can't even cast or scout for locations until you're *done* writing.

So what they do to kill time while you're creating the movie is to talk to you about how to write—like the baseball-hitting coach who never got out of the minors telling major leaguers how to hit a curveball.

A good director is worth waiting for.

Costa-Gavras, the director of *Z,* called me in 1977, after he'd read my script of *F.I.S.T.* He said, in very broken English, that he loved the script but that he couldn't speak English very well.

But he was taking Berlitz courses, he said, and when his English got better, he'd call me back and maybe we could do something together.

Eight years after that first phone call, he directed my script *Betrayed*.

Don't completely dismiss your director's ideas.

Director Costa-Gavras saved me from an ending to *Music Box* that, I think, in retrospect, would have hurt the movie. I will always be grateful for the way he slugged it out with me and convinced me that my ending was wrong.

On the other hand, dismiss most of your director's ideas.

Costa-Gavras had an idea for the ending of *Betrayed* that, I was convinced, would destroy the movie.

We slugged it out for two days and, at the end of those days, he reluctantly agreed with me that he was wrong. I will always be grateful for that, too.

LESSON 13

Every Good Director Is a Sadist!

If you argue with your director, go for the jugular.

Sam Spiegel, arguing with Elia Kazan, said to him, "What the hell do you know? You only know about testifying on your friends."

On *An Alan Smithee Film: Burn Hollywood Burn*, I said to Arthur Hiller, "You don't know what the fuck you're doing, you doddering old fuck." (I apologized later.)

Are you masochistic?

Producer David Merrick: "All good directors are sadists. I won't put up with it from mediocrities, but for genius I'm willing to be a doormat."

Your disagreement with the director can get ugly.

Working on *Lawrence of Arabia*, screenwriter Carl Foreman and director David Lean got along so badly that they were even arguing about whether a character would scratch his face or not.

Foreman accused Lean of being "an art house director." "You have made only small British films," Foreman said. "You have no experience of the international market."

Lean attacked Foreman in an eight-page letter to the film's producer, which began: "This is not meant to be an attack. But when one gets into the

244

scenes in detail, they are awfully rough and ready, and in many cases cheap and derivative."

In a creative discussion, use any lethal weapon you can.

Director Jack Garfein (*The Strange One*) had survived concentration camps, and when a screenwriter wasn't listening to him about the scene he wanted, Garfein asked, "Why are you arguing with me? Don't you know I am an Auschwitz victim?"

The way to talk to a director . . .

Producer Robert Evans: "I don't want a director to talk with me and then leave and say, 'Gee, what a nice guy.' I want him to say, 'That bastard.' 'That son of a bitch!' Because then they always come back and say, 'You were right. Let's talk.'"

To Do a Terry Malick

To acquire a towering international reputation for very little work.

Break his ribs.

When screenwriter/actor Sylvester Stallone had a creative disagreement with director Ted Kotcheff (*The Apprenticeship of Duddy Kravitz*) on the set of *First Blood,* Sly smashed a jarring left hook into Ted's rib cage, breaking three ribs.

Brass-knuckle him.

If a director insisted that Frank Sinatra do more than two takes of a scene, the director got a visit at home that night from Frank's pal Jilly Rizzo.

Jilly carried a pair of brass knuckles given to him by Frank and inscribed "To Jilly with love from Frankie." Jilly would show the director he visited these brass knuckles.

Shoot him.

Screenwriter Abraham Polonsky about director Elia Kazan: "I'll be watching, hoping somebody shoots him."

Yes, I know, I know—Abe *might* have had personal issue with him: Kazan testified in front of the House Committee on Un-American Activities; Polonsky refused to testify and therefore became a blacklisted screenwriter.

Spit in the producer's face and call him a pig.

That's what Katharine Hepburn did when she finished the last shot of *Suddenly Last Summer.*

She spit in the director Joe Mankiewicz's face and called the producer "a pig in a silk suit who sends flowers." Then she spat on the floor.

Seduce his wife.

I was introduced to Martin Scorsese a few years after I publicly fired his good friend and agent Michael Ovitz. Marty looked at me superciliously, barely taking my hand.

I knew he was the King of the Auteurs, while I was the auteur-slayer. I knew how seriously he took himself, while I prided myself on being the "rogue elephant" of screenwriters.

I knew all those things about him and I knew a whole lot more that he didn't know I knew, things I had learned from one of his wives, things she had told me after we'd made love on the kitchen floor of Marty's house while Marty was off on location, shooting, being the auteur.

Throw something in his face.

Angry at Roman Polanski, Faye Dunaway peed in a coffee cup and threw it into his face.

Did poor Francis lose his marbles?

When studio head Mike Medavoy arrived on the set of *Apocalypse Now* in the Philippines, director Coppola spoke to him mostly in the language of the natives he'd been living with.

Coppola said to Medavoy, "Maybe it should be a perpetual work in progress. I don't know if I want to finish it this year. I might want to finish it next year. Or maybe I should just start improvising and see where it goes."

Francis can teach you how to write a screenplay, though.

He can do this for you, even though he hasn't written anything in decades, even though he spends most of his time these days greeting tourists at his Napa Valley winery.

If you pay Francis $3,250 plus air fare to Belize, you can stay at his Blancaneaux Lodge, sleep in teak cabanas, drink wine shipped from Francis's vineyard, and talk about writing a script—not with Francis, no, since he'll be back home in Napa greeting tourists, but with the editors of his *Zoetrope* magazine.

Francis who?

Accepting her Oscar for Best Original Screenplay, Sofia Coppola thanked no writers for inspiring her. She did, however, thank a long list of directors.

Not among them, however, was her father, Francis Ford Coppola.

She did thank her mother "for inspiration."

No wonder Francis went bankrupt.

ABC offered Coppola $10 million for the TV rights to *Apocalypse Now.* He held out for $12 million. After the film came out and failed commercially, he sold it to ABC for $4 million.

The gods get angry sometimes.

Because he was the director, Francis Ford Coppola was able to hire his father, Carmine, to do the score for *The Godfather.*

Carmine did the score so well that he won the Oscar for Best Original Score.

But on the way back from the stage to his seat, he dropped the Oscar and it shattered.

Were they also screenwriters?

When two studio executives from Columbia Pictures showed up on the set of *The Cincinnati Kid,* director Sam Peckinpah had them stripped, hog-tied, and left in a seedy motel far away from the set.

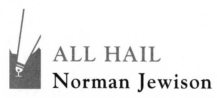

ALL HAIL
Norman Jewison

Yes, I know he's a director, but he's a man I admire, and he's also a friend of mine.

A male star threw a punch at Norman on the set, then came back and apologized and said he was ready to go back to work.

Norman said, "After you apologize."

"I just apologized," the star said.

Norman said, "You have to apologize to everybody. The whole crew. You insulted them."

The star apologized to the whole crew.

Directors are human.

Director Victor Fleming suffered a nervous breakdown during the shooting of *Gone with the Wind*. Francis Ford Coppola had a near breakdown/heart attack during the shooting of *Apocalypse Now*.

Director Robert Harmon suffered a heart attack while reading a memo I'd sent him, questioning his ability to direct *Nowhere to Run*. Harmon recovered and went on to botch the movie, just as I knew he would.

I swear, though, that I didn't know—didn't know, did not, did not *know*—that Harmon had a preexisting heart problem when I sent him my near-lethal memo.

Directors are feminists.

Sam Peckinpah: "Women have very complicated plumbing that I'm fascinated with."

Another romantic director . . .

Director Blake Edwards said about his wife, Julie Andrews, "She has lilacs for pubic hairs."

A director is a visual artist.

More than anything, he's a painter—but he likes to think of himself as a writer.

Gus Van Sant did oil paintings before he began to direct films, and he still paints. Peter Weir says he wishes he could "cram my trailer full of Gauguins and van Goghs and all the great art in history." Paul Verhoeven is a comic book artist who actually draws images of the scenes on the pages of the screenplay. Adrian Lyne knows more about modern painters than most art critics. Howard Zieff, Jerry Schatzberg, and Stanley Kubrick all began their professional careers as photographers.

In theory, to have a man who is a visual artist direct a script written by someone who works with words sounds like the perfect combination. Except that the director always tries to tell the writer what to write, while the writer never tries to tell the director how to compose his images on the screen.

Director Michael Mann is an especially brilliant visual stylist.

Gusmano Cesaretti, a respected still photographer, has been Michael Mann's associate producer since the 1970s. After he reads the script of whatever Mann's upcoming film is, he goes out and shoots thousands of stills of images that might work in the film.

As Mann shoots the movie, he tries to fit photographer Cesaretti's images into "his" film.

Some directors love torturing the actors.

Walter Salles (*The Motorcycle Diaries*): "We asked the actors to arrive four months prior to the shoot in Buenos Aires and then we started to do a series of seminars on Latin American history; on the cinema of the 50s. We did seminars on Incan history; we studied the music of the 50s in Latin America, with the help of professors from Buenos Aires University—all this was done to create a collective starting point, where the actors and the technical crew could have a really ingrained sense of what this journey was about."

Orson Welles was a liar.

Welles said he wrote the character of Harry Lime in *The Third Man*. "I wrote everything to do with his character, I created him all around," Welles said. "It was more than just a part for me. Harry Lime is without doubt part of my creative work."

The Third Man was written by Graham Greene. Welles *played the part* of Harry Lime. He wrote no dialogue for the character.

Orson Welles was a big fat liar.

The only film I wrote from the first to the last word," Welles said, "is *Citizen Kane*."

Welles directed *Citizen Kane*, but he didn't write it. It was written by Herman J. Mankiewicz.

You'll meet all kinds.

When Joe Mankiewicz was on the set directing, he always wore white cotton gloves. He had eczema, which broke out on his hands whenever he was nervous. He was always nervous on a set.

Director Jack Clayton (*Moby Dick, The Innocents*) chain-smoked on the set, drank brandy and sodas nonstop, and wore a Bedouin knife strapped to his right leg. He once said to his producer, "Don't speak while I'm talking or I'll have you thrown off the set."

You might even run into some Hungarian hack.

Legendary director Michael Curtiz, who was Hungarian, was often used by the studios to replace other directors. He was famous for getting the script on Saturday and beginning to shoot on Monday.

Hitchcock was a great auteur.

In a letter to the head of MGM after he'd written the screenplay of *Strangers on a Train,* Raymond Chandler wrote, "Are you aware that this screenplay was written without one single consultation with Mr. Hitchcock after the writing of the screenplay began? Not even a telephone call. Not one word of criticism or appreciation. Silence. Blank silence then and since. There are always things that need to be discussed. There are always places where a writer goes wrong, not being himself a master of the camera. There are always difficult little points which require the meeting of minds, the accommodation of points of view. I had none of this. I find it rather strange. I find it rather ruthless. I find it almost incomparably rude."

To Do a Jim Cameron

To have the kind of huge success that frightens you out of doing any more films.

Robert Altman is an asshole.

That's what producer Don Simpson, a friend of mine, thought: "We made *Popeye* and we hated Altman. He was a true fraud . . . he was full of gibberish and full of himself, a pompous, pretentious asshole."

Don Simpson was right about Robert Altman.

Ring Lardner wrote *M*A*S*H* and director Altman praised his script in early interviews.

After the movie was a hit, Altman said that he had tossed out Lardner's script and written it himself.

The movie's producer, George Litto, said, "Bob was never one to acknowledge a writer's contribution. The movie was ninety percent Ring Lardner's script, but Bob started saying he improvised the movie. I said, 'Bob, Ring Lardner gave you the best opportunity you had in your whole life. Ring was blacklisted for years. What you're doing is very unfair to him and you ought to stop it.'"

Howard Hughes's masturbatory vision . . .

He took over directing *The Outlaw* from Howard Hawks. His camera angles were always in dominant positions over Jane Russell, who was nineteen years old during filming. His biographer Charles Higham wrote, "No other individual in commercial Hollywood had so completely released his sexual urges on screen."

Directors are occasionally self-aware.

Abook published in Holland about director Paul Verhoeven is entitled *Verhoeven: Poet or Pervert?* Paul told me that he came up with the title.

Never mind everything else, Billy Friedkin is an honest man.

Friedkin: "The day after I won the Oscar was the only time I ever went to see a psychiatrist. I was profoundly unhappy. I told him I won an Oscar and didn't think I deserved it."

Beware of English directors.

The English were supposed to be so nice," Marilyn Monroe said. "But they treated me like a freak, a sex freak. All they wanted to know was whether I slept without any clothes on, did I wear underwear, what were my measurements. Gosh, don't they have women in England?"

It's tough for a director to share credit with Henry James.

Woody Allen had lunch with Peter Bogdanovich shortly after Bogdanovich wrapped *Daisy Miller.*

Allen: "He spent the whole meal agonizing. He didn't know what the credit should read. A Peter Bogdanovich Film of Henry James's Novella? Henry James's Novella Directed by Peter Bogdanovich? Henry James's *Daisy Miller,* a film by Peter Bogdanovich? Peter Bogdanovich's *Daisy Miller*, from Henry James's Novella?"

Directors have taste.

Costa-Gavras directed two of my scripts—*Betrayed* and *Music Box*—showing, I think, great taste in choosing them.
I don't know why he passed on directing *The Godfather.*

First-time directors are piglets.

On HBO's *Project Greenlight,* directors Kyle Rankin and Efram Potelle did the following things on-camera:

1. Tried to fire a boom-mike operator because he had "a bad attitude."

2. Wasted most of a day's shoot talking to producers as cast and crew stood around doing nothing.

3. Asked that the screenwriter and the producer communicate with them through index cards.

4. Demanded a free car when learning that the screenwriter had been provided a car to use.

After all, they were first-time directors.

Don't hold your breath.
Eventually," wrote screenwriter/novelist Raymond Chandler in 1951, "there will be a type of director who realizes that what is said and how it is said is more important than shooting it upside down through a glass of champagne."

If you consider yourself a writer, don't direct.
Playwright Robert E. Lee: "Becoming a director diminishes the writer. He may have more control and more power, but he loses the writer's perspective, the chance of looking at something with a broad, objective eye."

"More and more writers are becoming directors," wrote Raymond Chandler in 1957. "But in essence they cease to be writers, because a writer creates his own world on his own terms, in his own way."

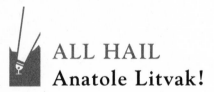

ALL HAIL
Anatole Litvak!

Yes, he was a director . . . but we're hailing him anyway for creating one of old Hollywood's legendary moments.

One night at Ciro's—as fancy and celebrated then as Spago is now—Anatole Litvak sank to the floor, put his head in Paulette Goddard's lap, and did naughty things there.

Don't be so sure you can direct.
After a week's production on *Personal Best,* screenwriter turned director Robert Towne was a month behind schedule.

Directors know *there are screenwriters out there who hate them.*

Steven Spielberg, Bob Zemeckis, and Michael Mann describe themselves as "weapons enthusiasts" and can sometimes be seen at various L.A. "shooting clubs."

All three also describe themselves as liberal Democrats who "believe in gun control."

Let's hope David Benioff doesn't hate any directors.

Screenwriter David Benioff (*Troy*) describes himself as a "weapons enthusiast," too; and according to gun club owners, he can outshoot Spielberg, Zemeckis, and Mann.

Was he a screenwriter?

Police arrested a man trying to break into Steven Spielberg's Pacific Palisades mansion. The man had a gun, a knife, rolls of duct tape, whips, a dildo, and various objects described by police as "torture instruments."

The man told police he wanted to rape Spielberg and kill him.

PART EIGHT

WORKING WITH THE PRODUCER

LESSON 14

Is His Heart Full of Shit?

Your producer can be your greatest ally.

When a woman got up at a *Betrayed* screening and started yelling about how much she disliked the movie, producer Irwin Winkler, a literate and sophisticated man, yelled this at her: "Shut up! Sit down! Throw her out! Get her the fuck outta here!"

Pray for a good producer.

I got very lucky with two of my scripts—*Betrayed* and *Music Box*. Irwin Winkler produced both of them.

I saw what made him a great producer on the *Betrayed* set. He was there from seven in the morning until seven at night every day. It was a hundred degrees outside, and under the bright lights in a suffocating barn, it was much hotter than that—but Irwin was there for every single day of the shoot.

One day he was so exhausted and dehydrated that he got dizzy and had to be driven back to his hotel. I warned him about his health, and Irwin said, "I know. But all directors are a little nuts. The best directors are more than a little nuts. I want to be there to make sure we don't experience any unexpected improvisations or unwarranted flights of frenzy."

Irwin was talking about Costa-Gavras, a man we both loved and greatly respected, but still . . . *he was a director.*

The definition of a good producer . . .

Novelist/screenwriter John Gregory Dunne: "If Don Simpson didn't like something, he hit you right between the eyes with it; he did not send eleven pages of notes to an agent, with orders not to show them to the writer, and then go pissing and moaning to the studio. Okay, he said, let's fix it, and we would sit down and do it. What the really good producers do is make you enthusiastic by the sheer force of their personalities about the most problematic ideas.

If your producer is pissing you off, remember that you've got him by the balls.

Playwright/screenwriter David Mamet: "The problem for them is, the story is the one thing that producers can't do."

The most respected producer.

Sam Spiegel is admired by today's producers as the "producer of all producers." He produced *The African Queen, The Bridge on the River Kwai,* and *Lawrence of Arabia.* He won *three* Oscars.

When he first came to America from Europe, he told his sister, "I'll either become a very rich and famous man or I'll die like a dog in the gutter."

He bounced checks constantly. He even pimped for a while. He even went to jail in San Francisco for fraud.

Sam Spiegel's résumé . . .

Before Sam Spiegel produced any movies, he had an affair with a wealthy divorcée. He stole her George Bernard Shaw first editions, he stole her car, and he stole her ex-husband's walking stick.

He was arrested in England for fraud: the nonpayment of his apartment bill. He went to Brixton Prison and was allowed one phone call.

He called a studio executive in Hollywood and tried to set up a film deal.

If your producer asks you to send him your script before you send it to the studio.

Don't do it. Your deal isn't with the producer; it's with the studio—and by contract, you have to deliver the script to the studio. What the producer is trying to do is to get a free draft of the script from you.

If you send it to him first, he will tell you how you can make it "better" before the studio sees it. Chances are, if you listen to his ideas, your script will be worse than it was before he told you his ideas.

"Tell me everything you have in mind."

This is William Goldman's spin on what to say to a producer. Take out a notebook and say this to the producer, who will have nothing to say that he would want written down . . . so your meeting won't last long.

Producers want to get paid, too.

If you're a screenwriter, you're paid when you start writing the script or when you sell it. But if you're a producer, you're paid only when the movie starts shooting.

Consequently, the producer will do everything he can to get you moving along on the script as fast as possible—so he can get paid.

You're better off ignoring his notes.

Screenwriter/novelist James Brown: "The producer is an articulate, intelligent man, and during the course of our meeting he gives me several pages of notes, all of them insightful. I want to do a good job, and once more I'm willing to mercilessly cut and chop, create new scenes and eliminate others. Inside of six months we have a strong screenplay with the original vision of my novel still intact. The producer shops it around to actors, directors, and studio executives. A year passes. No luck. The call comes from Vermont, where he is vacationing, and I can sense by the tone of his voice that he's given up. 'You wrote a good script,' he tells me, 'but they're all saying that it's too soft.'

"My phone stops ringing. My book mysteriously disappears from the bookstores. I think it's all over and then out of the blue he phones again to tell me, in short order, that I'm fired."

ALL HAIL
Gore Vidal!

Screenwriter and novelist Vidal (*Myra Breckinridge*): "I was having a meeting with a producer and I said to him, 'Look, I'm tired shitless of your complaints. You don't know what you're talking about. You know marketing, you may know how to make deals, but you don't know how to make movies, and you intrude on other people who are talented and do.' He exploded. 'How can you say that to me?' he said. He was halfway across the room. 'I will hit you!' he said. Then I started toward him and said, 'I am going to throw you out of this window.' And I came at him. We were about three feet apart and he was running toward me and he couldn't stop because of how much he weighed—he was very heavy. He veered off to the right and ran into a wall. I heard his nose crack against the wall."

A producer today isn't what a producer was yesterday.

Mike Medavoy: "Producer credits today are given out like lollipops in a pediatrician's office—to managers, wives, girlfriends, lawyers, and development executives. They are the ego badge of the business.

Schnorrer

A flimflam man who can talk you into and out of anything ... especially your wallet. It's a term usually applied to producers.

You, too, can be a producer today.

The Assassination of Richard Nixon boasted *sixteen* producers.

That sound you just heard was Sam Spiegel and David O. Selznick rolling over—and over and over—in their graves.

Beware of producers' offices that are in fancy buildings but have no furniture.

I had a meeting once with a well-known producer in an office like this and called my agent as soon as the meeting was over to tell him that I didn't trust the fact that there was no furniture in the office.

"They just moved in," my agent said; "the furniture is on the way."

Two weeks later, the producer declared bankruptcy and closed his office.

Producers are intellectuals.

I con producer Sam Spiegel said his two favorite things in life were "great food and very young girls."

Producers are honorable people.

S aid writer/director John Huston about producer Sam Spiegel, the winner of three Oscars for best picture: "If you had committed murder, a totally unjustified act of which you were guilty as hell, Sam would be one of the two or three friends you would turn to, certain that Sam would help."

Take it from zsa zsa

You don't want to seduce your producer.

Actress and Hungarian femme fatale Zsa Zsa Gabor: "Everyone thinks that the one kind of man you find most in Hollywood is the ugly, vulgar producer who smokes big fat cigars. This image is, of course, exaggerated. Some of these ugly, vulgar producers smoke little thin cigars, and nowadays some of the producers are young bearded men who smoke pot."

Producers are demanding.

P roducer Charles Evans advanced me $2 million to write the script of *Showgirls*. When I was more than a month late turning it in, he threatened to sue me unless I agreed to rewrite for free a script that he owned called *Bloodlines* (after I finished writing *Showgirls*).

When I finished *Showgirls* and Carolco agreed to finance the project, Charles Evans received $3.7 million—a $1.7 million profit on his $2 million investment.

But even after he made such a whopping profit, he still insisted that I had to rewrite *Bloodlines* for free.

My lawyers told me I had no choice but to rewrite it. I did.

But my rewrite somehow wasn't very good. *Bloodlines* was never made.

No one can force you to write anything.

Alas, as hard as I worked on that free and forced *Bloodlines* rewrite—as much of my heart and soul and guts I put into it— alas, alas, alas, my rewrite was god-awful. But I completed it and Charles Evans couldn't sue me.

Joel Silver is demanding, too.

What do you want out of life?" someone asked the producer Joel Silver.

Joel said, "*Everything!*"

So was the great Selznick.

Producer David O. Selznick, looking back at his career: "I was a pig. I worked so hard and waited so long, I got piggish and wanted everything."

How to deal with a European producer . . .

Quote Paddy Chayefsky to him in your first meeting. Paddy said, "You America-haters bore me to tears. Europe was a brothel long before we came to town."

The Nipple Check

A producer's role at the casting call.

A powerful producer like my friend Robert Evans can change the course of history.

Evans told me this story: "I called Henry Kissinger and invited him to *The Godfather* premiere in 1972. I needed Henry there for the publicity. Henry said he couldn't come—something about the war and the Paris peace talks and having to fly to Moscow the next morning. I reminded Henry how often he'd stayed in my guest house. I didn't hear any more about the Paris peace talks. Henry didn't fly to Moscow the next morning. He flew to *The Godfather* premiere."

TAKE IT FROM ZSA ZSA

Actress and famed Hungarian femme fatale Zsa Zsa Gabor: "I was in Boston, touring in Blithe Spirit, *and Henry Kissinger made a date with me to fly down and take me out. But on opening night, he called and canceled. A trifle piqued, I asked why. And Henry gave me the reason—a reason that even I couldn't quibble with: 'I can't fly down because we are invading Cambodia tomorrow. It is a big secret, you are the first person outside the White House who knows about it.'"*

It's all about whose is bigger.
Producers have big egos.
    The first time that producer Sam Spiegel met director David Lean's girlfriend, he tried to seduce her.

ALL HAIL
Irwin Shaw!

The novelist and Sam Spiegel didn't get along and Spiegel criticized Shaw's work behind his back to other Hollywood producers—thereby stopping Shaw from getting screenwriting jobs.

    To get even, Shaw began having an affair with Spiegel's wife.

ALL HAIL
Irwin Shaw!

Sam Spiegel dumped the wife that Irwin Shaw had seduced and remarried.

And one day Irwin Shaw was having lunch with a mutual friend and the friend said that Sam Spiegel's new wife was supposed to be "great in the feathers."

So Irwin Shaw seduced Sam Spiegel's new wife and began an affair with her.

ALL HAIL
Marion Shaw!

Shaw's wife, Marion, found out about the affair and, at a dinner party, she stuck her foot out and tripped Spiegel's wife, who broke her ankle.

ALL HAIL
Omar Sharif!

Sam Spiegel discovered Omar Sharif in obscure Egyptian films. He made him an international star.

In return, Sharif seduced Sam Spiegel's wife and had an affair with her.

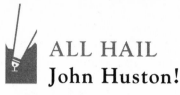 ALL HAIL
John Huston!

Angered that Sam Spiegel's wife was flaunting jewels while he was broke, *African Queen* director John Huston began an affair with her.

"John was very cruel to her," a friend said. "He really abused her.

Sam Spiegel's was bigger than Mike Todd's.

Sam Spiegel took his new wife to the Lido in Venice. Producer Mike Todd went over to their table.

"Hey, angel face," Todd said to Spiegel's new wife. "Do you know where you were last year on this exact same date at this exact same time?" Sam Spiegel said to his new wife, "Never mind."

But Mike Todd continued: "You were sitting right here, at this exact same table, with me, angel face."

Don Simpson admired Sam Spiegel.

Don didn't date; he fucked," said a former assistant.

Simpson said, "When you meet a lady and she says, 'Would you like to make love?' well, the first thing I like to do is fuck, not make love."

Because they're all empowered . . .

Screenwriter Nick Kazan: "Why is it that, in Hollywood, every producer, studio executive, and development person just out of college feels entitled to make suggestions on every script they receive? How can they be so confident of their opinions? Are they truly unaware of the damage they can do?"

What's it really like being a producer?

Sam Spiegel, who had escaped from Hitler's Germany, said, "It's better than being a lamp shade."

"Some producers have hearts full of shit."

Director Elia Kazan said that about Sam Spiegel.

Because we're scared to speak up . . .

Screenwriter Nick Kazan: "Why do we writers accept notes (from producers, studio executives, development people) which will destroy what we have so painstakingly created?"

Don't throw the damn thing back at 'em.

Producer William Sackheim was known for throwing across the room scripts that he didn't like.

If someone throws your script across the room, pick it up, tear off the first page, and make whoever threw it eat it.

Producers have impeccable taste (oh yeah!).

Respected Broadway producer Cheryl Crawford turned down a new play Arthur Miller offered her.

She wept bitterly at the opening night of *Death of a Salesman*.

These are the kind of people who give you notes on your script.

Jed Harris was Broadway's most famous stage director when he saw Arthur Miller's *Death of a Salesman*. Harris called it "a stupid play" and said "there is no drama in an ass like Willy Loman."

It takes one to know one.

Otto Preminger, the director, and Sam Spiegel, the producer, met in Hollywood for the first time—they had known each other previously in Europe.

Preminger said to Spiegel, "You are the greatest, most treacherous son of a bitch that every lived. . . . You end up in Mexico where you get involved in selling dope. You also get arrested on a white slavery charge. You get thrown in prison. Somehow or other you bribe yourself out of prison and you sneak illegally into the United States at Tijuana."

Spiegel looked at him sorrowfully and said, "It wasn't Tijuana."

R E E L S P E A K

Showman

The highest praise for a producer whose name, identified with a project, immediately gives it status: Sam Spiegel, Mike Todd, David Merrick, Irwin Winkler, Alan Carr, David O. Selznick, Jerry Bruckheimer, Joel Silver, Brian Grazer, Scott Rudin, Steven Spielberg, and Cecil B. DeMille are showmen.

Nazis yes, producers no . . .

Screenwriter/playwright/director David Mamet: "It occurred to me that there are films about good Nazis, but there are no films about good producers. Every producer in every movie is bad. Of course, that makes sense, because all of the films about bad producers are written by writers."

Don't bugger any boys in the backseat of the Porsche, either.

Producer Don Simpson, on why he was fired by Paramount as vice president of production: "They fired me for doing coke. They fired me on a fucking morals clause in the contract. They had executives buggering boys in the backseats of their Porsches and they fired me on a fucking morals charge."

Some producers really know how to hype their films.

Executive producer Robert Redford, discussing *The Motorcycle Diaries*: "There's a lot that's touching, there's a lot of humor, there's a lot of comedy, but it's real. It's honest comedy that comes out of real experiences, particularly with the young guys on what starts as an adventure. But there's also a lot of poignancy, and a lot of powerful emotional stuff in it, that's also real, and for that reason, it's all the more powerful."

Some producers really, really know how to hype their films.

Executive producer Robert Redford, discussing *The Motorcycle Diaries*: "When you see the film, you'll see that they really went through something to tell their story. Exactly what the characters actually went through. They followed the path that was absolutely authentic—the actual path they took on the motorcycle. They went to all the same places. And you see it, but more importantly you feel it. And if you feel it, then you're going to feel how Ernesto Guevara was affected by it."

Some producers really, really, really know how to hype their films.

Executive producer Robert Redford, discussing *The Motorcycle Diaries*: "This is a great story. This was not an easy film to make. They went to some really extreme locations that were next to impossible in some cases. The weather, you had the threat of violence along the way, political violence. You didn't know how things were going to go. You were going to go into some pretty hot areas. So that's all evidenced in this film."

Some producers know how to hype the directors who work for them, too.

Executive producer Robert Redford, discussing Walter Salles, the director of *The Motorcycle Diaries*: "Walter's work draws you in because, first and foremost, he is a natural storyteller. He blends, in a visually compelling manner, a specific world of characters, places and struggle that subtly reveals larger threads of shared human experience and emotion that link us all."

Robert McKee took producer Don Simpson's film course.

Producer Lynda Obst: "Don created the three-act structure that we all use, the one that Robert McKee and Syd Field [another screenwriting teacher] use and take credit for. Don made up this logarithm. There is the hot first act with an exciting incident, and the second act with the crisis and the dark bad moments in which our hero is challenged, and the third act with the triumphant moment and the redemption and the freeze-frame ending."

Some producers are true liberals.

During the South Central riots of 1992, producer Bert Schneider said, "I wish they'd come up here [to Bel Air] and burn my house down."

Some producers really respect screenwriters.

Producer Bert Schneider walked past writers' offices on the Columbia lot, banging on their doors and yelling, "Get out from under your desk, motherfucker! I know you're in there. Why don't you go write something, turn something in, you jerkoff!"

ALL HAIL
Charles MacArthur!

In the middle of a script dispute, MacArthur (*The Front Page*) knocked producer David O. Selznick over a bed.

Selznick's agent brother, Myron, jumped on MacArthur's back to try to stop him, but MacArthur hurled himself on Selznick and bit him in the leg.

"Dracula!" Myron Selznick screamed.

A Pisher

An old term used by producers for a nobody.

Many producers are happy and well adjusted.

T he secret to happiness is whores," said "the producer of producers," Sam Spiegel.

If he speaks Hungarian, he's not all bad.

S am Spiegel spoke fluent Hungarian.

Unfuckable

A producer's term for an actor or actress whom he doesn't want to cast in the movie.

Because they can't do what we do.

Screenwriter Nick Kazan: "If we refuse to make destructive changes, why are we considered 'difficult' rather than 'principled and passionate'? Why are we not considered experts, both in general and, most especially, on the distinct universe of the script which we have written?"

A powerful producer can even move the White House.

When I needed serious government help with a personal problem (a psychotic brother-in-law), I went to Robert Evans, who was walking around his house those days with a commander in chief ball cap from the Bush White House.

Evans got the government involved for me and solved my problem.

Press secretary Marlin Fitzwater had been a guest in Evans's guest house.

Bring 'em a towel from the rest room.

A producer and I met in the little bar at La Scala on Little Santa Monica. He proposed a deal and it sounded good to me. We shook hands on it.

I told my agent about the deal and the agent said, "Forget it. There's no way I'll let you make that deal."

The producer went ballistic when he heard we had no deal.

Six months later, he asked me to dinner. His wife joined us. We went back to La Scala on Little Santa Monica.

We had a couple of martinis at the bar. He said to his wife, "You see this stool I'm sitting on? He fucked me right here on this stool. Right here."

She laughed and laughed. The producer sort of smiled, but he wasn't laughing. I was laughing, but I was forcing it.

I went into the bathroom and got a paper towel. I took it out to the bar and told the producer to stand up a second. He did and I put the paper towel under him on the stool.

Now he started to laugh. He laughed and laughed, and so did his wife and I.

"You son of a bitch," the producer kept saying, sitting on the paper towel, but he was still laughing.

To Do a Burt Weisbourd

He was the hottest producer of the early eighties, the producer of *Raggedy Man* and *Ghost Story.* He was working with Robert Redford on *Red Headed Stranger* when, word is, he went up against Redford and got into a major battle with the star. He went from being one of the hottest producers in town to getting out of the business.

Give 'em music lessons.

Screenwriter Nick Kazan: "The next time someone reads your script and either really hates something that you know works or makes cavalier and foolish suggestions . . . perhaps you should ask them: Did you ever hear a song for the first time and hate it and then two weeks later find yourself singing it?"

Producers outbid themselves sometimes.

Producer Charles Evans bid on a house that he wanted to buy. He forgot that he'd already made a bid; then heard about another bid, which was really *his* bid.

So he made another bid, bidding against himself, and bought the house.

Creative Parasite

A wannabe producer who pals around with you and cultivates your friendship in the hope that if you sell your script, you'll get him the job of associate or executive producer on the movie is guilty of creative parasitism.

Producer Don Simpson was the reincarnation of David O. Selznick.

Screenwriter Nunnally Johnson, who turned down working on another project with Selznick: "Working with you consists of three months of work and three more of recuperation."

Joel Silver stopped when he was seven.

Screenwriter Ben Hecht to producer David O. Selznick: "The trouble with you, David, is that you did all your reading before you were twelve."

This producer's a real clown.

David Nicksay was once employed as a clown by the Ringling Brothers and Barnum & Bailey Circus. He even graduated from clown school.

Producers have to start somewhere.

Irwin Winkler, the Oscar-winning producer, once worked as a "laugher" for live television.

Nobody messes with Sean Connery.

Producer Peter Guber was going to tell Sean Connery about a new ending needed for a movie.

When Connery poked his finger in Guber's chest and said, "Now what's all this shit about not shooting the ending we want?" Guber backed off and said, "No, I just came by to wish you luck."

David Geffen is tougher than Michael Ovitz.

Said Ovitz to producer Geffen: "You're so smart, so bright, so aggressive. . . . I wish to God you could take all your venom and turn it into something positive. Your whole life is so negative. It's not enough for you to win. You have to have everyone else do poorly around you. They have to do badly. I don't get that, David. If you keep saying bad things about me, I'm going to beat you up."

In the end, it's all BS.

Producer Peter Guber: "Success is more attitude than aptitude."

Some studio bosses can't read very well.

One studio head hated reading so much that he sat with an assistant for an hour a day as the assistant told him the plot summaries of the scripts the agencies had submitted.

That's the sound of one hand clapping.

Peter Guber: "The perception of power is power."

Stay away from hands-on producers.

I will not work for dominating people like Selznick or Goldwyn," said Raymond Chandler. "If you deprive me of the right to do my own kind of writing, there is almost nothing left."

The producer was a pimp.

David Merrick defined producer Robert Evans this way: "He's Paramount's vice president in charge of procurement."

Robert Evans's role model.

Joe Schenck, powerful studio head and producer, was known for discovering and "sponsoring" women in Hollywood. He prepared them for other men and even marriage to other men. He took care of them and asked for "a little consideration along the way."

One of the women Joe Schenck discovered and sponsored was Marilyn Monroe.

Don't take any meetings at a producer's house.

Marilyn Monroe: "He had me come over to his house. It was a mansion. I had never been any place like that. He had the greatest food, too. That's when I learned about Champagne. What I liked was hearing about all the stars I had seen in the movies. He knew them all. He seemed to have this thing about breasts. After dinner, he told me to take my clothes off and he would tell me Hollywood stories as he played with my breasts. What could I say? He didn't want to do much else, since he was getting old, but sometimes he asked me to kiss him—down there. It would seem like hours and nothing would happen, but I was afraid to stop. I felt like gagging, but if I did, I thought he'd get insulted. Sometimes, he'd just fall asleep. If he stayed awake, he'd pat my head, like a puppy, and thank me."

Producers can be assinine.

On my film *Jagged Edge,* producer Marty Ransohoff kept trying to get rid of Glenn Close, claiming, "Her ass is too big."

After lunch with Helen Mirren, producer Sam Spiegel said she was wrong for the part in his film. "Her ass is too big," he said.

A Truffle Nose

A nose that can find a treasure (truffles) hidden in the brush.
  A nose only a successful producer can have.
  A pig's nose, since it is pigs that discover truffles.

Powerful producers can afford to wear dirty, smelly toupees.

Producer David Merrick ordered a toupee from the man who made Fred Astaire's. But Merrick never cleaned his toupee. It smelled. He didn't even put it on carefully, letting it look like a dirty, smelly napkin atop his head. It was Merrick's way of showing contempt for the people he worked with. He had so much power, he could walk around in a dirty, smelly wig . . . and not even bother about how he looked.

And they call Thalberg a genius.

Irving Thalberg passed on a movie and said to his boss, Louise B. Mayer, "Forget it, Louis. No Civil War picture will make a nickel." He was talking about *Gone With the Wind*.

In need of producorial stimulation . . .

Screenwriter Eleanor Perry and her director husband, Frank, wrote this note to a producer: "I'm afraid that both of us seem now to require your direct stimulation before we embark or agree on truly significant changes, in short, we need you."

Don't steal the crumpled paper.

English screenwriter Ivan Moffat (*Giant, Black Sunday*) on working with an internationally acclaimed producer: "He was crablike and all-controlling. He would hold on to everything. I had idly taken a crumpled piece of paper from his desk. He said, 'What is this, Ivan? No, please.' And I had to put it back. On Saturday or Sunday, he would call up, saying, 'Ivan, where are you going? Please leave a number. We might have to work.' There was never any question of our working. I said something flippant at dinner with him once. He said, 'Ivan, hold the humor.'"

Not only can you get snorted; you can get chomped, too.

Director Robert Parrish (*Casino Royale*), speaking about a well-known producer he had worked with: "He never chomped on a cigar. It wasn't his style. He was too much of a gentleman to be caught 'chomping' anything, except maybe a script or a screenwriter."

Murder is always an option.

At 3:30 A.M., screenwriter Budd Schulberg's wife awoke, to find him not in bed.

He was in the bathroom, shaving.

She said, "Why are you shaving so early?"

He said, "Because I'm driving to New York to kill the producer."

He would've loved Heidi Fleiss.

A Fox executive welcomed producer Sam Spiegel to New York. "I proposed showing him places like the Metropolitan Museum," the executive said, "and all he wanted to go and see was Polly Adler's—the best whorehouse in town. Sam spent the whole night there. I had to buy the place out—it was over nine hundred dollars."

The best producers are the best liars.

Director Elia Kazan said producer Sam Spiegel could lie "without betraying a tremor of his facial muscles. He kept me intrigued just to see how he got away with everything."

David Geffen is refined.

When producer David Geffen went to a high-toned reception for Princess Margaret, he wore blue jeans.

He went up to her and said, "Hi ya."

I'm not going to mess with David Geffen.

Writer Tom King did—in his book, *The Operator*. Only a few years after writing the book he died at a young age—of natural causes, of course.

Did you say that to Tom King, David?

Whenever producer David Geffen gets angry at someone, he says, "I hope you die!"

You have to love David Geffen a lot.

David Geffen said this to screenwriter Robert Towne about why he wouldn't work with him again: "You just didn't love me enough, Robert."

I always liked Michael Eisner.

"Michael is a liar," David Geffen said about Disney chief Michael Eisner. "And anybody who has dealt with him—genuinely dealt with him—knows he is a liar."

But what if David Geffen is lying?

I worked with Michael Eisner on *Flashdance* and enjoyed working with him. He disagreed with me sometimes, but he never lied to me—as far as I know. It is possible, therefore, that David Geffen is lying when he calls Michael Eisner a liar.

On the other hand . . .

I've dealt with David Geffen, too, and he never lied to me, either.

But he obviously wanted to fuck Tom Cruise.

After he read the script of *Risky Business,* producer David Geffen told the director, "I want you to cast someone in the role of Joel that I would want to fuck."

Who's that holding Ron Bass's Oscar?

Peter Guber produced *Rain Man* with his partner Jon Peters, even though director Barry Levinson rarely saw them on the set.

Yet Peter was photographed with "his" Oscar after the Academy Awards.

Alas, it wasn't his Oscar; it was *Rain Man* screenwriter Ron Bass's Oscar—Peter and Jon had asked Ron to "borrow it for the photographers."

Why weren't the photographers taking Ron Bass's picture with his Oscar?

Because photographers aren't interested in taking screenwriters' photographs.

They're not *all that* interested in taking producers' pictures, either, but they are more interested in producers than screenwriters.

Peter Guber doesn't exist; Peter Bart invented him.

Peter Guber produced *Flashdance,* though I never once saw him during the making of that movie. He also produced *Midnight Express,* though the director, Alan Parker, said that he rarely saw him during the making of that movie. And he produced *Rain Man,* though the director, Barry Levinson, said that he rarely saw him during the making of that movie.

Don't be a pawn in these games.

Powerful producer Irwin Winkler once asked me to write the "true story" of media baron Rupert Murdoch. I turned him down.

Powerful producer Scott Rudin once asked John Gregory Dunne and his wife, Joan Didion, to write "the true story" of entertainment mogul Barry Diller. They turned him down.

Tough-guy producers are easier to work with.

John Gregory Dunne: "In general, we prefer doing business with the bully boys than with the smoothies. The clout of the bully boys allows them to act as a buffer between you and the studio, shielding you from those mind-deadening omnibus meetings at which everyone present feels the necessity to say something; the bully boys do these meetings, and give you only the notes they think are worthwhile. If you let them know you will yell back at them when they yell at you, then they are more prone to listen—or else they fire you quickly; the smoothies just jerk your chain and smile as they measure your rib cage—for the ribs between which they will slip the stiletto."

At all cost, even if you're secretly writing a tell-all, appear loyal.

Producer Peter Guber: "In Hollywood, even the appearance of disloyalty can shoot down even the most promising future."

Avoid the producer who is a wannabe director.

Watching the filming of *Duel in the Sun*, producer David O. Selznick interrupted filming, dashed over to Gregory Peck and Jennifer Jones, and splashed more makeup blood on them.

The director, King Vidor, got up off his chair and said, "David, you can take this picture and shove it," and left the set.

Producers know how to cheer themselves up.

On days when he was depressed, producer Robert Evans said to his staff, "Go out there and find me some money!"

Producers are survivors.

Before he became my friend and, on several films, my producer partner, he had worked in a bookstore in Mill Valley, California, and owned an art theater with its own restaurant in Sonoma County. After he and I parted ways, he partnered with someone else—this time in a new Italian restaurant in Beverly Hills, where he also became the maître'd.

If a producer gets bored, he can always change his name.
My friend Howard Koch, Jr., a very successful producer and truly nice guy, decided one day that he didn't like his name anymore.

So he changed it. He became "Hawk" Koch.

He asked his friends to call him that, and he called himself that on all of his future film credits.

Everyone called him Hawk. Everyone liked Hawk better after he became Hawk.

A Velvet Octopus

A producer who wraps his arms around you with great affection and takes from you for free what you should be paid for: idea, outline, option, or script.

Don't ever let yourself be caught by a velvet octopus.

Make the producer swim for your script.
John Huston wrote the first eleven pages of his script and handed them to producer Sam Spiegel. Spiegel started reading the pages, but Huston's pet monkey grabbed the pages from him and threw them into the swimming pool. Siegel jumped into the pool and swam underwater to retrieve the pages.

Make him hire armed guards to keep you at bay.
Producer David Geffen hired armed guards to keep screenwriter Robert Towne out of those theaters in New York and L.A. that were showing Towne's *Personal Best*.

One way to get even with a producer.
Actor Timothy Bottoms disliked Dino De Laurentiis so much that he pissed on his shoes during the production of the movie.

If you're a writer, don't be a producer.

I never wanted to be a producer, but I had more movie ideas than I had the time to write them all. Plus, I was intrigued by the notion of setting up a production company that would give screenwriters more control over their scripts and more participation profit than they'd ever had before. And I had two good producer friends—I'll call them Ben and Bill—whom I enjoyed hanging out with.

So the three of us started to set up our own production company. We even had the name for it: Renegade. We had the company icon all worked out, too. Our films would begin with a steel door slamming shut and then being sprayed by bullets that spelled out R-E-N-E-G-A-D-E. We even designed and ordered three beautiful varsity jackets with the Renegade logo on the back and the names Joe, Ben and Bill scripted on the front. We also had office space picked out and—*get this*—studios ready to begin bidding against one another to make a deal with us.

And then, suddenly, in the Hungarian way, with a great big bang (not a whimper) Renegade *imploded*.

Ben and Bill, I noticed, didn't like each other and were trying to score points against each other—with me—behind each other's backs. I finally realized that it was normal behavior—because they weren't friends; they were—individually—*my* friends. I liked hanging out with Ben and with Bill—*individually.* There were serious strains in the subtext when *all three of us* were together. Each guy was jealous of the other's friendship with me.

That was one good reason to forget about Renegade.

The other was that I fell in love with Bill's wife and married her.

PART NINE

DEALING WITH THE STUDIO

LESSON 15

You're a Jackass in a Hailstorm!

Barry Diller ruined movies.

According to producer/studio boss Mike Medavoy: "Barry Diller's Paramount regime was the beginning of the movie by committee syndrome that pervades Hollywood today.

"Diller and his lieutenants began setting the agenda at the script stage. Previously, it was left up to the director and the screenwriter to work out what the movie would say and how it would be said, and then run it by the studio for input. But at Paramount, the executive would get involved with the first draft of the script, typing up voluminous notes for the filmmakers.

"Next, they would hold story meetings so the executives and filmmakers could float their ideas, many of which were undoubtedly in conflict with one another. It was then left up to the filmmakers to cut and paste it all together."

Killer Dillers

Executives hired by Barry Diller in whatever enterprise he is involved in.

Ingratiate yourself with your superiors.

In an effort to convince me to change the ending of my script, a studio head listed for me all the television series that he had written, worked on, or supervised.

I said, "I know you've done all those things. That's exactly the problem."

Insult their pampered white asses.

I am extremely allergic to big shots of all types wherever found," said screenwriter/author Raymond Chandler. "I lose no opportunity to insult them whenever I get the chance."

They begrudge you the money they have to pay you.

Playwright/screenwriter David Mamet: "In my experience, almost every financial interchange with Hollywood ends with an accusation by the corporation of theft. 'You didn't do what I wanted, you didn't work hard enough, you intended to defraud me.' These are the recurring plaints of industry. They may be translated as: You forgot to work for nothing."

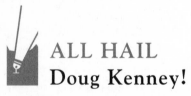

ALL HAIL
Doug Kenney!

Doug Kenney, the screenwriter of *Caddyshack*, hated the poster for the movie so much that he confronted studio head Mike Medavoy outside his office and the two wound up grappling on the ground.

The poster was changed.

The Green Light

The decision by a studio to film (green-light) a script.

Until recently, this was the decision of the studio head—he took the blame when the movie failed, or got the credit when it was a hit.

Today, though, many studio heads have figured out that they'll last longer in the job if they alone don't make the decision to green-light.

So, at many studios today, a committee makes the decision to green-light a script. The committee is made up of the top execs on all levels— even publicity, advertising, and marketing.

Since you can't fire the whole committee (*all* the executives) and have a studio left, *everybody* holds on to their jobs.

Thanks to The Mummy, *we got Graham Greene.*

*T*he Quiet American *was green-lighted by Intermedia Films only when Brendan Fraser agreed to take the supporting role. Brendan had just starred in* The Mummy Returns *and the studio felt he was a big-enough star for it to be able to take a chance on Graham Greene.*

Sherry Lansing speaks doublespeak.

Director Phillip Noyce, discussing *The Saint*: "At the end of the first screening, Sherry Lansing, the head of the studio, was genuinely crying. She said it was a brilliant film and it was *Doctor Zhivago*-ish. . . . Later I did feel resentful that Sherry Lansing had initially been so enthusiastic about the movie, only to eventually talk me into cutting those things which had most moved her when she first saw the film."

REELSPEAK

A Bomb Thrower

A studio executive who disagrees with a reader's coverage of a script will be known as a "bomb thrower."

To Do a DeLuca

To be caught publicly in flagrante delicto—as was then New Line head Mike De Luca at a party at then agent Arnold Rifkin's house (with the sister of a William Morris agent). To trip on your own dick.

With ding-a-lings like this in charge . . .

David Picker, the former head of United Artists, MGM, and Paramount, looking back on his career: "If I would have reversed all my decisions—if I hadn't made the pictures I did and made the pictures I didn't, the results would have been exactly the same."

A studio boss is an orchid.

Studio mogul Louis B. Mayer: "You see, wherever I go there are girls who want to become actresses. I have a sixth sense for it. She would follow me into my stateroom, if I snapped my fingers, and stay all night. Just for a bit role in any picture. But I am not interested in fast affairs. I am interested in *relationships*. I am a human being. I need warmth—like an orchid."

To Sweat Dollars

To wait for the box-office results from your film's opening weekend.

It's not about money, it's about getting laid.

An agent told Hedy Lamarr this story: "Phil Kamp has had an office at a major studio for four years and he has never made a picture. He's a distant relative of the president of the studio. He just auditions girls. That's his whole life. He gets a salary but he's a producer who doesn't produce. Phil is so dedicated to his art that he occasionally goes to another city and there he tries another variation. He puts in ads for a secretary to a movie producer—if he were to advertise for an actress it would look suspicious. As a producer, girls who are really secretaries often want to be actresses. Phil does well both in and out of town."

They'll want you to write dishonest stories.
Paramount studio head B. P. Schulberg: "We can't afford to alienate our movie audience by telling them the truth about themselves."

Creative Executive

There's no such thing. It's an oxymoron, like "lady producer."

The barbarians are inside the gates.
Frank Pierson, screenwriter (*Dog Day Afternoon*) and president of the MPAA: "We had been having too much fun to notice: the barbarians were inside the gate. . . . We began to see Harvard Business School MBAs sit in on our story conferences. Lawyers multiplied."

They don't like to say no.
Columbia studio exec Peter Guber was instructed by his boss, Leo Jaffe, to tell the once-powerful Jack Warner, now an old producer, that his movie *1776* was being canceled.

Guber went to see Warner but didn't have the guts to tell him.

Leo Jaffe didn't have the guts to tell him, either.

1776 was made . . . and bombed.

Dumb Fuck Films

The late director Hal Ashby's movie company, generally thought by Hollywood cynics to be the best name of a production company ever.

Lew made a big boo-boo.
Not long before his death, former Universal tycoon Lew Wasserman said, "Sold the company to the Japanese. It wasn't the price that was wrong, but the sale itself."

What if he had hemorrhoids?

Harry Cohn, the Columbia czar, said, "If my fanny squirms while I'm watching it, the movie is bad. If my fanny doesn't squirm, it's good."

A Civilian Question

A stupid question asked at a story meeting—the kind of question asked by someone outside the industry, a "civilian," who doesn't know anything.

Those poor scared studio execs . . .

Screenwriter/novelist Raymond Chandler: "Sometimes I feel kind of sorry for the poor bastards. They are so damn scared they won't make their second or third million. In fact, they are just so damned scared, period."

We've all got a spiritual side.

The wife of a studio exec said to me, "Jack was so wound up, we really needed a relaxing evening. We went to a séance for Henry Fonda and Katharine Hepburn."

Hollywood Sperm

The children of studio executives.

Lew had a big problemo.

Lew Wasserman said, "I was unfortunate not to have a son, only a daughter."

They're all sleep-deprived.

The wife of a studio exec told me that he woke up many nights yelling things in his sleep.

Things like:

"He's going to hand *me* my head on a platter? I'm going to hand him *his* head on a platter!"

"He wants to see a professional? I'll show *him* a professional!"

"The hat has been thrown in the ring! So he better be ready!"

"If he tries to take credit for this movie, I'll fucking kill him."

Three-Piss Picture

Jack Warner felt that if he had to go to the bathroom during a screening, the movie would fail. A movie that would be a disastrous embarrassment was "a three-piss picture." Nobody could ever convince him that he had a weak bladder.

They live in the reel world.

Sony had financed the ill-fated Roland Joffe–directed *City of Joy*, set amid the dire poverty of India.

A few months later, Mark Canton, Sony's head of production, was showing me around the studio lot, which was in the midst of massive construction. Bulldozers were everywhere; much of the lot seemed to be in ruins.

"This," Mark Canton greeted me, "is our *City of Joy*."

Dick Zanuck's dad "passed" on Marilyn.

Studio chief Darryl Zanuck refused to cast Marilyn Monroe in any "serious" roles.

Marilyn said, "I would have been happy to do anything—*you know*—to get him to let me try something different. He wasn't interested at all. Every other guy was. Why wasn't he?"

Suckfish

The junior executives who scuttle the corridors at a movie studio. Also known as "hall mice."

I hope he got Bill Goldman's next job.

James Ryan, adjunct professor of playwriting at the New School in New York City, writes in his book *Screenwriting from the Heart,* "Most executives who run Hollywood, in my experience, are incredibly bright and often very well educated."

Sorry, but this won't work.

Discussing the making of his *Blue Dahlia,* Raymond Chandler said, "I threatened to walk off the picture, not yet finished, unless they stopped the director putting in foolish dialogue out of his own head."

A Halfway Girl

A studio executive who slept her way not to the top, but to the middle.

They're all fans of Robert McKee.

Screenwriter Dan Pyne (*Pacific Heights*): "Maybe that's who's taking all these screenwriting courses—story editors or producers who want to write one. I met up with a guy yesterday, a very nice guy from Disney. He wants me to read something . . . if he writes it. For them, it's all about writing that one script and then cashing in on it. Whereas, I think, for the real writers, it's about a career."

Bob's lucky he's still alive.

In a disagreement with Universal titan Lew Wasserman, director Bob Rafelson said, "What's this fuckin' bullshit?" and swept all of Wasserman's medals and awards off his desk.

A Total Fucking Disaster

The worst kind of disaster, a movie that does such a belly slam that it clears all the water out of the pool, a movie like my *Showgirls* (before it became a cult classic).

Make 'em show you theirs first.

I f you're sitting in a meeting with a young studio exec who says, "Tell me what you've done," reply this way: "You first."

Michael Eisner's is bigger than yours.

S creenwriter John Gregory Dunne ran into Disney chairman Michael Eisner at Morton's.

Dunne: "I asked him how his heart was, and Michael said it was fine. He had come through his bypass surgery in good order. 'You know,' I said, 'I had the same operation,' and without missing a beat, Eisner replied, 'Of course, mine was more serious.' I have rarely been struck dumb, but this seemed to be 'mine is bigger than yours' Hollywood-style."

Putting Your Dick on the Table

What studio bosses do when they agree to pay a big star $20 million to do a movie. They put their "dicks on the table"—ready to be chopped off if the movie fails.

Harry Cohn had big balls.

M y fellow Hungarian, actor Tony Curtis: "Some people were glad the studios were disintegrating, because they hated the moguls, Harry Cohn in particular. I always liked Harry, myself. One day I got an inside look at the way he operated. He liked to see me, and I'd stop by now and then, just to talk. One day I'm in his office with a friend, just sitting there, talking, and Harry's buzzer rings. He says to the secretary, "Well, send her in." And in walks this beautiful girl, maybe twenty years old, just a magnificent young woman in a beautiful silk summer dress. . . . She takes a look around, nervously, and says, 'Harry, I have to talk to you.' He says, 'So talk.' She looks at us and says, 'Harry, I'd rather not talk in front of these gentlemen.' He says, 'Anything you've got to say, you can say in front of them.' She takes a deep breath and says, 'Harry, I can't go on this way. You promised to take care of me, put me in a movie. It's been eight months now, and it just can't keep on like this. You have to do something, or I'm going to have to call your wife.' He looked at her, picked up the telephone, dialed the number, held out the phone to her, and said, 'Tell her yourself.' . . . She just slowly walked out. After a silence my friend had the nerve to ask, 'Harry, was that really your wife?' Harry Cohn just looked him straight in the eye and said, 'You'll never know.'"

ALL HAIL
Ben Hecht!

This is the advice screenwriter Ben Hecht gave to a director who had been asked by Columbia chief Harry Cohn if he was a member of the Communist party.

"Tell him to go fuck himself," Hecht said. "It's none of his goddamn business. Ask him if he's a Jew."

Hecht didn't call Cohn by name. He called him "White Fang."

Perry King gave birth to Sylvester Stallone.

Arthur Krim, the respected octogenarian head of United Artists, signed Sylvester Stallone up for *Rocky* after he saw *The Lords of Flatbush* and was impressed by the actor he thought was Sly in that movie. It was only when *Rocky* was released that Krim realized he'd confused Sly in *Flatbush* with another actor in that film, Perry King.

Without Perry King's acting ability, the world today would be without *Rocky* and Sylvester Stallone.

Spitballing

Usually used as "just spitballing," as in "We're just spitballing here." Often used in creative meetings by studio execs who (1) are trying to write your story for you and (2) know that what they're suggesting is stupid. Therefore they cover themselves by saying, "We're just spitballing here, right?" or "This isn't a very good idea, probably but we're just spitballing here, aren't we?"

Ingratiate yourself with your superiors.

Jack Valenti, the head of the Motion Picture Academy of America, and I were on the *Today* show.

Jack was berating me (I deserved it) for telling teenagers to use their fake IDs to see *Showgirls,* an NC-17 movie.

Jack, exasperated and angry with me, said, "Oh, you're just here publicizing your movie."

And I said, "So are you, Jack."

Stereotypes

A word used by directors, producers, and especially studio executives to get you to rewrite a character. If you force them to admit that a character is acting in a realistic manner, then they tell you that while the behavior is realistic, it's also stereotypical.

The word is frequently used when discussing black or gay characters.

Jack Valenti is not an Oliver Stone fan.

Said Jack about Oliver's *JFK*: "Young German girls and boys in 1941 were mesmerized by Leni Riefenstahl's *Triumph of the Will* in which Adolf Hitler is pictured as a newborn God. Both *JFK* and *Triumph of the Will* are equally a propaganda masterpiece and equally a hoax. . . . Does any sane human being truly believe that President Johnson, the Warren Commission, the CIA, the FBI, the Secret Service, local law enforcement officers, assorted thugs, weirdos, all conspired together as plotters in Stone's wacky sightings?"

Studio execs feel no pain there.

A Warner Bros. executive who didn't think *Bonnie and Clyde* was releasable said this after a preview audience got up and cheered it at the end: "Well, I guess Warren Beatty just shoved it up our ass."

Send Me Some Pages

What producers, directors, or studio execs say when they are worried your script won't be any good. Don't ever send anyone pages from your script until you are finished with the script—then send the script in toto. Their hope is that if you send pages before you're finished, they can tell you where to take the story from there . . . or tell you to start all over again.

DBTA

Dead by the third act . . . this usually refers to the protagonist's best friend or partner, killed off by the third act . . . usually to motivate the protagonist to take revenge for his pal's death.

Studio execs have impeccable taste.

I still think *Pinocchio* is a perfect movie," said Dreamworks coboss Jeffrey Katzenberg. "Perfect story, perfect characters and stunning animation."

Off Point

A scene that doesn't work.

Lew tells me it ain't so.

When I was a young screenwriter, I ran into Universal potentate Lew Wasserman and his wife, Edie, one morning near the deli Nate and Al's on Beverly Drive. I introduced myself and said that I knew that both Lew and Edie were from Cleveland, like me.

Then I said that I had a gangster friend in Cleveland named Shondor Birns, who'd told me that Lew had worked handling the racing wire across the street from the Theatrical Grill on Short Vincent Street (before he became a mogul).

Lew Wasserman looked at me, smiled, and said, "You got some bum information. I never did that."

Then he said, "Is Shondor Birns still alive?"

I said, "No, he got blown up in a car bomb on the West Side."

Lew Wasserman smiled and said, "There you go," and walked away with Edie into Nate and Al's.

That Doesn't Work

Usually uttered by producers and studio execs, it means "I don't like it."

What does Mike Medavoy know?

Director Bob Rafelson went to studio head Mike Medavoy's office to tell him that Arnold Schwarzenegger would be perfect in *Stay Hungry.*

Medavoy said to Bob, "I've known you were crazy for years and now I'm sure of it. This guy has an Austrian accent and he doesn't look anything like a traditional movie star. Get out of my office."

Your Script Is Too Soft

By this, they mean it's too arty, too lyrical, not dramatic enough, lacking enough violence for a box-office hit.

Studio execs are very busy people, too.

Louis B. Mayer and his executives spent weeks trying to figure out how many times the MGM lion should roar on-screen at the beginning of a film. They finally settled on two loud growls followed by a yip.

Tweaking Your Script

If a director, producer, or studio exec tells you that your script is "terrific" but needs "a little tweaking" it means you are about to be paid off and another writer will soon come in and rewrite everything you've written.

In short, it means they hate your script.

You're a jackass in a hailstorm.

Jack Valenti did give screenwriters some good advice.

Jack: "I do get frustrated; in fact, I do get depressed from time to time. But I've learned something. If I just hunker down, as LBJ used to say, like a jackass in a hailstorm and wait till the storm passes, it's going to be all right. If I look down on a day or two, I know on the third day I'm gonna start rising again."

A Round Conversation

One that is going nowhere.

Give studios you've been in business with before a first chance to read a brand-new script.

Just make sure the brand-new script doesn't have too many coffee stains on it.

They have to pay you, but they don't have to thank you.

Columbia studio boss Harry Cohn: "The word gratitude is not part of the Hollywood dictionary."

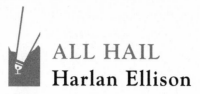

ALL HAIL
Harlan Ellison

When screenwriter/novelist Ellison felt that a studio executive
had lied to him, he messengered the man a dead gopher.

Bullet Points

What studio execs call their most important notes on a screenplay.
Screenwriters say they're called "bullet points" because these are the
points that will kill the script.

This Is the Best First Draft I've Ever Read

Producers and studio execs say this when they know that an awful lot of
work will have to be done on the script and when they want to cajole
you into doing more drafts than what your contract calls for.

Garbage

This is what studio executives call the dialogue of a screenplay.

Sweet Jesus . . .

Academy Awards producer and former studio chief Joe Roth
had this idea to start the show the year after *The Passion of the
Christ* was released: "I say, bring Billy Crystal out in a loincloth,
carried on a cross through the Academy."

PART TEN

INSPIRING THE ACTORS

LESSON 16

Their Shorts Have Skid Marks, Too!

Don't star-fuck.

William Goldman, on the making of his *Marathon Man,* starring Laurence Olivier: "But that moment—when the actor of the century asked me would I mind if he switched six words around—is the most memorable incident of my movie career. Olivier. Calling me 'Bill.' Olivier. Asking *me* would I mind. That's high cotton."

Actors have a social conscience.

Shooting *Viva Villa* in Mexico, Lee Tracy took a piss off of his hotel balcony while Mexicans beneath him were marching to celebrate their national independence.

In order to avoid an international incident, Tracy had to be replaced.

Do not genuflect before stars.

William Goldman: "Stars do not—repeat—do not play heroes— stars play gods. And your job as a screenwriter is to genuflect, if you are lucky enough to have them glance in your direction. Because they may destroy your work, will destroy it more often than not—but you will have a career."

Listen to me carefully: I am my own best example. You don't have to genuflect to anyone to have a lengthy and profitable screenwriting career.

You'll pick up a lot of rug burns and need to carry mouthwash with you. (We already know that Bill used to carry bottles of Kaopectate.)

Aw, come on, their shorts get skid marks, too.

Screenwriter John Gregory Dunne: "I have a confession to make: I have a hard time calling Robert Redford 'Bob.' He is younger than I am, and yet I would let his diminutive cross my lips only if I could not get his attention by catching his eye or clearing my throat. To me, he is Robert Redford. In an era of faux egalitarian familiarity, when presidential contenders pass themselves off as Bill or Phil, 'Bob' is somehow diminishing; it would be like calling Woodrow Wilson 'Woody.'"

ALL HAIL
The Old Scum-Sucking Swine!

Hunter S. Thompson was the only writer I've ever known who could make groupies out of movie stars.

Johnny Depp slept in a little room, which was filled with brown spiders, in Hunter's basement.

Sean Penn, Jude Law, and Benicio Del Toro were all friends who tried to cheer Hunter up when he was depressed by reading to him . . . from his own writings.

I asked Hunter once how he was able to do this to actors.

"They're actors," he said, "I show 'em my guns. I let 'em play with 'em. Actors like to play with guns."

Actors ruined everything a long time ago.

Producer David O. Selznick: "I don't mind spending money, but there's no more reason to believe that Marlon Brando is a producer than Karl Malden is. We always have difficulties but actors used to accept discipline. I've called Jack Barrymore into my office for not knowing his lines; he was contrite and apologetic. I had to speak to Leslie Howard, who was embarrassing Vivien Leigh by not being prepared for a scene. But you never had to speak again. They recognized their fault and corrected it."

TAKE IT FROM ZSA ZSA

Don't marry an actor.

Actress and famed Hungarian femme fatale Zsa Zsa Gabor: "When you are married to an actor, you have the feeling you are nothing but an understudy to him. He only has eyes for himself. It is really the one situation I know of where, with just two people, you have a triangle! Both of you, madly in love with him. They probably have these big ego problems because deep inside, they are not secure, like little boys. There is a saying that an actress is something more than a woman and an actor is something less than a man."

Please, Bill, you're embarrassing me.

Screenwriter William Goldman: "I have worked with Redford. I have been in a room with Beatty. They are brilliant men, passionate about what they produce, and boy are they not dumb. Well, Michael Douglas is their equal. And Douglas did something no other actor did with me—he spent *time*. On the script. Going over it and over it. Actors just don't do that. They are simply too busy. But Douglas spent literally days locked in a room with me and with Stephen Hopkins, who did a wonderful job directing the movie."

Oh boy, Bill, I know you think it's about *the next job,* but you don't have to be this *desperate* to get one, do you? You "have been in a room with Beatty"? Hallelujah, man! They're "brilliant" and "passionate" and "wonderful"? Have you no gag reflex left?

Michael Douglas, in my experience, is not brilliant and may very well, in some cases, be dumb. This is the guy who wanted to change the ending of *Basic Instinct* because he said it wasn't "redemptive." Pressed, he said he was the star of the movie and "she one-ups me at every turn." The ending he wanted was for himself to shoot Sharon in the final scene. Even when the movie came out and was a huge hit, he kept bellyaching and asking, "Where's the redemption?"

If he's so brilliant, then why doesn't he understand that not every movie has to end (especially in film noir) with redemption? And that ambiguity is a much more interesting way to go than redemption, which is, at the same time, a disguised way of soothing a star's ego.

You don't want theater tickets, do you?

Agent Swifty Lazar: "The actor Jacob Adler induced some actress to sleep with him, only to have her hit him up for money. 'Mr. Adler,' she told him, 'I need bread!' To which he replied, 'Then fuck a baker. Fuck an actor, you get theater tickets.'"

This means Robert McKee is a great actor.

The better the actor," said screenwriter/novelist Truman Capote, "the more stupid he is."

Billy Friedkin agrees.

Friedkin: "I'd rather work with tree stumps than actors."

To get actress Angie Everhart into the right frame of mind for her character in *Jade*, Friedkin slapped her. He also slapped a bit actor, a priest, on the set of *The Exorcist*.

Mike Nichols agrees, too.

Asked how many smart actors he knew, Nichols said, "One and half—Anthony Perkins is smart, and Richard Burton is something."

Barbara Kingland, who had an affair with Richard Burton when she was thirteen, was impressed by all the wise things Burton was always saying to her—until, when she was older, she found them in *Bartlett's Familiar Quotations*.

Drew Carey studies Robert McKee.

Comedian Drew Carey has taken Robert McKee's screenwriting course twice—which means he's spent sixty hours listening to him.

John Cleese studies Robert McKee.

The comedian John Cleese has taken the Robert McKee screenwriting seminar three times. In other words, he's spent ninety hours listening to McKee.

Joan Rivers studies Robert McKee.

Comedian Joan Rivers has taken Robert McKee's screenwriting course—but only once.

Actors can be smart.

Debra Winger called me at midnight in California from the *Betrayed* set in Canada. She said she had a script idea.

I listened. Then I told her why her idea was uninspired.

She listened. Then she said, "You're right, damn you!" and hung up.

An Immersive Actor

An actor who never steps out of the part, a potential Oscar winner, a phony, a pain in the ass.

But actors aren't geniuses.

Montgomery Clift turned down the Marlon Brando role in *On the Waterfront*, the William Holden role in *Sunset Boulevard*, the Paul Newman role in *Somebody Up There Likes Me*, and the James Dean role in *East of Eden*.

Actors aren't narcissistic, either.

Jennifer Aniston: "The last thing we think about is our looks, even though people think we do, because our wardrobe and hair are so great."

Actors are human; they're insecure, too.

If an actor says, "My character wouldn't do that," it usually means the actor is afraid he can't act that scene.

Jim Carrey: "When the camera's on, I'm a desperate motherfucker."

Actors are dumb.

For many years, Robert De Niro, always brilliant on-screen, couldn't even say two words on his own. He'd sit there, not speaking, stuck inside the mannerisms of the last character he'd played on-screen—woefully, miserably, pathetically lost without the words of a script.

But actors are no dummies.

When she was in her midforties, Sharon Stone legally adopted a woman as her grandmother.

The woman was a multizillionaire wife of a New York City parking magnate.

Actors are sensitive.

Sharon Stone told the English press that she was so "traumatized" by having to do killing scenes in *Basic Instinct* that during

those scenes, she asked that paramedics be near with a tank of oxy-
gen and a mask in case she passed out.

It was a complete crock. She was as ruthlessly efficient in her killing scenes
as she was in her sex scenes.

Actors are so very sensitive.

Sharon went up to the *Basic Instinct* cinematographer with a gun
in hand and waved it in his face.

"If I see one ounce of cellulite on-screen," she said, "you're a dead motherfucker."

You, too, can create a monster.

Sharon Stone: "People who have seen *Basic* stand two feet away
from me. They speak to me in careful tones. They don't condescend to me at all anymore."

Beware of "ach-trusses."

Sharon Stone put a clause in her *Diabolique* contract that she
wouldn't do any nudity.

Here's my two bucks.

Sharon Stone to Carrie Fisher: "I've often thought that if I could
get a 900 number and charge all the people who say they've had
sex with me—or say they know someone who's had sex with me—
two dollars a call, I'd never have to work again."

Maybe it's not such a good idea to sleep with your leading lady.

Actor James Woods to actress Sharon Stone: "Look, Sharon,
maybe everyone can't wait to get in there, but once they get it
in, the big problem is getting it out again."

Some actors have guts.

As feminists everywhere were trashing *Basic Instinct* after the
movie's release, actress Demi Moore, who had been offered the
Stone part, told the press that she was upset at herself for having
turned it down.

She particularly liked the scene where Catherine Tramell is interrogated by a
roomful of policemen. Demi thought it was "the best female empowerment
scene in movie history."

The Suicide Years

Used in reference to actresses who are in their thirties.

Actors are nutcases.

Marlon Brando's contracts for many years specified that he could leave the set in the midafternoon to see his shrink.

Actors can't write.

Hudson Hawk, one of the great total disasters of our time, was cowritten by Bruce Willis, who also cowrote the title song, which also bombed.

Not even Warren can write.

John Gregory Dunne: "Warren Beatty does not write as much as he supervises, in the manner of an architect. *Teams of writers* in effect work under the pseudonym Warren Beatty."

Be careful making suggestions to actors.

Said George C. Scott to Paddy Chayefsky when Paddy tried to give him some acting tips: "You do your fucking writing! And I'll do the acting!"

But actors can be mellow.

George C. Scott (*Patton, The Hospital*): "I've always been mellow. I have been the most mellow son of a bitch you've ever seen."

Actors will do anything to upstage one another.

Zero Mostel always ate a big dish of black beans and onions before the premiere of a play he was appearing in. He did that so he could fart easier (and louder and smellier) to distract the other actors.

Actors can be cheap.

Two actors I've worked with—Ryan O'Neal and Maximilian Schell—*took* all the clothes that they wore in the film they had just finished shooting.

Ryan O'Neal left the set so quickly with his new Armani suit that he had to be chased across town to bring it back—Arthur Hiller, the director, wanted to do another take.

Actors can be pissy.

This is especially true on a set, where they're pumped full of diuretics like Diazide, which make them go to the bathroom three times an hour (that would make anyone irritable).

They take the pills to look lean and hollowed out for the camera. Some actors—like Jeff Bridges and Michael Douglas—put twenty pounds on between movies and have to go on a rigid crash diet before the shoot. And *then* they have to gobble their piss pills on the set.

To Do a Pee-Wee

To be caught in a dark place playing with it.

Actors are somewhat competitive.

Anna Magnani watched Marilyn Monroe accept a prize from the Italian industry and yelled this from the audience: "*Putana!*" (Whore!)

They're so worried about wrinkles.

When Marilyn Monroe died, hair designer Sydney Guilaroff, one of her best friends, said, "I'm glad she died young. She could never have stood getting a wrinkle on her face. All she had was her beauty."

HOLLYWOOD PARABLE

Dr. Haing S. Ngor worked as a gynecologist in Cambodia. When the Communists took over the government, he and his wife were taken to a prison camp as slave laborers.

He was crucified in the camps and had part of his right little finger chopped off. His wife, pregnant with his child, was beaten to death.

He escaped to a Thai refugee camp. The director Roland Joffe met him and asked him to play a lead part in his film The Killing Fields. He agreed to do the part only because he had promised his wife that he would do his best to tell the world of the horrors that had taken place in Cambodia.

He received a Golden Globe Award and an Academy Award for his performance, the first nonprofessional actor in nearly fifty years to win the Oscar. He played other roles in film and television but spent much of his time involved in Cambodian relief efforts.

In February 1996, he was standing in the driveway of his Los Angeles apartment when he was shot to death by three young men. They were members of the Oriental Lazy Boyz street gang and were trying to rob Dr. Ngor.

He resisted. He didn't want to give them the locket around his neck. Inside it was a photograph of his dead wife.

If an actor has good lines, you'd better believe that he improvised them. Director Richard Marquand and I loved Robert Loggia's performance in *Jagged Edge* because he was the ultimate pro. He hit all his marks, said all his lines, never asked a question about his character's motivation, and never improvised.

When the movie became a big hit, Bob Loggia told his many interviewers that he had improvised *most* of his lines.

He stopped saying it when Richard told him that if he said it one more time, "I'm going to tell the press that you're a bloody bald-faced liar."

Robert Loggia was nominated for an Academy Award for his performance in *Jagged Edge*. He thanked neither me nor Richard.

In the beginning was the word.

Actor Chris Cooper (*Adaptation*): "Last night I tried to make a little bit of a joke at the very opening of a speech. I'm a guy that always needs a script. I can't talk off the cuff and be witty."

Who do you want me to be?

Actor John C. Reilly (*Chicago, Gangs of New York*): "I don't know who I am unless you tell me who I am—or who you want me to be. I'm still figuring out who I am, you know?"

Sometimes it's up to you to convince an actor to take the part.

Director Phillip Noyce (*Sliver*) describes a meeting he and I had with Sharon Stone to convince her to take the part of Carly Norris in *Sliver*: "On that occasion, which was quite tense going in, Sharon asked Joe if he'd like a massage. . . . It's true that I stopped talking. But not because I was sexually moved by the sight of a fifty-year-old man lying on the floor moaning as Sharon Stone was massaging him while sitting astride him. I stopped talking simply because he was so grotesque in the sounds he was making that it seemed ridiculous to continue trying to convince Sharon to do the part. And so I stopped talking and let the two of them play with each other on the floor. After massaging Joe, Sharon agreed to take the part of Carly."

If you have actor friends, try to get them to do a reading of your script.

Screenwriter Nicholas Kazan: "A reading won't always validate the writer's view . . . and that's its beauty. It simply exposes the text, usually revealing problems of some sort."

You don't want Edward Norton starring in your movie.

He was so disgusted by the quality of the scripts he was getting that he took Robert McKee's course, too, and he now *rewrites all the scripts he agrees to act in.*

Since he is a star, directors and studio execs try to flatter him into starring in their film by letting him do whatever he likes to the screenplay.

Try to stop Dustin Hoffman from being cast in your film.

Dusty is a huge fan of improvising a script. He will take a scene in the script that takes a minute and use it as a basis of improvisation with the other actors. They'll improvise for a half hour and then ask the writer to rewrite it in a way that they discovered while they were improvising.

Penis Extension

A Robert Evans phrase for a male star with "eruptability and swagger."

If Warren Beatty has anything to do with your film, stop working on it.
The joke in Hollywood is that Beatty, the great auteur, can turn a "go" movie into a development deal.

He'll get involved, work with six writers, rewriting your script, then *pull out of the project*.

He wanted to play the lead in my film *Jade,* but the director knew that if Beatty got involved, he (the director) would be out of a job. So he blocked Beatty from getting involved by making sure the studio didn't make Beatty's very expensive deal. The way he made sure of that was by discussing it with his wife, who ran the studio.

The director was Billy Friedkin, his wife Sherry Lansing.

Beware the unprepared actor; he could give you the performance of a lifetime.
Marlon Brando arrived on the set of *Apocalypse Now* without having read either the script or the novel on which it was based. He was so overweight that he could be shot only from the neck up.

Oh, but to be a star.
Hedy Lamarr: "To be a star is to own the world and all the people in it. A star can have anything: if there's something she can't buy, there's always a man to give it to her. Everybody adores a star. Strangers fight just to approach her. After a taste of stardom, everything else is poverty."

If an actor is looking for you, run!
Keanu Reeves was looking for a writer on the Academy Awards show.

"You're one of the writers, right?" he said to Bruce Vilanch, holding a script.

"This is really important. In this line 'This shocking, brutal, hilarious adventure is called *Pulp Fiction.*' "

Keanu looked at Vilanch.

Vilanch said, "So?"

Keanu said, "I want to change it."

Vilanch said, "You want to change it?"

Keanu said, "Yeah."

Vilanch said, "What do you want to change it to?"

Keanu said, "Can I say 'entitled' instead of 'called'? 'Entitled *Pulp Fiction.*' "

Vilanch said, "I don't see why not."

Keanu said, "Okay, good."

Maybe you can learn to eat glass.

Agent Swifty Lazar: "One night a well-respected French writer named Joseph Kissel was a guest at the home of Lewis Milestone, a fine director who did *All Quiet on the Western Front.* Kissel, a monster of a man, had mastered the art of eating glass.

"Humphrey Bogart had never met Kissel. . . . It was early in the evening when Kissel encountered Bogart in the foyer and asked him if he could eat glass. Bogart admitted he could not.

" 'I can,' the writer boasted.

" 'Well, eat this,' Bogie said, pointing in the direction of an eighteenth-century mirror. And before you knew it, Bogie had smashed the mirror and handed a piece to Kissel. And Kissel immediately swallowed half the piece Bogie had given him.

" 'If you can do it, I can do it,' Bogie said.

"He tried, but all he did was cut up the inside of his mouth."

Actors bring their own strengths and weaknesses to the part.

Robert Redford belches a lot, one reason he's mostly so cool and poker-faced on screen.

If Redford gets interested in your script, delete any scenes where he might be laughing.

Actors live their parts.

Hedy Lamarr: "How deeply do actresses become involved in their roles? Very deeply. I know when Ida Lupino did a string of neurotic characters, it had a definite effect on her. The doctor recommended happier pictures. The same thing happened to Bette Davis. I remember that during the making of *Samson and Delilah* my libido was definitely aroused."

Sometimes, very rarely, very very rarely, once in a blue moon, hardly ever, an actor will improvise a line better than any writer could have written it.

At the Academy Awards, after a streaker crossed the stage, actor David Niven said, "Isn't it fascinating to think that probably the only laugh that man will ever get in his life is by stripping off his clothes and showing his shortcomings?"

Actors really do respect, um, the screenwriter.

Tim Robbins: "There are the scripts you don't want to touch at all, that are so brilliant that you just have to figure a way into the character, and that's your job. There's other stuff that you have to fill out on your own and flesh out on your own. I try not to get involved with rewriting. I don't think it's necessary for an actor to do that. I think it's necessary for an actor to say, 'This doesn't really ring true. Is there something else we can do here?' But only after really trying. Sometimes actors can be wrong about their instincts and, without trying to go to a place emotionally out of some kind of reluctance, think they need a rewrite. But I trust—99 percent of the time—the writer's instinct."

I wasn't a dirty old man then, but maybe I am now.

When she was cast as the lead in my film *Jade*, Linda Fiorentino told *Daily Variety*, "It's an absolutely brilliant screenplay."

When *Jade* failed, Linda Fiorentino told reporters, "I had a lot of doubts about the script. It reads like it's written by a dirty old man."

Actors are ingrates.

I asked Paramount to cast Tom Berenger in *Sliver*. Tom and I were friends—we had met on the *Betrayed* set.

Paramount didn't want to cast him—he hadn't had any hit movies and he was drinking too much.

I finally went to Brandon Tartikoff, the head of production at the time, and asked him as a personal favor to me to cast Tom.

Brandon finally agreed—but told me I owed him a big one.

During the shoot, I discovered on the set that Tom was indeed drinking too much—he had vodka bottles in his trailer that he was sucking on, but I stood by him. The studio didn't replace him.

When the movie was released (and failed), Tom told *USA Today*, "Yeah, well, Joe can be real sleazy sometimes."

Actors have short memories.

Asked at a New York political fund-raiser what children should say no to, Arnold Schwarzenegger, whose movies have included more than five hundred shootings, maimings, or knifings, said, "How about violence? We should say no to violence."

Actors are loyal.

David Caruso, about my film *Jade*: "You'll see. *Jade* will be rediscovered by audiences in the future. In fact, I will make a prediction that this film will have a resurgence."

Gina Gershon, about my film *Showgirls*: "I'm not embarrassed saying I was in that movie. And I can't tell you how many people still come up to me and tell me how much they liked that movie. I think the *Showgirls* phenomenon has to do with the media. There were such high expectations that by the time the movie came out, it was bound to fail. And then when the critics started blasting it, people were scared to have their own opinion. I don't think it was as bad as some people said."

Shit happens to actors, too.

Hedy Lamarr: "At times, sex has been a disruptive factor in my life. The men in my life have ranged from a classic case history of impotence to a whip-brandishing sadist who enjoyed sex only after he tied my arms behind me with the sash of his robe. There was another man who took his pleasure with a girl in my own bed, while he thought I was asleep in it."

It ain't easy to be a star.

I stopped believing in Santa Claus at an early age," said Shirley Temple. "Mother took me to see him in a department store and he asked me for my autograph."

To Do a Garry Shandling

To sue, as Shandling did, your own agent or manager—an absolute no-no in the business. Look at what's happened to Shandling's career in the past five years: nada.

No hobbies, no kids, no nothin' . . .

Christopher Walken (*The Deer Hunter, King of New York*): "I hardly turn down anything, that's true. I don't have hobbies. I don't have kids. I really like to go to work. And when you're working, you want to stay a little bit fit and thin—so you look nice and your diet's better."

Macho Isn't Mucho

Said first by Zsa Zsa Gabor. In today's industry, macho definitely isn't mucho.

Try to avoid Method actors.

My fellow Hungarian Tony Curtis: "At the studio's urging I made a stab or two at the Method school of acting. . . . They called it sense memory. You had to recall the feeling of an icebox, or the exact sensation you had when you held a glass ball in your hand or felt the fabric of your tie. It was valid enough for some young actors, because it gave them something to do. But the truth is, acting was the only profession *people thought about a lot* and *did* very little. . . . It was a mind fuck: Go off in your head somewhere and find some other reality for what you were doing, *regardless of what the script intended.*"

Poor Victor Mature . . .

Hedy Lamarr complained to director C. B. DeMille that in every scene she had with Victor Mature, her back was to the camera.

De Mille said, "Do you think there are any men in America who would rather look at Victor's face than your ass? Up to this point in your life, every man in the audience wanted to marry you. After this picture every man will want to go to bed with you. I have taken you out of the living room and brought you into the bedroom."

To Do a Jennifer Grey

To get the kind of plastic surgery that destroys your career.

It helps if the director is your ally and not the star's.

Director Phillip Noyce, discussing *Sliver*: "We were only a few weeks from shooting and basically Sharon was saying she wanted to start back with the script at square one. My own loyalty to Joe Eszterhas, as well as the practicality of the situation, meant that I had to say 'No, we're not gonna do that.' That was the issue—whether we were going to rewrite the script from the first page, and that was the issue on which I took a stand. I gave her the appearance of submitting, whereas in fact we did shoot Joe Eszterhas's script. But I allowed Sharon to feel she had won—that she was the most powerful person in the relationship. Joe Eszterhas has failed to understand that you can often achieve exactly what you want to by appearing to let the other person win."

The star is not your script's ally.

Producer Mace Neufeld described Harrison Ford's contribution to the script of *Patriot Games* this way: "He's always looking to eliminate false notes, writer's directions that look good on paper but just don't work."

Some screenwriters hate actors.

Author/screenwriter William Saroyan hated Marlon Brando. He had his reasons.

1. When he was a young man, Saroyan discovered that Brando had seduced his wife, Carol.

2. When he was an old man, Saroyan discovered that Brando had seduced his daughter, Lucy.

Why Marlon Brando could seduce both Mrs. and Miss Saroyan . . .

An actor friend of Robert Duvall's told him that as far as sex is concerned, "acting is the greatest leg-opener in the world."

You're lucky you're you and not Tom Cruise.

Screenwriter William Goldman: "It's shitty work. Not the money, not the power, that's all neat. But have you ever been on a movie set? Death. It's all mechanical stuff. Done in quick snippets. Sure, there's craft involved in sustaining a character over a four-month shoot—but most stars only play themselves, so even that isn't so hard. Ask anyone—movie acting is the snooze of all the world. So it's shitty and it's phony and the fame doesn't last. No wonder they're crazy. Maybe the real wonder is that they're not crazier than they are."

Actors are bullies.

Ryan O'Neal, sometime producer, played a studio executive in my film *An Alan Smithee Film: Burn Hollywood Burn.*

The script called for him to hit a *National Enquirer* reporter named Alan Smith, played by a real *National Enquirer* reporter named Alan Smith.

O'Neal, a Hollywood lothario, had reason not to like the tabloids . . . and Alan Smith, who had written about him in the past.

So when the scene was being filmed, Ryan hit the real Alan Smith so hard that he almost broke the man's jaw.

"Score one for us," Ryan O'Neal said.

If you're really pissed off at an actor, touch him or her.

What's awful about being famous and being an actress," said famous actress Winona Ryder, "is when people come up to you and touch you. That's scary, and they just seem to think it's okay to do it, like you're public property."

ALL HAIL
Mercedes de Acosta!

The screenwriter/playwright seduced both Greta Garbo and Marlene Dietrich.

A friend said she looked like "a Spanish Dracula with the body of a young boy."

She was known in society circles as "the dyke at the top of the stairs."

You're too smart to learn anything from actors.

Professor James Ryan in *Screenwriting from the Heart*: "Having worked early in my career as a professional actor in stage, film, and television, I tried an experiment. I got my writing students on their feet doing improvisations. It helped enormously even if they were lousy actors. They began to understand that good dramatic writing is acting on the page and there must be truthful moment to moment behavior for their characters. I devised 'simple-stupid' exercises to get all their 'learning' out of the way, so that they could access their deeply felt imagination and find that place in themselves that would give them a sense of prowess—a feeling of being alive and true."

H—E—L—P!

Forehead

One of Arnold Schwarzenegger's favorite words—it means a stupid person or a person who argues with Arnold. Most of the legislators in California are "foreheads."

Lame-o

Jack Nicholson's version of "forehead."

Their PR person will decide about your script.

Actress Sally Field said, "I hesitate to say that Pat Kingsley does my public relations. It's way beyond that. I send her material, the scripts I'm thinking of doing or developing. And I'm not the only one who does. Jim Brooks, Goldie Hawn—a whole bunch of people ask her about scripts, about writers."

Oh, wasn't Jim Brooks a writer once?

The screenwriter/director, according to Sally Field, sends his scripts to Pat Kingsley, PR person, for advice.

A writer who sends his script to his PR person? *For advice?*

This is the meaning of "star power."

Screenwriter/director Billy Wilder: "There was an actress named Marilyn Monroe. She was always late. She never remembered her lines. She was a pain in the ass. My Aunt Millie is a nice lady. If she were in pictures, she would always be on time. She would know her lines. She would be nice. Why does everyone in Hollywood want to work with Marilyn Monroe and no one wants to work with my Aunt Millie? Because no one will go to the movies to watch my Aunt Millie and everyone will come out to watch Marilyn Monroe."

You, too, can leave your wife.

Mike Medavoy said this to Kevin Costner after meeting him for the first time: "You know, I have this sense that I'm sitting here with someone who is going to become a great big star. You're going to want to direct your own movies, produce your own movies, and you're going to end up leaving your wife and going through the whole Hollywood movie-star cycle."

Stars are better with their mouths closed.

Screenwriter Robert Towne: "What was once said of the British aristocracy, that they did nothing and did it very well—is a definition that could be applied to movie actors. For gifted movie actors affect us most, I believe, not by talking, fighting, fucking, killing, cursing, or cross-dressing. They do it by being photographed. The point is that a fine actor onscreen conveys a staggering amount of information before he ever opens his mouth."

Work with actors who are unknown.

Producer Sam Spiegel: "When actors are still comparatively unknown, they are easygoing and amiable. When they lose their sense of proportion, they become lionized and begin to believe their own publicity."

A complete unknown can be better in a part than Robert De Niro or Gene ("the Hack") Hackman.

Director Phillip Noyce: "Between a beginner and an experienced actor there is a huge gap. And often it's better not to fill that gap, because someone with absolutely no experience, and therefore no technique, can be just as good as the most experienced actor. With experience come actorly tricks, acting techniques that can make a performance false."

If you marry an actress, don't write a script for her.

Arthur Miller wrote *The Misfits* for Marilyn Monroe. This is what she had to say: "Arthur did this to me. He could have written anything and he comes up with this. If that's what he thinks of me, well, then I'm not for him and he's not for me. Arthur said it's his movie. I don't think he even wants me in it. It's all over. We have to stay with each other because it would be bad for the film if we split up now.... I think Arthur secretly likes dumb blondes. Some help he is."

Find your own Marilyn Monroe and have a fling with her.

Mexican screenwriter José Bolaños found the actual Marilyn. He was one of her last lovers. This is what she said about him: "He's the greatest lover in the whole wide world. I heard he writes some of the worst movies in Mexico. Silly romances. But what do I care? Everything else he does is incredible."

ALL HAIL
Mercedes de Acosta!

Truman Capote designed a game that he called the International Daisy Chain. Its goal was to connect people through the people they had slept with.

Capote said that the best card to have in the game was screenwriter Mercedes de Acosta because she had slept with so many people, "you could get to anyone from Francis Cardinal Spellman to the Duchess of Windsor."

You, too, can marry a movie star.

Paul Bern wrote screenplays for German films directed by Ernst Lubitsch and Josef von Sternberg.

That's not what made him famous. What made him famous was marrying sex bomb Jean Harlow.

When Harlow married him, she said, "He doesn't talk fuck, fuck, fuck, fuck all the time."

He was just another impotent screenwriter.

Screenwriter Paul Bern killed himself after two months of marriage to Jean Harlow.

The studio wanted to make sure the public didn't blame Harlow in any way for her husband's suicide. They made up a story that Bern killed himself because he was suffering from "underdeveloped genitalia"—a real problem, considering he was married to the world's greatest sex bomb.

Keep your casting ideas to yourself.

Novelist Margaret Mitchell suggested that Groucho Marx be cast as Rhett Butler in the film version of her novel, *Gone With the Wind*.

Don't fly on the same plane with actors.

We were flying from Dubuque, Iowa, to Chicago in a puddle jumper after the *F.I.S.T.* premiere—Norman Jewison, the director, and I and the actors Kevin Conway and Cassie Yates.

We got caught in a thunderstorm and the little plane started to be buffeted about in the wind.

"Oh shit," Norman Jewison said to me. "If this thing crashes, I'm only going to get the second paragraph. The actors always get the lead—and you, the screenwriter, will be mentioned somewhere deep in the middle of the story."

Don't have a movie star for a friend.

Remember that the word *star* spelled backward is *rats*.

LESSON 17

Just Say the Fucking Words!

Even Bill Goldman wrote a tell-all.

Bill Goldman wrote about going bikini shopping with Elizabeth Hurley; Norman Mailer wrote about his great lust for Marilyn Monroe; Arthur Miller wrote a play about Marilyn Monroe, his wife; and then there was the screenwriter who wrote about rolling around on the floor with Sharon Stone.

Movie stars are right not to trust writers.

Warren Beatty shouldn't ever be without his watercooler.

When studio head Frank Wells denied director and star Warren Beatty's request for a watercooler in his office, Beatty took *Heaven Can Wait* away from Warner Bros. and went to Paramount.

Actors are teenagers undergoing a sexual identity crisis.

Sir Laurence Olivier: "To oneself inside, one is always sixteen with red lips."

TAKE IT FROM ZSA ZSA

Actors are like children and children are simple.

Stallone fights like a sissy and Sean Penn can't fight.

When Sylvester Stallone claimed in interviews that he had written *F.I.S.T.* (it had taken me years to research and write the script), I challenged him to a fistfight by saying I'd been in more barroom brawls and claiming that he "fought like a sissy."

My father, who loved me, said "I've seen *Rocky*. I've seen him fight. Challenge him to fight, yes, but do not under any circumstances fight him. He will beat you bloody." I took my father's advice.

At dinner one night, screenwriter/novelist Charles Bukowski told Sean Penn that his wife smelled "like she'd been sucking donkeys off all day."

Sean jumped up and challenged Bukowski to fight. Bukowski, then in his seventies, said, "Sit down, Sean, you know I can take you."

A Blood Star

An action star like Van Damme, Stallone, Seagal, or the governor of California.

Don't get caught in a cross fire between two superstars.

When Sly Stallone was directing John Travolta in *Staying Alive*, they got into a hellacious battle royal over the script.

Sly wanted me to do a rewrite incorporating both of their thoughts. I had a meeting with the two of them in Sly's trailer and saw that they were a thousand miles apart.

Sly and I had had a previous battle over *F.I.S.T.*, so I said to him now, "Sly, you fucked me with a tree trunk on *F.I.S.T.* What do you want to fuck me again for?"

Both Sly and Travolta laughed—they thought that was really funny.

I didn't do the rewrite.

You, too, can be a star maker.

Jennifer Beals, Sharon Stone, and Gina Gershon became stars playing the characters that I created.

All three of them denied it and said they became stars thanks to their own talent.

But none had any explanation for why they didn't become stars after playing other screenwriters' parts.

Actors know how to flatter you.

An actress in a Harold Pinter film said that saying Pinter's words was like "blowing air into yeast when making bread."

Liv Tyler is obsessed with me.

Liv Tyler did an interview in which she said *she* was the inspiration for *Showgirls*. She said I had become obsessed with her after seeing her play a stripper in an Aerosmith video.

She said, "Joe Eszterhas thought the video was brilliant. It gave him the idea for *Showgirls*. He tried to get me to take the lead in the movie, but I didn't want to get into that kind of thing."

It was news to me.

I'd never seen the Aerosmith video; neither had Paul Verhoeven, the director of *Showgirls*.

I'd never met or spoken with Liv; neither had Paul Verhoeven.

I didn't even know that Steven Tyler had a daughter named Liv; neither did Paul Verhoeven.

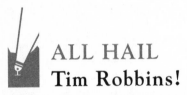

ALL HAIL
Tim Robbins!

The actor thanked novelist Dennis Lehane and screenwriter Brian Helgeland "for the writing of this amazing script" before thanking the director and producers as he accepted his Oscar for *Mystic River*.

THE HELL WITH TIM ROBBINS

In The Player, *he plays a sleazy studio executive who murders the screenwriter.*

Actors, like writers, don't like to think of themselves as liars.

Actress Melina Mercouri: "My colleague says that all actors are liars. But my colleague is an actor. So he is lying, yes? So therefore actors are not liars. Therefore he speaks the truth and therefore actors are liars, so therefore he lies and so on and so on."

You, too, can get even with an actor who treats you badly.

John Barrymore already had an opossum, a kinkajou, a mouse deer, and six dogs, which had been born during an earthquake—it was his theory that dogs born during earthquakes are more alert than others.

And then, as a gift from an English actress, John was given a monkey, which bit everyone in the house except him. The monkey would sit next to his feet for hours, gazing at him fondly. It was only after he'd been forced to give the monkey to the zoo that a vet told him the monkey had been transfixed not by his personality but by the booze he'd smelled on him. So John made weekly visits to the zoo to breathe on his monkey.

And then a screenwriter who secretly despised him gave John a vulture. Not just any vulture, but a king vulture, which became John's best friend. He named the vulture Maloney. He'd take Maloney out on the yacht, and the crew would be horrified as the big vulture sat on John's shoulders, nibbling at John's eyeball, holding his beak out for a kiss. They sailed happily up and down from Santa Monica to Santa Barbara, but one day John realized that Maloney wasn't happy. Maloney wasn't eating properly. John realized he wasn't able to feed Maloney what he required: partially but not *completely* decayed meat.

So he took Maloney ashore, kissed him farewell, and sailed away.

From then on, for the rest of his life, thanks to a diabolical screenwriter who hated him, John Barrymore did little but drink, a brokenhearted old actor pining for his vulture.

You can get even with an actress, too.

On the set of one of her earlier movies, Sharon Stone's prima donna act pissed off the crew so badly that *they pissed* into a bathtub before Sharon got into it for her scene.

What you write can destroy someone's career.

They told her she was going to be a big movie star and she almost believed it. She had done the television and the stage work, and here she was, at twenty-seven, costarring in a big movie with a big star at a cheap hotel out in the middle of nowhere, with only her pills and her little Baggies of coke to keep her company, to make her forget how much she hated the script. (They weren't such little bags, really; they were pretty big bags, a last-minute gift from her agent in L.A.)

She had a 5:00 A.M. wake-up call, and here it was, 2:00 A.M., and she couldn't get to sleep. She kept thinking about how awful this script was. She went out on her patio and practiced deep breathing for a while, noticing the balminess of this Iowa summer night, the softness of the corn-scented air.

She went downstairs, her pills and her Baggies in her purse, and got into her rent-a-car. Just a little drive around the blacktop and dirt roads was what she had in mind. But somehow she found herself flying down the interstate, popping another pill.

She lost track of much of the next couple of days. She woke up in the desert sun, out of pills, out of coke, trembling, knowing that it was over, that everything she had worked for was gone, knowing now that she would never be a star.

Beware of "serious" actors.

Laird Cregar was the best fiend you've ever seen on-screen. He was a talented actor with a weird, off-kilter face and a swollen body. Playing monsters and freaks, he'd go into makeup at the start of each film and ask them what they were going to do to his face, and they'd smile and say, "Nothing."

He read a sensitive book about an inward young guy with an inferiority complex. At his suggestion, a studio bought the book, but then the people there turned the inward young guy into a rapist and a murderer and cast Laird in the part.

When the shoot ended, Laird had plastic surgery done on his eyes, his nose, his jaw, and his ears. He wouldn't ever allow himself to be cast as a fiend again.

He was going to turn himself into a romantic lead. All he had left to do was to lose the weight.

He lost thirty pounds. Then he suffered a heart arrhythmia from the weight loss and died.

The pain, the pain . . .

Marlon Brando to Mike Medavoy: "Can you imagine going to work every day and pretending to be someone else?"

Just say the fucking words!

Faye Dunaway asked Roman Polanski about her character's motivation in *Chinatown*.

Roman said, "Say the fucking words. Your salary is your motivation."

Sharon didn't like Billy.

Sliver director Phillip Noyce: "Billy Baldwin knew that Sharon Stone hadn't wanted him in *Sliver* and their relationship was always tense. I ended up having to shoot many of their close-ups with only one of them in the room at a time, because they didn't want to look at each other."

Why didn't Sharon want Billy to costar with her?

Because she wanted Billy's older brother, Alec. Sharon said, "Alec can put me over a table anytime he wants."

What did Billy Baldwin have to say about that?

Billy called Sharon "a paean to lipstick lesbianism."

Comedians can kill you.

Producer Bernie Brillstein: "The words of comedy are death—'I killed them, I laid them in the aisle, I blew their head off, I murdered them'—it's all death—it's how far you can take a human being."

Who the hell is Hedy Lamarr?

Hedy Lamarr: "I enjoyed the location trips to desert towns in Arizona. The nights were mellow and romantic. Making love out of doors is so much more thrilling. Add a cowboy who never heard of Hedy Lamarr and the situation is ideal."

My friend Phillip Noyce fell in love with Angelina Jolie.

Director Phillip Noyce, discussing *The Bone Collector*: "In the second half of the schedule I was shooting predominantly with Angelina Jolie. Usually in the morning when I woke up, I couldn't wait to get to the set to work with her. I was impatient to continue what became a sort of love affair, being connected in this weird manner, through the lens, through the story, through the strange relationship between performer and director. I had the same connection with Nicole Kidman. I loved her, adored her; she was the angel who couldn't do a thing wrong."

The Crack of the Ass

The line at which most actresses stop when it comes to shooting nudity. There is usually a clause in their contracts that specifies that in a scene in bed, the bedsheet will be high enough so that a "crack of the ass" is visible.

My friend Phillip didn't just fall in love; he went stark raving gaga apeshit.

Some directors can fall gaga apeshit over their actors.

Phillip Noyce, discussing Angelina Jolie: "When I first met Angie I felt a sense of discovery, of being there when something wonderful is being formed. You could see tremendous talent as well as hunger, a hunger for work, good work, a love of trying things, a love of giving herself up to the character, to the lens, to the moment.... Porcelain isn't fine enough to describe how fragile she is. She's not burned out with the joy of performing. She's in her element because she can set parameters for a character, whereas I suspect she doesn't know her own boundaries emotionally and physically. She's very courageous as an actress. Angelina will go anywhere, or at least she'll try going anywhere that the director suggests."

Clint is Marilyn in drag.

Clint Eastwood's ex-lover said that Clint listened to hours and hours of audiotapes of Marilyn Monroe—to get his hushed voice just right.

Dustpan Hoffman, movie star . . .

As a young actor, Dustin Hoffman was known to his friends as "Dustbin" and "Dustpan." But after he was cast in *The Graduate*, all of his friends called him "Dusty."

Dennis Quaid asked God to take it all away.

Actor Dennis Quaid (*Far from Heaven*): "I wasn't really prepared for the sort of attention I got. When it started happening, it was just too much—and I was also fueling it by getting loaded a lot. There was so much coming at me at one point that I remember just asking God to take it away from me."

Tom Thumb's boots . . .

Tom Cruise didn't mind being cast with Brad Pitt in *Interview with the Vampire,* but he demanded that his costumer be allowed to make him boots that made him look taller than Pitt.

Her acting teachers killed Marilyn.

Marilyn Monroe's drama coach, Michael Chekhov, told her to spread her arms wide and stand with her legs apart so she could imagine herself becoming larger and larger.

She had to say to herself, "I am going to awaken the sleeping muscles of my body. I am going to revivify and use them."

Then she was to kneel on the floor and imagine herself getting smaller and smaller, until she became a speck on the floor.

She did these exercises every day for six hours.

Bogie was a wuss.

At a party he was attending with Lauren Bacall, his wife, Humphrey Bogart got angry when a sailor pinched Bacall's butt.

Bogie and some friends locked the sailor in the bathroom and called the Shore Patrol to come and arrest him.

Billy Wilder, who witnessed it all, said, "That was Bogie, the hero of *Casablanca.*"

Michael Douglas looks better with Botox and surgery.

Bogart once said to his cinematographer, "I like my lines and wrinkles, so don't try and light them out and make me look like a goddamn fag."

Dustpan is a hypocrite.

He starred in *Straw Dogs,* one of the bloodiest of all the films directed by Sam Peckinpah. Years later, he first turned down *Captain Hook,* the Peter Pan remake to be directed by Steven Spielberg, because, as Dusty's agent said, "The script is too violent."

Montgomery Clift in The Bridge on the River Kwai . . .

Producer Sam Spiegel was interested in casting Montgomery Clift in *The Bridge on the River Kwai.* He asked him to dinner in New York.

Clift arrived sky-high on pills. He would say things out of the blue, like "The sky is blue." He ordered a martini and then ordered two more. He ordered both steak and lamb chops—rare. He ate the steak and the chops and spit meat and blood all over the table. Then he lay down in the booth and went to sleep.

The producer changed his mind about casting him.

Only if it's a real honker . . .

While nose jobs hurt the careers of Jennifer Grey, Carol Burnett, and Roy Scheider, Peter O'Toole had such a beak of a nose that he would always have been a character actor without surgery.

Brando was stupid.

Brando not only sold off his gross points in *The Godfather* for $100,000 but then asked for $100,000 to attend the twenty-fifth-anniversary party of *The Godfather*'s release.

He didn't get it and didn't go. He would have received at least $8 million had he not sold his gross points.

Kate Nelligan was too smart.

Screenwriter/playwright Harold Pinter: "The porter called to say that a young actress named Kate Nelligan was on the way up to meet us and I can always remember Mike Nichols saying 'I feel sorry for young actresses. Can you imagine coming up to meet Sam Spiegel, Harold Pinter, and me—it must be terrifying.' And the next thing we knew, she walked into the room and took us to the cleaners. She was totally self-possessed, absolutely on top of everything, and made us feel that we didn't know what we were doing. *She didn't get the part because of that.*"

TAKE IT FROM ZSA ZSA

Zsa Zsa killed Clark Gable.

Zsa says that Clark's favorite food in the whole world was the artery-busting Hungarian favorite kolbasz, *smoked and dried sausage.*

She introduced Clark to it and he loved it so much that she would take a bunch of it over to his house each week—even the week that he died of a massive heart attack.

Elizabeth Taylor killed his dream.

Richard Burton, who said he was "a pockmarked boyo from Wales," didn't want to be an actor. He said he should have been a coal miner.

His dream was to own a big house filled with books and little else. He wanted to spend his life reading his books.

The Italian dwarf, movie star . . .

He is the actor whom Paramount executives referred to as "that Italian dwarf" before they cast him in *The Godfather.*

George C. Scott was George Lincoln Rockwell.

George C. Scott hated black people so much that *Islands in the Stream* had to be shot in Hawaii, on Kauai, where there were no black people—so Scott wouldn't get into trouble in the bars at night.

The few blacks necessary for scenes in the movie, set in the Caribbean, had to be flown in.

Vacuum the Dustpan.

Dusty went to story meetings for years with his own personal "dramaturge"—the playwright Murray Schisgal. Dusty wanted screenwriters he was working with to "work with Murray" as they wrote their scripts.

After they had worked with Murray and the script was finished, Dusty often brought in another personal pet writer just to rewrite his character's dialogue—that's how Malia Scotch Marmo wound up getting a shared screenplay credit on *Hook.*

The moral of the story: After Dusty and Murray and Malia are done with you, you might not recognize your own script.

Kim Novak almost killed Sammy Davis, Jr.

Columbia studio czar Harry Cohn once asked mobster Mickey Cohen to kill Sammy Davis, Jr., because Sammy was having an affair with Columbia star Kim Novak.

Cohn worried that if the affair became public, Novak's career would be finished.

Drew's father was an actor, too.

Actress Drew Barrymore: "My father said, 'Hey, Drew, you want to give me an autograph, too? How about putting it on a check?'"

David Caruso sleeps with a mirror.

My lead actor in *Jade,* David Caruso, said, "I'm nowhere near as sexy as I come off on-camera. Film just loves me."

Sandra Bernhard defines whores.

I cast her in *An Alan Smithee Film: Burn Hollywood Burn.* I think she's a brilliant actress.

She once said, "I find people in the porn world are very lively and animated. So what if they screw for a living? I like a lot of them better than the actors in Hollywood—who are the real whores, to be perfectly honest with you."

I wonder if Grace Kelly ever slept with Joe Mankiewicz.

Gary Cooper told friends that Grace Kelly liked going to bed wearing nothing but white gloves.

Coop said, "She gave the impression that she could be a cold dish until you got her in bed . . . then she could really explode."

Tim Robbins is full of . . . himself.

Actor Tim Robbins: "The best directors I've worked with would never consider themselves auteurs or experts or anything. Those experiences taught me that the open ear, the open mind, the open heart can produce such great work from the actor. If an actor comes on the set and the director is viewing themself [sic] as the person who knows everything, the person that has all the answers, then you're not going to create an organic performance. You're going to create someone's idea of a performance. And the really great directors know that and are able to inspire their actors to create by giving them a confidence in themselves and a worth in themselves. Then actors feel like they belong there. They feel like they are contributing something significant, that they aren't just saying lines, that they are bringing who they are as people to the project and are fully appreciated for that."

A Quality of Eruptibility

Absolutely necessary for a lead male part, making every female viewer believe that the actor playing the part would go to bed with her.

A Quality of Availability

Absolutely necessary for a lead feminine part, making every male viewer believe he could bed the starlet playing the part.

Val Kilmer is an imbecile.

Asked by the Academy to nominate the three best film moments of the century, Kilmer nominated three of his movies (one of them was *Batman Forever*). He enclosed a postcard to the Academy that said, "I can't help it, these are my three favorite movies."

The Pesci is beginning to stink.

Actor Joe Pesci, after winning Best Supporting Actor for *Good-Fellas,* went offstage and collapsed on the floor, clutching his Oscar and mumbling, "I can't believe this! I can't believe this!"

Yes, but did she clean the blood off the coat hangers?

Joan Crawford had all of her furniture and even her walls coated in plastic so she could clean them better.

Is that why he changed professions?

Harrison Ford, carpenter, was hired by John Gregory Dunne and Joan Didion to remodel their Trancas house.

Julia Roberts's virgin eyes . . .

When she moved into an apartment complex, Julia Roberts had notices sent to the other tenants, telling them they were not to speak to her or even look at her if they ran into her in the corridor.

Barbra Streisand did the same thing when she was doing a gig at a hotel in Vegas.

And Hillary Clinton did the same thing with Secret Service agents in the White House.

Is Tom Thumb the new Burt Reynolds?

Mimi Rogers, discussing soon-to-be-ex-husband Tom Cruise: "Here's the real story on why we broke up. Tom was seriously thinking of becoming a monk. At least for that period of time, it looked as though marriage wouldn't fit into his overall spiritual need. And he thought he had to be celibate to maintain the purity of his instrument. My instrument needed tuning. Therefore, it became obvious that we had to split."

James Woods's Krazy-glued penis.

When she broke up with actor James Woods, actress Sean Young put mutilated voodoo dolls on his front porch and told friends she was going to Krazy-glue his penis to his thigh.

The one-sheet tells all.

If the stars' faces aren't on it, their careers are fading. Check out Harrison Ford and Michelle Pfeiffer, missing from the *What Lies Beneath* one-sheet, and Sylvester Stallone, missing from the *Cliffhanger* poster.

He, too, was a big-mouth Hungarian.

Hungarian screenwriter Andrew Solt told his friend Zsa Zsa Gabor that Ingrid Bergman, on *Joan of Arc*, the picture he had written, slept with everyone on the set, including the electricians, and that when she was through with the electricians, she had them fired.

If Bruce Willis is a real asshole, then say he's a real asshole.

At a writer's seminar on Maui, Shane Black (*Lethal Weapon*), who was sitting next to me, said, "Okay, I'll say it, Bruce Willis is a real asshole."

Okay, maybe my physical proximity to Shane made him say it.

PART ELEVEN

SURVIVING THE CRITICS

They Want to Kill You, Rape Your Wife, and Eat Your Children!

The definition of a critic . . .

Ben Hecht: "A person who smiles when he calls you a son of a bitch."

Comedian Dick Shawn: "A critic is someone who comes in after the battle is over and shoots the wounded."

Don't read your reviews.

William Faulkner never did. "Who knows the faults of my work better than I do?" he said.

His brother said, "He was simply protecting himself from hurt."

Never mind the damn critics; maybe you've just written Dr. Zhivago.

Dr. Zhivago was hammered by the critic when it was released. It is now considered perhaps the greatest movie of all time by many writers, directors . . . and critics.

The best way to deal with a bad review . . .

When critic Louis Kronenberger panned one of Ben Hecht's plays, Hecht threatened to castrate him.

Bruce Willis might be an asshole, but he's got a pretty good idea here.

Bruce Willis: "What I had hoped for her [the critic] was that she became so famous that she had to start worrying about her life, that she had to start feeling that she was threatened, and then had to sleep with a gun by her bed every night because she thought that she was so famous someone was going to do something to her or attack her. And then one night she finally realized the sick life she was living, and she just put the gun in her mouth and blew her fucking brains out."

They have a (tawdry) living to make.

Most film critics also do filmmaker interviews for the publications they work for. Their income depends on their access to stars.

So let's say Steven Spielberg has directed a new movie starring Julia Roberts and written by John Doe.

Let's say this new movie is awful. The critic for your local metropolitan paper or TV station knows he will need interviews with Spielberg and Roberts in the future. He reviews the film nevertheless and says that the movie isn't very good. He knows that if he says a bad movie is good too often, his readers will dismiss him as a street-corner hooker.

But if the movie isn't very good, then whom should he blame? Spielberg? Roberts? Or the screenwriter, John Doe, whom he will never need to interview because (A) the public could give a flying fig about who the screenwriter is, and (B) because there are almost no screenwriters who are stars (and whom he will ever need to interview).

This, more likely, will be the critic's capsule review: "Julia Roberts shows flashes of brilliance with some of her obviously improvised lines of dialogue. But Spielberg, who has given it a heroic try, is ultimately brought down by John Doe's hackneyed and cliché-ridden screenplay."

Now you're talking, Billy boy!

William Goldman: "Directors have no vision. . . . One of the reasons the media gushes about them is this—they don't know shit about the movie business. They are filling columns or minutes for circulation or ratings. And since they want to feel important, the people they interview have to be fabulously important. The *hottest* young star, the *most brilliant* director. That kind of madness."

They want to kill you, rape your wife, and eat your children.

No critic working today compares the first draft of an original screenplay with the finished movie.

Doing this would show the critic—especially in a misfired movie—who is to blame.

What if the script was brilliant and a moronic director destroyed it?

Critics claim that it would take too much time for them to read the script of a movie, but I'm convinced they don't want to know if a director has butchered a brilliant script.

Critics *purposely* blind themselves to any information that would force them to praise the writer and damn the director or the star.

This is because their bread and butter depends on access to the directors and the stars. And because they hate you—because they want to *be* you.

Aw, come on! Rape your wife and eat your children?

Yup.

Because you're a screenwriter and they're self-styled "film experts" who can't write screenplays.

Because you make big bucks and they make peanuts, even in comparison to what you make if you write *unsuccessful* movies.

And because they don't think it is fair that they know all this movie trivia and you don't, and still you're the one writing screenplays!

They want to be you!

Consequently: If you've written a good movie, don't expect them to praise you. They might not even mention you in their review, and they'll certainly heap lavish praise upon the director for "creating" a great movie.

If, however, you've written a movie that winds up being bad on-screen, they'll not only mention you; they'll blame you for *everything*—even bad acting. The actor, they'll say, just couldn't do anything with your lame lines of dialogue.

Some critics are so shamelessly biased that they'll even praise an actor's performance while bashing your script—as if the performance were created by the director's notes and not your story, character, and lines of dialogue.

Who are these miscreants?

Hollywood Reporter columnist Ray Richmond, himself a some-time film critic: "They are at once heavily ego-driven and desperately insecure. Film critics are movie geeks who write as much to impress other critics as they do to inform their audience. They're obsessed with being taken seriously, which can manifest itself either via quotes in movie ads or their anointing by the critical intelligentsia as one of their own. Yet while critics sport the iconoclast's soul, it's mitigated by an almost child-like need to be loved—not necessarily by the public but by their peers. They pine to be members of the club and at the same time somehow outside it, but not so much that they appear to be snobbish. This is why most would never be caught dead lavishing too much worship on a mainstream blockbuster . . . unless of course their contemporaries did too (such as in the case of *Spider-Man 2*). Then it would be cool."

How these miscreants see themselves.

Film critic A. O. Scott in *The New York Times*: "Criticism always contains an element of autobiography, and it is not much a leap to suggest that more than a few have seen themselves in *Sideways*. (Several have admitted as much.) This is not to suggest that white, middle-aged men with a taste for alcohol are disproportionately represented in the ranks of working movie reviewers; plausible as such a notion may be, I don't have the sociological data to support it just yet. But the self-pity and the solipsism that are Miles's less attractive (and frequently most prominent) traits represent the underside of the critical temperament; his morbid sensitivity may be an occupational hazard we all face."

Critics are hustlers who want to be screenwriters.

Consider James Agee, Peter Bogdanovich, Barbara Shulgasser, Paul Schrader, Jay Cocks, Paul Attanasio, among others—all critics who made it to be screenwriters or directors.

What better way to advertise that you know something about writing screenplays than to pick apart the screenplays of the movies you're reviewing—knowing that producers and studio execs will read your review if it's coming from a relatively prominent place.

They'll hang you by your themes.

I've always been fascinated by the notion that we don't ever know one another—that lovers and family members may not really know their mates or parents.

I played with that theme in *Betrayed, Music Box, Jagged Edge, Basic Instinct,* and *Sliver.*

According to the critics, though, screenwriters aren't allowed to have themes. However, novelists and directors are.

But the critics said there was no theme to my work. I was, they said, "plagiarizing myself."

If you write witty dialogue . . .

Be prepared for the critics to call you not a witty writer, but a wordsmith.

No matter what you do, the critics will define you.

Critics have defined me as the man who writes about sleazy sex.
To reach that conclusion they have ignored most of my films: *F.I.S.T., Checking Out, Big Shots, Hearts of Fire, Betrayed, Music Box, Nowhere to Run, Telling Lies in America,* and *An Alan Smithee Film: Burn Hollywood Burn.*

You, too, can laugh all the way to the bank.

In every bad review I got for *Basic Instinct, Showgirls, Sliver,* and *Jade*, the amount of money I received for the script was always in the review—often in the first paragraph.

William Goldman, speaking about *Butch Cassidy and the Sundance Kid*: "My very late great agent, Evarts Ziegler, had secured $400,000 for the screenplay. A lot of money today. Back then, record-shattering. It made all the papers, not just *Variety*. And a lot of people wondered what the world was coming to, a western selling for that. It's my belief that the reason the reviews were so shitty is because of the money I got. A lot of people were pissed, a lot of these people were critics. For them the title of the movie really turned out to be this: *Butch Cassidy and the Sundance Kid $400,000.*"

If they were pissed about Bill Goldman's $400,000, imagine how apoplectic they must have gotten when I got $2.5 million for *Jade,* $3 million for *Basic Instinct,* and $3.7 million for *Showgirls*. Or how insane they must have been when the movie they'd unanimously trashed, *Basic Instinct,* became the biggest-grossing film of the year wordwide!

In the old days, they openly took bribes.

Syndicated columnist Jimmy Fiddler revealed that he was offered $2,500 for a favorable review of Errol Flynn's *The Prisoner of Zenda* and turned the money down because the movie was so bad that he felt he couldn't take it without looking like a simpleton.

Running into Fiddler at a party later, Flynn decked him—at which point, Fiddler's wife stuck a fork in Flynn's ear.

They can be bribed? You damn betcha!

Martin Kaplan, associate dean of the USC Annenberg School for Communication and former Disney executive: "Studios know that many in the entertainment press don't have the budgets or the scruples to turn down all-expenses-paid junkets to Disney World, to New York, or the set in New Zealand. A bag of swag, or a signed photo of the reporter in a bear hug with a smiling superstar, isn't a guarantee against a critic's pan, but it can't hurt."

They're just damn whoors.

Many listen to the studio publicity people who call them and ask, "Couldn't you say this about the movie?" and then tell them what to write.

The reason many critics listen is because they like going on those press junkets, where the studio pays for everything.

They like the Christmas gifts they'll receive if the studio is pleased with the things they write during the year.

And they like to see their names in big letters in full-page ads paid for by the studio in *The New York Times* or *USA Today*.

Harlots, harlots everywhere!

Mike Medavoy: "Back in 1971 *The New Yorker*'s Pauline Kael could anoint a picture like *Last Tango in Paris* simply with a review. But by the end of the eighties, there were so many movie critics that their impact had become watered-down as their opinions piled up. Every small town has its own movie critic, and there are reviewers out there working for dubious-sounding organizations who will say something great about any piece of junk just to see their names in the ads."

Liar, liar!

A reporter named Lenny Traube, writing for the *Western Queens Gazette* in Astoria, New York, described an interview he did with me at a place called Mary McGuire's restaurant on Broadway.

He wrote: "Joe Eszterhas, the bearded millionaire screenwriter, turned up at Mary McGuire's on Broadway following a script session at the Kaufman-Astoria studios and passed on the following to his eager interviewer, yours truly."

Lenny Traube then quoted me at length about my past movies and future projects.

The only problem was that I'd never spoken to anyone named Lenny Traube or anyone else from the *Western Queens Gazette*. I had never been in Astoria, New York. I had never been at the Kaufman-Astoria studios. I had never been at Mary McGuire's restaurant.

Lenny Traube had made the whole thing up and had plagiarized other interviews I had done during the previous six months.

When I threatened to sue, the *Western Queens Gazette* apologized and admitted that Lenny Traube had made it all up. They begged me not to sue. They even offered to do a lengthy (this time real) interview with me.

I didn't do the interview.

I didn't sue, either, although I should have.

Let's make critics real people, not cinema geeks.

Here's how to clean up film criticism—how to take the corruptions out of it, how to stop the payoffs and the junket swag and strip critics of their power.

It's easy, really. In the interest of fairness, newspapers should rotate their film critics every six months. Film critics should not be people who have seen ten movies a week for years and years.

Their expertise should not be in the technique of moviemaking. They shouldn't be cinema geeks who spend most of their time in dark theaters.

They should be reporters from the newspaper's other beats—sports, news, the style sections, the obituary pages—who, for six months, get to review movies—not from a technical viewpoint, but from a human point of view—and who aren't afraid to tell us without mincing words (for fear of antagonizing studios) how they feel about the movie they've just seen.

Take their names away from 'em.

I said this to a studio executive: "If you think critics are supreme egotists who like to see their names displayed in full-page newspaper ads, why don't you leave their names out of the ads? Just go with the publication they work for. If all the studios did that, maybe critics would write less grandstanding reviews."

She said, "No, we need their names, even if nobody's ever heard of them. Because if we get thrashed by all the major media outlets, we will still have reviews from John and Jane Doe from obscure radio stations around the country, who will give us the review we need to plaster on a full page."

Be patient—once they kick the holy hell out of you, they just might praise you.

While, after its release, feminists bashed *Basic Instinct* unanimously (Tammy Bruce, the then president of the L.A. chapter of NOW, even stood in a picket line), months later feminist author Naomi Wolf wrote, "What was so cathartic about *Basic Instinct* was here was not a cartoon villainess like in *Fatal Attraction*— not a misogynist two-dimensional nightmare—but a complex, compelling Nietzschean *Uberfraulein* who owns everything about her own power. She's rich. She's not ashamed of being rich, which is transgressive in the ideology of femininity."

Yale lecturer and revisionist feminist Camille Paglia wrote, "Woman is the bitch goddess of the universe. . . . Sharon Stone's performance was one of the great performances by a woman in screen history."

When my film *Jagged Edge* was released, it was panned by the critics, dismissed in a few paragraphs by *The New York Times*. Ten years later, in an article about modern classic thrillers, the *Times* included *Jagged Edge*.

Pauline was the worst!

Canonized as "the Divine Redeemer" of film critics, Pauline Kael viewed James Toback (*Fingers*) as a creative genius.

That's all you really need to know about her.

Plus the fact that she stopped writing criticism when Warren Beatty hired her to become part of his production company. Then, when he fired her about a year later, Pauline started writing reviews once again.

A Feedable Critic

Screenwriter/director Buck Henry: "Everyone knew that Pauline Kael was feedable, that if you sat next to her, got her drunk, and fed her some lines, you could get them replayed in some other form."

Pauline liked to hang out.

To Pauline Kael, Altman was a cinematic god. She called *M*A*S*H* "the best American war comedy since sound came in."

Screenwriter Joan Tewksbury, who worked with Altman, said, "Bob could cultivate Pauline. She would come to the sets, go out to dinner with him, hang around his office."

How did Mailer know this?

He called Pauline Kael "the first frigid of the film critics."

A Paulette

Disciples of Pauline Kael.

Was he talking about Pauline or Roger Ebert?

No, Raymond Chandler was referring to Edmund Wilson, the top literary critic of his day, when he called him "a fat bore . . . who made fornication as dull as a railroad time table."

The next time you listen to Ebert . . .

Remember that he is a failed screenwriter, whose sole credit is *Beyond the Valley of the Dolls*.

Gene Shalit is a circus clown.

Paddy Chayefsky called NBC's Gene Shalit "a professional clown" and added that TV critics are "frustrated actors who try to be cute in ninety seconds."

Charles Champlin was a good friend.

When *F.I.S.T.,* my first movie, was released, Norman Jewison, the director, told me that the film critic of the *Los Angeles Times* had seen it and loved it.

"That doesn't really mean a whole helluva lot, though," Norman said.

"What do you mean?" I said. "It's the *Los Angeles Times*. Who's going to write the review it?"

"Charles Champlin," Norman said.

"He's a very respected guy," I said.

"Sure he is," Norman said. "But he's a good friend of mine. I even blurbed his last book."

"So what," I said. "He liked it."

"He certainly did," Norman said, and grinned.

"But he's a friend of yours," I said.

"He certainly is," Norman said, still grinning.

If Rex Reed gives you a bad review . . .

Ben Hecht and his writing partner, Charles MacArthur, saw a critic in a restaurant who had trashed their latest film. Hecht encouraged MacArthur to go over and punch the critic out.

MacArthur said, "It's not worth it—I'll just send him a poison choirboy."

They gave me my props.

Many critics said *Basic Instinct* was written "from the crotch . . . from his loins . . . by his penis."

Those reviews obviously impressed many women who read them and then, after reading them, sought me out.

A Popcorn Movie

They are movies like *Flashdance* and *Jagged Edge* that overcome negative critics and wind up doing huge business. In other words, they are movies that people who've seen them tell other people about. Mike Medavoy: "Studio owners have been known to tell production people, 'Make popcorn movies; that's what people want.'"

Maybe he thought Mike Ovitz would help him sell his script.

A reporter working for *Details* magazine asked me how I felt about the distress I was causing Michael Ovitz "and his family" by telling the world that he had threatened to destroy my career unless I continued to let him represent me.

From a writer's point of view, who is the best film critic working today?

From a writer's point of view, there are no good film critics working today.

There weren't any good film critics working yesterday, either (except for maybe Graham Greene).

And there won't be any good film critics working tomorrow, either.

From a writer's point of view, as my late director friend Richard Marquand advocated, "All critics should be taken into the backyard, lined up alongside the garage wall, and shot."

Forget about critics.

Marilyn Monroe said: "I don't care about the critics. I don't care about anybody. The only people I care about are the people in Times Square, across the street from the theatre, who can't even get close as I come in."

They even beat up on Arthur Miller.

A 1991 *New Yorker* article referred to Arthur Miller (*Death of a Salesman, After the Fall, The Misfits*) as "a critic's punching bag."

Leave the sons of bitches hanging.

Many film critics supplement their income by teaching film classes at various schools around L.A. and New York. Their salaries depend to a great extent on being able to get "stars" to do free Q and As sessions for their classes.

If, while doing an interview with you, they ask you to make a guest appearance in their classes, always say yes. The interview with you or their review of your movie will appear long before your scheduled appearance in one of their classes.

Then, a day before your scheduled appearance, call the person and, faking a hoarse voice, tell him you've got the flu.

Since my throat cancer, I don't even have to fake my hoarse voice.

It pays to be friendly with Daily Variety.

Getting great coverage from *Daily Variety* translates into dollars and cents. If a studio knows that your profile and your relationship with *Daily Variety* can get it positive front-page coverage, that studio is more likely to make a deal with you.

You can use Variety to close your deals.

Another way to profit from a good relationship with *Daily Variety*: When a deal isn't quite done, leak the story as a fait accompli to *Daily Variety*—it will make the deal more likely to get done if everyone is already talking about it.

It worked when I leaked that Paul Verhoeven was directing *Showgirls,* before he'd actually decided to direct it. Everyone told Paul what a great idea it sounded like, and he closed his deal.

It didn't work when I leaked that Cuba Gooding, Jr., would play Otis Redding in my script *Blaze of Glory.* Cuba got pissed that *Variety* was writing about something he hadn't yet decided to do, and he immediately pulled out of the project.

I had outfoxed myself.

This *Variety* device to get deals done was something I called "the Mike Fleming Net," after the *Variety* writer who wrote all the stories about new deals.

Columnists like Cristal.

If you want her to mention you and to mention you nicely" producer Irwin Winkler said to me about entertainment columnist Marilyn Beck, "send her a bottle of great champagne each Christmas."

I did . . . and she did.

A Chatter Chippie

A Hollywood gossip columnist.

Disrupt traffic, break windows, and slit tires.

A group of Writers Guild officials sat in my dining room in Malibu, telling me how awful it was that the *Los Angeles Times* was increasingly giving the "Film by" credit or simply the "by" credit to directors.

I said, "What are you guys doing about it?"

One of the Guild people said, "We're setting a series of cocktail events up where *Los Angeles Times* and other journalists can come by and meet screenwriters once a week."

I said, "Why are you doing that?"

One of them said, "So they can get to know screenwriters, write about them, and elevate their profile."

I said, "That won't do any good. Those journalists are jealous as hell of screenwriters. Those bastards would die to make the kind of money a lot of screenwriters make."

One of them said, "Well, what would you do?"

I said, "I'd set up a picket line outside the *Los Angeles Times* building to protest the 'Film by' credit. I'd make a lot of noise, disrupt traffic, break some windows, slit some tires, and get our feelings on the front page of every newspaper in the country. SCREENWRITERS RUN AMOK—that'd be a great headline."

The Writers Guild people got out of my house very quickly.

Isn't there something wrong here?

Many newspapers are already using the "by" credit.

Here is what it looks like: *Daisy Miller* by Peter Bogdanovich; *The Color Purple* by Steven Spielberg; *Gone With the Wind* by Victor Fleming; *The Godfather* by Francis Ford Coppola; *War and Peace* by King Vidor; *Huckleberry Finn* by William Desmond Taylor; *The Ten Commandments* by Cecil B. DeMille; and *The Bible* by John Huston.

PART TWELVE

THE HAPPY ENDING

LESSON 19

Fight, Write, Throw Up, and
Keep Writing!

It's okay to be jealous of other screenwriters.

Novelist and screenwriter Gore Vidal: "Every time a friend succeeds, I die a little."

Robert McKee can get jealous, too.

McKee: "Would you rather get paid $25,000 to have your story on the screen exactly as you wrote it, or get paid a million dollars by a studio and have your script butchered by development executives? Nine out of ten screenwriters want the latter. These people are not artists. They have no integrity and they get what they deserve—to have their names associated with bad films."

You don't get it, Bobby. The name of the game is to get the million bucks and *still* get it made exactly as you wrote it . . . which is exactly what I have done with many of my movies.

Your movie needs a little luck.

The advance word on *The China Syndrome* was bleak. The movie lacked any buzz; everyone expected it to bomb.

Three days before it was released, a nuclear catastrophe at Three Mile Island got the attention of the whole world. *The China Syndrome,* a movie about a nuclear catastrophe, was a smash hit.

You need a little luck, too.

A reporter for ABC television did a lengthy *20/20* piece about my screenwriting success. I had just sold several scripts for millions of dollars and I had just fallen head over heels with the love of my life. I was floating when I did the interview.

ABC's correspondent Judd Rose told me off-camera in the course of our day together that he felt like his luck in life had run out. He was a young man and he had recently been diagnosed with an inoperable brain tumor.

For luck, I gave him a beautiful antique Hawaiian walking stick, one of my most treasured objects.

But a couple of years later, Judd Rose died.

Avoid the gods of irony.

Mike Medavoy: "The gods of irony wield a lot of power in Hollywood."

Don't let it kill you.

Producer Alan Carr died as a result of the failure of his Academy Award telecast; director Richard Marquand died as a result of the failure of his film *Hearts of Fire*; Paddy Chayefsky died as a result of his directorially butchered film *Altered States*.

If you fail, don't kill yourself.

Writer and producer Dominick Dunne: "For me, the pain of failure exceeded by far the joys of success. My plight was hopeless. I almost jumped in front of a train in Santa Barbara. At the last second I let it pass me. I had a major flirtation with a kitchen knife that I took to bed with me. The love that I felt for Los Angeles turned to hate. I ran from there."

Creatively Reliable

A person who is so screwed up on drugs or booze that he is personally unreliable . . . but can still function as a screenwriter.

Remember that chicken shit can turn into chicken liver.

My film *Showgirls*, trashed as one of the worst movies ever made when it was released, is now a cult classic.

A sequel and a Broadway show are planned.

Remember that chicken liver can turn into chicken shit, too.

Titanic, the world's most successful film in history, winner of God knows how many Academy Awards, was voted one of the worst movies of all time in 2003 by the viewers of England's BBC.

You don't want to turn into Joe Gillis.

In *Sunset Boulevard,* Joe Gillis, screenwriter (played by William Holden), wound up as the kept man of a broken-down movie star who hadn't made a movie in decades. She spoiled him, belittled him, and finally killed him. In the last scene of the film, we see him floating facedown in her swimming pool.

Someone asks him in the film, "Don't you sometimes hate yourself?"

Joe says, "Constantly."

This is the way Joe Gillis describes himself: "Nobody important, really. Just a movie writer with a couple of B pictures to his credit. The poor dope."

Don't let this be your self-portrait.

William Goldman: "Everybody knows that writers are miserable—the line between novelists and alcoholics is constantly talked of. But we're weird. We're antisocial, and if you've seen us on the tube, you know that, except for Gore Vidal, we're not a whole lot of fun. You expect the unhappiness."

If you're a boozer, go clean yourself up.

I did. I was the complete functioning alcoholic. I never staggered or slurred or passed out. I rarely even had hangovers.

But I started drinking when I was fourteen, and by 2001, I was drinking a fifth of tequila, bourbon, or gin a day and two bottles of white wine or two six-packs of beer.

I developed throat cancer and had to detox before the surgery. After the surgery, to have a chance to live, I had to stop smoking and drinking.

I did. I've been sober five years. It was the most difficult thing I've ever had to do in my life, but I did it. So can you.

Remember that first and foremost you're an entertainer.

Director Phillip Noyce: "I first became interested in movies as a result of my fascination with the traveling tent shows that came to my small country town when I was a child. And my fascination with the tent shows was an attraction to the ability of the performer to engage the audience. So I've always seen myself as an entertainer of the public. Nothing gives me greater pleasure than to sit in a cinema where one of my films is screening and to feel the pleasure that I'm giving to the audience. That's what makes it all worthwhile. I'd make films for nothing if they told me there was no other way of getting a film financed, just so that I could continue to feel the thrill of that contact with a satisfied public as you take them into the make-believe world that you've created for them."

Hold on to the magic.

I liked the cinema better before I began to do it," said Orson Welles. "Now I can't stop myself from hearing the clappers at the beginning of each shot; all the magic is destroyed."

You can become an echo.

I f your script doesn't sell, there's still hope for the future. My script about soul singer Otis Redding, *Blaze of Glory,* wasn't made for eight years—until the Ray Charles biopic, *Ray,* became a hit movie—and then suddenly my phone didn't stop ringing. People were now showing interest in *Blaze.*

Screenwriter Larry Gross bought the rights to and adapted two Andre Dubus short stories. He couldn't sell his script for *twenty years*—until another Dubus piece, *In the Bedroom,* became a hit movie.

"My partner and I dusted off the script," says Gross, "did a couple of more changes, and all the reasons people had passed on it now were ignored because it was from the author of *In the Bedroom.*"

And you can create an echo.

W hen I wrote *Flashdance,* there hadn't been a hit musical in many years; after the movie's success, there was suddenly a vast variety of musicals being filmed.

Ditto with *Jagged Edge.* There hadn't been a hit courtroom mystery in a long time; after *Jagged Edge*'s success, one after another were released.

If everybody passes on your script . . .

P roducer Robert Evans's favorite saying is "Aw, fuck 'em. Fuck 'em all!"

If you get discouraged . . .

R emember that while *Confederacy of Dunces* is now hailed as the funniest novel ever written and won the Pulitzer Prize, every single publisher passed when it was first sent to them.

You're in good company: Screenwriting almost killed Raymond Chandler, too.

"The last picture I did at Paramount," said the novelist/screen-writer, "nearly killed me. The producer was in the doghouse—he has since left—and the director was a stale old hack who had been directing for thirty years without once achieving any real distinction. Obviously he never could. So here I am, a mere writer and a tired one at that screaming at the front office to protect the producer and actually going on the set to direct scenes—I know nothing about directing—in order that the whole project might be saved from going down the drain. Well, it was saved. As pictures go, it was pretty lively. No classic, but no dud, either."

The film Chandler was talking about was the noir classic *The Blue Dahlia*.

Don't look to Marilyn for inspiration.

John Kennedy Toole, unable to sell his novel *A Confederacy of Dunces*, drove to California and visited Marilyn Monroe's grave.

He then drove back home to Louisiana and killed himself.

Be philosophical about life.

While the PC police were organizing posses everywhere to lynch me for the sex in *Basic Instinct, Showgirls,* and *Sliver,* the president of the United States and his intern were practicing analingus in the Oval Office.

Don't get bitter.

Screenwriter and author John Fante (*Ask the Dust*) was sixty-nine years old and a resident of the Motion Picture and Television Hospital. He was blind. Both of his legs had been amputated.

He said, "The most horrible thing that happens to people is bitterness. They all get so bitter."

If you get discouraged . . .

Remember that fabled (and smart) studio head Frank Price had first crack at a Steven Spielberg project and passed. The project was *E.T.*

Come on, you've only had one cable movie made, Bobby.

Robert McKee: "What I teach is the truth; you're in over your head, this is not a hobby, this is an art form and a profession, and your chances of success are very, very slim. And if you've got only one story, get the fuck out of here. . . ."

Try not to burn out.

Screenwriter Dalton Trumbo: "For several years I have disliked motion pictures and planned tentatively to get out of them. . . . I have an overpowering desire never again to have anything to do with this depraved industry, and an equally overpowering desire to get what cash I can and blow."

Analysis Paralysis

The definition of Hollywood burnout. For example:

The writer who has writer's block.

The director who wants to himself rewrite the script.

The studio head who is afraid to say yes or no to a movie.

The agent who drives out to Joshua Tree in his new Porsche and sits in the car for three days drinking vodka and popping pills, watching the sunsets and sunrises.

The superstar actor who becomes a shoemaker's apprentice in Italy.

The actress who gets a nose job that ruins her career.

The producer who decides, at the age of sixty-two, that he's gay.

There are a thousand other symptoms of the same malaise.

The only cure? *Get the hell outta Dodge—now!*

If you get discouraged . . .

Remember that when a screenwriter changed the title to something else, put his own name on it, and sent it to most of the production entities in Hollywood, there were no takers.

The original title of that script was *Casablanca*.

If you can't sell your script, enter the competitions.

Some agents read the scripts of competition winners and some producers assign readers to the winners' scripts, too.

There seem to be more and more of these competitions each year, but some of the more established ones are the Nicholl Fellowships in Screenwriting, the Chesterfield Film Company's Writer's Film Project, and the Writer's Network Screenplay and Fiction Competition. Check the Internet for others.

If things go bad screenwriting, you can always try to write a novel.

There is no director, producer, star, or studio head to work with. You will get no "notes" from anyone. You will have an editor who will make "suggestions" to you. You can take those suggestions or leave them. No writer will replace you if you leave the publisher. You'll be paid whether you listen to the suggestions or not.

Sounds like bliss, right?

You can free yourself by writing a novel.

Screenwriter/director/novelist John Sayles (*Matewan*): "There's a basic structure to movies. It's rigid and reductive. In a movie, you only deal with core relationships: a protagonist, an antagonist. But in a novel you can do whatever you want. You can introduce characters that disappear for a hundred pages, you can have a dozen plot lines that interweave and overlap. In a novel, you get to be God. That doesn't happen in the movies."

Steven Bochco thinks writing a novel is fun.

Bochco (*Hill Street Blues, Death by Hollywood*): "Television and film are such streamlined story mediums. You can't really meander about, whereas a novel is an interior experience. Once you have your map, once you know your final destination, you can take all these pit stops along the way. You can take side trips and digress, riff on something and come back to the main road. It's so much fun."

If you write a novel, you gotta go platinum or else.

John Sayles: "Getting a second novel published is even harder than getting a first novel published. It's no longer enough to be a good writer; now you have to be a good writer whose first book went platinum."

It isn't bliss.

Publishing isn't what it once was. By their preorders, booksellers determine how many copies of a book a publisher will print.

In film terms, that's letting the exhibitors, the individual theater owners, determine how many prints a studio will make.

If you're already writing your novel . . .

Remember that booksellers have so much power that they can determine the jacket of your book. This is what often happens when Barnes & Noble doesn't like a cover. The publisher prints up a new one.

Another reason not to write novels . . .

One time when Irish author Carlo Gébler was doing a book reading, a group of drunken students in the audience started fighting.

"Do you want me to finish?" he asked.

"Not really," someone yelled.

Carl Hiaasen, my favorite mystery novelist, went to a book reading in Arkansas and discovered that an Arkansas Razorbacks game was taking place at the same time. He did his book reading for the few book salesmen who showed up.

Novelist William Trevor went to a reading, found no one there, and read for the cabdriver who'd brought him. He discovered after he finished reading that his cabbie had charged him for his reading time.

You might want to try gay porn.

Screenwriter/novelist Gigi Grazer (*Stepmom*, *The Starter Wife*): "Writers, or any artists, should constantly be reinventing themselves, whatever that means—plays to screenplays to novels and back again, or second wife to mistress to third wife to gay porn, whatever works. Life feeds us. If we stagnate, there is no material."

Be proud of being a screenwriter.

Don't take any shit from anyone who asks you why, if you're so unhappy being a screenwriter, you're not writing novels instead.

Paddy Chayefsky: "I consider writing novels déclassé. After all, drama has been around since the Orphic rites; the novel has been around only since Cervantes or thereabouts."

If you wind up writing television because you can't get a film job . . .

You're in good company.

David O. Selznick, the greatest creative producer in the history of Hollywood, wound up working in TV after he went broke.

If you can't write screenplays, then take over the studio.

That's what the legendary studio boss Darryl F. Zanuck did.

When he began his career, he was a screenwriter on the Warner Bros. payroll, making a hundred dollars a week.

If you can't make it as a screenwriter, there's still hope.

If you're Tom Cruise or Jack Nicholson or Barbra—one of *those* people—what are you supposed to do? Stand out there on the side of the road on the 405 or I-10 and change the tire?

Yourself? Getting your hands dirty? Dirtying your new Gucci embroidered jeans?

That's what gave my friend Hank an idea. He had been writing and trying to sell screenplays for eight years, without success. One year, he even slept in his car; his office was the Kinko's on Lincoln Avenue.

Then, one beautiful socked-in L.A. day, he was driving along the 405 in his beater and there was a brother standing on the side of the road next to a Rolls-Royce. Hank saw that it was Eddie Murphy, and that got him thinking.

Hank had a friend who had a friend who was an accountant for people like Harrison Ford and Richard Dreyfuss and a lot of other big-time directors and producers. He went to his friend, who went to *his* friend, the accountant, and got Hank an appointment with him. And the accountant *loved* Hank's idea.

The accountant gave Hank's number to all of his clients and the clients gave his number to big-shot friends of theirs, and pretty soon Hank's phone started to ring.

If they needed to take any of their cars (some had six or seven) to be serviced, Hank took it for them—drove it there, had the work done, and drove it back home for them.

If they broke down on the road, or had any other difficulty, Hank drove to the scene, fixed the car if he could, or drove it to the shop if he couldn't and then waited with them while the limo he had called for them arrived.

Hank has a staff of four now. As a sideline, he's starting his own limo company. A good-looking guy, he's even dating a couple of his clients, sometimes even showing them one of his scripts.

You don't want to die like Clifford Odets did.

The world-acclaimed playwright was employed as a segment writer for the television show *Paladin,* starring Richard Boone, when he died of cancer at age fifty-seven.

A friend said, "He was miserable out there. All of his dreams were of escaping from it, of writing plays and coming back to the theater. He never made peace with his defeat."

Go get some rhinoplasties.

Trevor Mills, a screenwriter who lives in Austin, Texas, couldn't sell a script, so he spent nine thousand dollars on a chin implant and two rhinoplasties to make himself look like Keanu Reeves.

He still couldn't sell a script after his surgeries, but he was thinking about studying acting.

Jim Harrison wants to be Jack Nicholson.

Screenwriter/novelist Jim Harrison was on a Mediterranean cruise with Jack Nicholson. Harrison said later, "It would be a tiny port and there would be all these women screaming 'Fuck me, Jack! I love you, Jack! I'm yours, Jack!' I remember thinking, What does that do to your head?"

Kevin Costner does Jim Harrison a favor.

Jim Harrison and Kevin Costner were sitting together in a bar. Jim pointed out to Kevin after their third beer that Kevin had gotten a dozen notes from ladies in the bar and that he had gotten none.

To make him feel better, Kevin offered to give Jim some of his notes.

Your teeth can be discolored and you can still score big-time.

Paddy Chayefsky, by all accounts, was a singularly unhandsome man—small, overweight, his teeth discolored, his hair balding. He usually reeked of tobacco and garlic. Yet he got the sex symbol of his age to go to bed with him.

Does anybody think that had a little to do with the quality of his writing?

I don't flatter myself, either. In the period of my life when I bedded the sex symbol of my age, I, too, was an unhandsome man—overweight, my teeth discolored, my hair down to my butt. I usually reeked of tobacco, garlic, and alcohol. And yet the sex symbol of my age slept with me, too.

If you keep writing, if you don't give up, then you, too, can follow in our footsteps.

Billy Wilder was a gigolo.

If you can't sell your script, maybe you can sell yourself.

That's what Billy Wilder did when he couldn't sell his scripts in Berlin. He became a gigolo.

If you get discouraged . . .

Paddy Chayefsky said, "In spite of everything, screenwriting is better than threading pipe."

You don't want to get old in Hollywood.

Bert Fields, one of the most powerful attorneys in Hollywood, wrote this in a short story entitled *The Heart of the Matter*: "On his sixty-fifth birthday, the actor sits alone on his terrace finishing a bottle of Cristal. The city lights stretch out before him. Millions of homes, millions of families. Husbands coming home to wives, kids, even dogs. He's got his butler . . . and sometimes his lawyer. His agent has died. It doesn't matter. No scripts come in anyway. He shakes his head, smiling sadly . . . remembering. He wonders whatever happened to his wife. He feels the need for people, noise, something. He dials his lawyer, gets an answering machine. He dials his favorite restaurant. They're fully booked. For a few minutes, he stares out at the city. Then he rises slowly from the chair, blows a kiss to the lights, and climbs the stairs to the bedroom, where the .38 special lies waiting in the drawer."

Unless you're Clint Eastwood (who's Marilyn in drag). . .
Clint: "Some people glow really early, in their twenties and thirties, then in their fifties they are not doing as much. But I feel that growing up and maturing, constantly maturing—aging is the impolite way of saying it—I like to think there is an expansion going on philosophically."

A Chocolate Life

Hollywood retirement: champagne, caviar, fresh flowers delivered every day, and all the chocolate you can eat.

No matter how old you are, you can always learn more about film.
Director Akira Kurosawa, at age eighty-two: "I'm just beginning to understand what cinema can do."

Did I tell you to get the hell out of L.A.?
Raymond Chandler: "No doubt I have learned a lot from Hollywood. Please do not think I completely despise it, because I don't . . . but the overall picture, as the boys say, is of a degraded community whose idealism even is largely fake. The pretentiousness, the bogus enthusiasm, the incessant squabbling over money, the all-pervasive agent, the strutting of the big shots (and their usually utter incompetence to achieve anything they start out to do), the

constant fear of losing all this fairy gold and being the nothing they have really never ceased to be, the snide tricks, the whole damn mess is out of this world . . . it is like one of these South American palace revolutions conducted by officers in comic opera uniforms— only when the thing is over the ragged dead men lie in rows against the wall, and you suddenly know that this is not funny, this is the Roman circus, and damn near the end of civilization."

If you reach a certain point, quit screenwriting.

I mean it. I bartended for a while.

Screenwriter Jeffrey Boam: "I have a schedule, I have a secretary and a producing partner and a development person, and I feel like I'm no longer living the quiet, contemplative life of a writer. I'm not getting that benefit anymore, and I've gotten to the point where I'm losing my patience with directors and producers. I feel 'Why do I have to please these people? Why do I have to knock myself out to please them? Come back to them with idea after idea after idea. They're all good, but they reject them so often. I'm just sick of it.'"

Time to go bartend, Jeffrey.

You can get drunk and dance in your bare feet.

Screenwriter William Faulkner: "Anybody who can sell anything to the movies for more than $50,000 has a right to get drunk and dance in his bare feet."

Peter Bart doesn't have any balls. Or . . . Take notes for your Hollywood tell-all. Or . . . Sidney Korshak was a sleazeball.

Variety editor Peter Bart, in his book Shoot Out: "One night I wandered home, dead tired, and found myself leafing through the journal I had been keeping—notes that I would someday turn into my 'definitive' book about life at the studio. I was riveted as I relived these day-to-day experiences—encounters with Mafioso and managers, with the Roman Polanskis and the Sidney Korshaks. I'd even noted down one conversation with Korshak, the ever-somber attorney who had started out serving Al Capone and ended up mentoring stars and studio chiefs. 'Peter,' he said, 'do you know what's the best insurance policy—one that guarantees continuous breathing?' I thought this an odd question, but I asked for his answer. 'It's silence,' he intoned. He said it as though he had just imparted great wisdom, and in a sense he had. This was, after all, advice emanating from someone who was arguably the industry's most talented 'fixer.' I decided it was advice worth taking. I would stay at Paramount, but I would shred my notes."

That's crap. Moustache Pete Omertà stuff. Write everything down and keep your notes, and if you feel like it, write the book that tells all. I've written two of those already.

If they screw you over, write about it.

It's okay to bite the hand that feeds you.

Ben Hecht, the king of all screenwriters, wrote the scripts for three films that satirized Hollywood: *Actors and Sin,* in which an old actor kills his actress daughter so she will not wind up being a nobody like him; *I Hate Actors,* in which a celebrated and successful script is written by a nine-year-old child; *The Scoundrel,* in which a producer says, "Don't use that line; it's twenty-five years old." (The line is "I love you.")

I wrote a script called *An Alan Smithee Film: Burn Hollywood Burn,* which made fun of most of the players in town. In my first draft, I used real names, not made-up ones. I will sell that draft on eBay someday.

(Just kidding, I *think*.)

You're a writer, not the owner of a writing factory.

Ben Hecht hired writers to "block out and draft" scripts, which he then revised and called his own. Ernest Tidyman (*The French Connection*) did the same thing after he won the Oscar. While Ron Bass (*Rain Main*) denies that he runs a writing factory, he does hire assistants and researchers, who accompany him to studio meetings.

The trouble with doing this, of course, is that word spreads quickly, and that studios will think twice about hiring you if they think *you're* doing what *they're* doing: grinding out sausages.

Nobody ever accused William Goldman of running a writing factory, but he does write *quickly*. When he wrote three scripts in one year and none of them was produced, word spread that he was grinding out sausages. His phone didn't ring for years.

Don't die wearing a diamond ring.

Famed producer Mike Todd's remains were stolen from a Chicago cemetery so the thieves could get the big diamond ring he was famous for wearing.

Anthony Pellicano will unearth you, too.

The infamous Hollywood private eye's first claim to fame was finding Mike Todd's remains. Alas, when the Pelican found the body, the diamond ring was gone.

If you're asked for casting advice, take great care.

My first draft of *An Alan Smithee Film: Burn Hollywood Burn* called for Anthony Pellicano to play an infamous Hollywood gumshoe named Anthony Pellicano.

I called Anthony and sent him the script and he happily agreed to play himself in the film.

When I cast Sly Stallone in the lead part, Sly had only one demand: that Anthony Pellicano not be in the film.

I don't know why he made that demand and I was smart enough not to want to know. I didn't ask him.

I called Anthony and told him I had to write him out of the film or I'd lose Sly.

Anthony called Sly a bunch of names but said he understood that Sly's presence in the film gave us our financing for it.

I changed the Anthony Pellicano character's name in the script to the fictitious Sam Rizzo.

My agent called me a couple of weeks later and said he had a friend who had read the script and was desperate to play the Sam Rizzo part. It was Harvey Weinstein, then the head of Miramax and one of the most powerful people in town.

I cast Harvey and called Anthony and told him that Harvey Weinstein would be playing the part.

Anthony said: "*Harvey Weinstein?* Harvey Weinstein is going to *play me?* He's a fuckin' wuss. He can't play *me!*"

I said, "No, he's going to play Sam Rizzo."

Anthony said, "There is no fuckin' Sam Rizzo! Sam Rizzo is *me!*"

Anthony said: "I oughta get my baseball bat and go visit the set."

But Anthony laughed. He was making a little joke.

The joke was funny, but . . .

Anthony invited himself over to my house in Malibu.

"I've got a lot of stories you'd be interested in hearing," he said.

Something told me I wasn't interested in hearing Anthony's stories.

I never invited him over to my house.

That may have been the smartest move I've ever made in Hollywood.

Raymond Chandler was just jealous of writers who made more money than he did.

After I sold a four-page outline for $4 million, I tried not to think about what Raymond Chandler had said about screenwriting in Hollywood: "The big money still goes to the wrong people."

PERK OF SUCCESS:
OLFACTORY PLEASURES

You will know the smell of freshly baked croissants at the Four Seasons Hotel in Beverly Hills.

You can bury your friends.

Maxwell Bodenheim, Ben Hecht's poet friend, wrote Ben and begged him for some money.

Ben wrote him a letter, saying that he was enclosing two hundred dollars. But he "forgot" to enclose the money.

When Maxwell Bodenheim died broke, Ben said he would pay for his funeral, so that Max wouldn't be buried in a potter's field. Then he put fifty dollars into a fund for his friend's funeral.

TAKE IT FROM ZSA ZSA

If you make it and get divorced, share custody but keep the help.

"There is nothing harder to find than good servants. I remember when I was sitting in the Plaza Hotel in New York with Porfirio Rubirosa, and George Sanders called from California to say that finally he'd allow me to divorce him, but he also said that Albert, who'd served us for years, was going with him. I started to cry bitterly. Rubirosa said, 'You wanted to divorce him and now that he says "yes," you start to cry.' And I said, 'Don't be silly! I'm not crying for him, I'm crying for the butler.'"

You don't have to be a victim.

Oscar-winning screenwriter William Goldman: "I've never seen a rough cut of a picture I've written. And I rarely get invited to sneaks. *Marathon Man* is a good example, because there were two sneaks, in California. And I live in New York, so it's expensive to bring me out. Except I was in California at the time. Wouldn't have cost a whole lot to have [had] me along."

I've seen the rough cut of almost all of the fifteen films I've written.

I have often been sent by FedEx the tapes of the dailies as they are printed.

I attend all of the research screenings of my films.

I have been to every focus-group preview of my films, flying on the corporate jet along with the director, the producer, studio people, and sometimes even the star to sneaks in Chicago; Paramus, New Jersey; Washington, D.C.; and Kansas City, Missouri.

Why does the studio ask me to participate in these things while shutting out Bill Goldman?

One reason may be that everyone involved with the films knows that I care passionately about them—I am not already thinking about THE NEXT JOB (Bill's caps).

Another reason may be that everyone knows I'm perfectly capable of bad-mouthing the movie publicly—and getting lots of media attention—if I'm shut out of the process.

Keep on writing and writing.

Screenwriter Dan Harris (*Imaginary Heroes*): "Life is hard, and it often pulls no punches. Sometimes when you think it cannot get any worse, it does. Sometimes the light at the end of the tunnel dies just as you approach it. But sometimes there is healing in catastrophe. Sometimes people are given a second chance."

Don't let the bastards get you down.

Paddy Chayefsky, in a letter to a friend: "I'm out here in California trying to make a movie, which has been a horror show from the beginning. We started shooting the fucker last Friday, and the director not only has turned out to be a monster, but a monster with not enough talent to make it worthwhile. Man, I'm tired of battling. I truly am."

You have to be the toughest person in the world.

Screenwriter/director Ron Shelton: "You have to be the toughest person in the world. If writers take the passive role, they become victims. I tell writer's groups—don't complain. If you're good enough at your work and your craft, get a lot tougher. You have to be ruthless. Writers aren't tough enough."

Don' let anyone walk over you.

Screenwriter/novelist Raymond Chandler: "I have fought many hard battles in my life and I never found that there was any way to fight them except directly, accepting the risks, knowing that all I had to fight with was my brain and my courage, and that I could easily lose against much more powerful people than myself. But I did not become one of the three or four highest-paid writers in Hollywood by letting anyone walk over me."

Write messages from your soul.

Writer/producer William Froug: "In the final analysis of our lives, as well as our writing, what else do we really have to listen to but the messages from our own souls, psyches, guts, instincts, muses, whatever you call it? This is where our personal truth, our themes, our creativity lies. The writers who fearlessly kept writing what they truly believed, in my experience, are the ones who have gone on to the greater glory—not merely money or fame, but something far more basic: inner peace and genuine fulfillment."

Go see your movie in your neighborhood theater.

Columbia Tristar once released a film nationally—*The Bloodhounds of Broadway*—with a whole reel missing from it. No one noticed.

Develop a short memory.

Producer Ben Hecht: "They can screw you, and you can screw them, but if you want to keep on working, both of you need a short memory."

You can make God smile.

Dalton Trumbo: "Once in a while when God smiles and the table is tilted just slightly in our favor, something happens. It comes from inside and reveals what we really are."

Just keep writing.

And writing and writing . . . and if you are good to your fellow humans and if God smiles, the day will come when you are writing something and *you* will stop and smile and jump up and down because it is working, because you know that what you are writing is *good*!

But until that magical sun-kissed moment comes, hang in there and *just keep fucking writing*!

Keep writing even if you're hurling.

For the first couple of years that I wrote screenplays, I was so nervous about what I was doing that I threw up before I began writing each morning.

There's nothing wrong with that. It's much better than reading what you've written at the *end* of the day and throwing up.

PERK OF SUCCESS: FEAR

My biggest fear . . .

After thirty years of writing scripts, it's a fear that I know you don't have, thank God.

I can't operate a computer. Oh hell, I can't even work an electric typewriter—I hit the keys too damn hard.

I'm a two-finger typist and I slam away at my manual Olivetti with both middle fingers (a lot of critics have made too much about the significance of writing with my two middle fingers, thank you).

The trouble is that one of these days they're going to stop making Olivetti manual typewriters. The only reason they still make them is because there's a big market for them in retirement communities.

Well hell, I don't live in a retirement community. I've got four boys under the age of ten, for Christ's sake. And I've got a lot of script and book ideas for the future.

So what's going to happen to me when Olivetti manuals become obsolete? Well, I have ten brand-new (still in the box) Olivetti manual typewriters in my closet, ready to go. But they're made in all kinds of Third World places (like Hungary) and sometimes I beat these machines to death in a matter of months with my slamming middle fingers.

And, get this: I discovered recently that they have already stopped making Olivetti ribbons for manual typewriters. Naomi has patiently hunted the Internet and we now have sixty-three new Olivetti ribbons in the closet with the ten machines.

> But what happens when I've killed all the machines or used
> up all the ribbons for the machines? Do I then have to learn
> how to use a word processor or the dreaded computer?
>
> Or do I hang it up and say God (and all my critics) has
> silenced me?
>
> I tell you this story to put all your fears into perspective. All
> you have to do is write your script. All you really have to do is
> write the first page of your script, because then you'll already be
> rolling.
>
> I have to figure out my entire future!

No matter what, try to be optimistic.

Screenwriter William Faulkner said, "You have to live so that you can die."

TAKE IT FROM ZSA ZSA

"If you get depressed," said my Hungarian compatriot Zsa Zsa Gabor, "take a bath and wash your hair."

Don't give up.

Paddy Chayefsky's mother said to him, "Listen, you want to be a writer, you've got to write. You submit, and they'll reject. But you've got to keep writing."

Don't ever give up on selling your script.

Warren Beatty said this about trying to bed every woman that he met: "You get slapped a lot, but you get fucked sometimes, too."

You've still gotta believe in happy endings.

When he was an old man, several of producer Sam Spiegel's Oscars were stolen by the prostitute who frequently came to his home.

But it's never too early to consider your epitaph.

This is one Marilyn Monroe wanted: "Here lies Marilyn. No lies. Only lays."

If I made it, you surely can.

Consider the following:

English is my second language. Some critics have said I butcher it.

I stole cars and carried a knife when I was a kid; I almost killed another kid with a baseball bat and almost went to jail.

I flunked both algebra and biology in high school and had to go to summer school two years in a row.

I was a *C* student in high school.

I didn't graduate from college because I was on both academic and disciplinary probation.

I was a *D* student in college, although I won every writing competition I entered.

I started drinking when I was fourteen and was a functional alcoholic by the time I was in college.

I've never believed in chitchatting and networking—I've been a loner all of my life.

Naomi says I'm abrupt, direct, sometimes downright rude, occasionally antisocial.

For much of my life, I've looked and dressed like a Hell's Angel.

I've always preferred reading a book to seeing a movie.

But I've always preferred having sex to reading a book.

For many years, I preferred having a drink to *anything,* but I don't drink anymore.

I've named my company "Barbarian, Ltd."

Hollywood has paid "Barbarian" many, many millions of dollars through the years.

Don't let 'em take your mojo.

They'll try to beat it out of you—depress you, disillusion you, corrupt you.

Keep your mojo hidden deep inside yourself. It's your heart and soul. It's what makes you tick, what makes you write, and what makes you special. It's the source of your work, your worth, and your talent.

Fight the fuckers with every breath of your being. And if, after you've fought the good fight, you lose—if your movie stinks or you're rewritten by five other writers or you feel betrayed by people you thought were friends or thought cared about you—get a good night's rest and sit down at your laptop the next morning and start making up a brand-new story. And fight the fuckers all over again with every breath of your being.

Because *you're* a writer. And *they're* not.

And if you fight hard enough, and write enough stories, one of these days you'll see your work up on-screen just the way you wanted. And you'll change the lives and better the lives and make more enjoyable the lives of the people who see it.

Your film. Your *mojo*. Up there on the big screen.

Epilogue

I had a three-script deal with United Artists. The first script was *Betrayed*, the second was *Music Box,* and the third was going to be *Media Mogul,* a roman a clef about Rupert Murdoch. But as I started writing the third script, it didn't go anywhere for me, and I gave up on it. It had been producer Irwin Winkler's idea anyway to do a filmic assault on Murdoch, not mine.

I started writing another script instead without telling anyone that I was writing it—not even Irwin, who was going to produce all three scripts. The new script's genesis was my unwavering and no doubt naïve belief that someday America would have a president who would tell the American people the truth, no matter how difficult that truth was.

I wrote it as a black but Capraesque comedy. Sam Parr, in his late sixties, the liberal Democrat president of the United States, is running for reelection against a right-wing McCarthyite demagogue. Sam Parr has always screwed around on his long-suffering wife and he's the kind of man who enjoys his Jack Daniel's. One misbegotten day during the campaign when everything goes to shit, he finds himself on the Nebraska farm where he grew up, tilting his Jack Daniel's bottle, and dozes off in the barn. He wakes up more than a little randy and does what he did as a boy. He, um, pops the nearby cow. Yes, *cow*—literally.

A right-wing spy takes a picture of him *in flagrante.* First the right-wingers try to blackmail Sam Parr to drop out of the race and then they release the picture to the tabloids. Sam Parr decides to tell Americans the truth. "Yes, I popped that cow!" he says. And, *mirabile dictu,* every farm boy or suburban ex–farm boy who ever popped a cow or a chicken or a cat in a boot votes for him.

Because he told America the truth, he is reelected to office by a landslide.

I wrote the script in 1989, during the Bush, not the Clinton, presidency; during the era of "Read my lips—no new taxes," before Lewinsky's lips and news of that infamous cigar.

I sent Irwin Winkler the script with a title page that said in big letters, *SACRED COWS.*

He called me when he received it and said, "I thought we were going to call this *Media Mogul.*"

"Well," I said, "um, the piece, um, changed somewhat. You'll see when you read it."

When Irwin called me back, he was laughing. "You son of a gun," he said. But he also said, "No one will ever make it. Even though I think it's one of the funniest and most moving pieces I've every read."

"Maybe somebody will take a chance on it," I said.

"No," Irwin said, "mark my words. A lot of people will read it. A lot of people will love it. A lot of people will say they want to make it. But no one will make it."

"How do you think United Artists will respond?"

Irwin laughed again.

"They think they're getting a piece about Rupert Murdoch called *Media Mogul.* Where's Murdoch in this piece? Maybe he's the cow, I don't know." Then Irwin added, "I'm afraid they'll sue you for nonperformance."

He was serious.

So, in order to avert a lawsuit, I put a new cover sheet on *Sacred Cows.* It was now entitled *Media Mogul,* but it was still about a president who pops a cow and fesses up.

Dick Berger was the head of United Artists.

"I started reading the script," he told me later. "I got to about page twelve— where the president does the cow. I hurled the script across the room. I thought to myself, This son of a bitch Eszterhas! He takes our money to write this *shit?* He writes about fucking a cow and expects us to make the movie? I'm going to sue this son of a bitch!' I seethed for an hour or so. But something made me pick the damn script off the floor. I finished reading it. I sat there crying when I finished it. I *never* cry reading a script. And I thought, It's brilliant, but I still feel like suing the son of a bitch."

United Artists didn't sue me. Nor did they say they were making *Media Mogul,* as the script was officially called.

They left the fate of my script up to me. If my agents (or Irwin) could attract major elements—an actor, a director—United Artists would *consider* making it.

The first person Guy McElwaine, my agent, sent *Sacred Cows* to was Steven Spielberg. Steven read it and called Guy to tell him it was the funniest script he'd ever read.

He said he was directing it. He said it would be his next picture.

Steven called me and told me he was already working on the movie's sound track. He said he thought all the music should be done by the Marine Corps Band.

I called Irwin and told him Steven was directing *Sacred Cows*.

"Never," Irwin said. "Forget it. It'll never happen."

"He's already making plans for the Marine Corps Band," I said.

Irwin laughed again.

Steven called back a week later and said he anticipated "great flak" if he directed *Sacred Cows*. So, to cover himself, he had sent the script to Stanley Kubrick, asking that Kubrick produce it with Irwin.

"I know there's going to be flak," I said to Steven, "but you're the top director in the world. Irwin Winkler is an internationally respected Oscar-winning producer. What do we need Stanley Kubrick for?"

"Oh," Steven said, "having Stanley certainly wouldn't *hurt*."

Stanley Kubrick wrote Steven a note that said, "This may be the funniest script I've ever read, but I wouldn't want to get within a thousand miles of it."

Steven told me that the Marine Corps Band was still a great idea, but he didn't want to direct *Sacred Cows* anymore. He still wanted to produce it, though. And he had sent it to his friend Bob Zemeckis to direct.

Steven called a month later to say that Bob Zemeckis "loved it" and was considering directing it.

A year passed as Bob Zemeckis kept considering. Then Bob Zemeckis decided he didn't want to direct it.

Since Bob didn't want to direct it, Steven decided he didn't want to produce it, either.

Tony Bill, who had won an Oscar for producing *The Sting* and who had directed *My Bodyguard,* wrote me a note telling me that he had read *Sacred Cows* and thought it one of the funniest scripts he'd ever read.

David Anspach, who had recently directed the hit *Hoosiers* and whom all the studios wanted to work with, read *Sacred Cows* and flew up to Marin County to see me. I liked David, liked his affection for the script, and told him it was fine with me if he directed *Sacred Cows*.

He was so happy, he started to cry.

United Artists turned him down.

David may have been the hottest director in town, but he wasn't hot enough to direct *this* baby.

Michael Lehman had just directed *Heathers,* a big critical hit. *Everybody* wanted to work with him. He read *Sacred Cows,* flew up to Marin to see me, and asked to direct it.

I said great, we celebrated, and he flew back to L.A. to have a meeting with United Artists.

They turned Michael down.

Michael may have been the hottest director in town, but . . . a *cow*? *The president of the United States and a literal, not metaphorical, cow?*

Edward J. Olmos read it, loved it, wanted to direct it. We met at the Ivy. In the back room of the Ivy, because Eddie had pissed off some Latino gang bangers who were even now, as we spoke, looking for him so they could kill him.

United Artists said, "*Who?* Oh, that guy from *Miami Vice?*"

United Artists said no thank you.

Blake Edwards, in my opinion, was a creative genius who had made some of the funniest movies in Hollywood history. We had lunch at Orso's.

He loved *Sacred Cows*. He was desperate to direct *Sacred Cows*.

"I wish there was some way to avoid the cow fucking," Blake said. "You don't *show* it in your script. We wouldn't show it in the movie, either, of course, but that's not what I'm talking about. I wish we could somehow avoid the fact that the president of the United States actually fucks the cow. I wish we could somehow give people the perception that he'd fucked it but reveal that he really hadn't done it."

"You can't do that," I said, "it would vitiate the power of the piece. The whole point is that he fucks the cow and then tells the truth about fucking it."

"I know," Blake Edwards said. "You're right. I agree with you. But I still wish there was some way we could have it both ways."

Blake went to United Artists and told them he could bring the movie in at a low budget. He mentioned James Garner and Bob Newhart as possible cowpokes.

United Artists said no. Granted, they told me, Blake had once made great movies. But he was too old now. He napped on the set and didn't do enough takes of his scenes—the reason, they said, Blake always came in under budget.

It was the first time I'd heard a director bad-mouthed for coming in under budget.

Irwin got the script to Milos Forman, the Oscar-winning director of *One Flew Over the Cuckoo's Nest*. Milos said he liked the script very much and asked for a meeting at his apartment in New York.

United Artists said up front that if Milos committed to direct the movie, they would finance it.

I liked Milos and thought his ideas about the script were insightful. He wanted to broaden the scope of the piece and include a presidential trip to India, the home of the sacred cows.

I did a serious rewrite incorporating his ideas and thought the script was funnier and more poignant than it had been before. So did Milos. He thought I'd done an "extraordinary job" on the rewrite.

"Are you going to direct it?" I asked him bluntly.

"Give me two weeks to consider it," he said.

"What do you think?" I said to Irwin later. "Will he direct it?"

"No." Irwin smiled. "He won't direct it."

Two weeks later, Milos called and said, "I'll tell you the truth. I love the script and I like you, but as much as I'd like to direct this movie, I can't. My best friend in the world is Václav Havel, who is the president of the Czech Republic. How will it look if Václav Havel's best friend makes such fun of the American presidency? We're both immigrants, you and I—me from Czechoslovakia and you from Hungary. *Two* immigrants joining to make this kind of fun? If your name were Jules Feiffer, then I would direct this movie. But for *both* of us to be foreign-born? No, no, you must find an American director."

Jim Abrahams was an American director of broad farcical comedies like *Airplane* and he wanted to make *Sacred Cows* with Lloyd Bridges as the cowpoke.

I realized I was pretty well charging through a wild gamut of directors with this script: Spielberg, to Kubrick, to Blake Edwards, to Milos Forman, to Jim Abrahams!

Jim Abrahams committed to direct *Sacred Cows* as his next picture and United Artists immediately agreed to make it.

Then Jim Abrahams went off to Hawaii to vacation with his family.

When he got back, he changed his mind. He loved his children, he said, and he didn't want to direct anything his children couldn't see.

Shortly afterward, Lloyd Bridges died.

Paul Michael Glaser, the actor, was on vacation in Hawaii, too, and ran into Jim Abrahams. Jim told him he was thinking about directing this crazy script called *Sacred Cows*.

Paul asked to read it and loved it.

When Jim changed his mind, Paul went to United Artists and asked to direct it.

And United Artists said, "*Starsky and Hutch?*"

The script was being mentioned in the media now as "one of the most famous unproduced scripts in Hollywood history."

Even Michiko Kakutani mentioned it in *The New York Times*.

Somebody at United Artists sent the script to Robert Duvall, thinking of him for the part of Sam Parr. Robert Duvall passed.

Years later, when he met me and realized I had written *Sacred Cows,* Robert Duvall looked at me, shook his head, and kept laughing and laughing.

Betty Thomas was the newest directorial flavor of the month.

She read it, she loved it, and she wanted to direct it.

We had lunch and she asked me to tell United Artists that I wanted her to direct it.

I told Betty I'd tell United Artists that if she agreed not to change anything in the script.

"Anything?" Betty said.

"Anything."

"What if we improvise something great?"

"No improvising," I said. "You shoot the script. You change nothing."

She laughed.

"You're some piece of work, Esty," Betty Thomas said, and agreed not to change anything in the script.

I told United Artists I wanted Betty to direct *Sacred Cows* and United Artists said they'd think about it.

Chevy Chase called and wanted to get together. He'd read *Sacred Cows* and wanted to be the cowpoke.

We had lunch. I liked Chevy a lot and thought he'd make a wonderful cowpoke.

I set up a lunch for Chevy with Betty Thomas, who, I said, I hoped would direct the movie.

Betty and Chevy had lunch and Betty decided that she didn't want to work with Chevy.

United Artists decided that they didn't want to make the movie with Betty or with Chevy.

I was standing outside the front door of the Four Seasons Hotel in Beverly Hills with my wife, Naomi, when a black pickup truck drove toward me and stopped. Steven Spielberg was driving; Kate Capshaw sat next to him.

Steven said, "I was a real chickenshit not to do *Sacred Cows*."

I said, "You sure were."

We all laughed.

Steven waved and drove away.

Steven made an overall production deal with MGM/United Artists a few weeks later and walked into his first meeting with the studio to discuss projects he wanted to produce.

There was only one UA project he wanted to produce: *Sacred Cows.*

His friend Tony Bill, Steven said, who'd loved the script for a long time, would direct it.

A few months later, Steven informed United Artists that he wasn't interested in producing *Sacred Cows*—*again*—anymore.

He and Kate had become good friends with Bill and Hillary Clinton, and while it was true that the script had been written a long time ago, during the Bush era, some people might think—considering Paula and Gennifer and Monica—that the president popping this literal cow might be . . .

So because of his friendship with the president who wouldn't tell Americans the truth, Steven wouldn't produce the script about the president who did.

The producer Rob Fried was playing golf with President Clinton one day at Burning Tree and on the way back to the White House in the limo, Bill Clinton started bitching about Paula Jones's lawsuit.

"Jesus Christ," Bill Clinton said, "one of these days someone's gonna accuse me of fucking a cow."

And Rob Fried said, "Mr. President, Joe Eszterhas has already written a script about that."

He told Bill Clinton about *Sacred Cows* and Bill Clinton asked to read it. Rob Fried sent it to him. He never heard from Bill Clinton again.

Irwin Winkler, all those many years ago, was right. A lot of people have read *Sacred Cows*. A lot of people have loved it. A lot of people have said they want to make it. But no one has made it. And I don't think anyone will.

You can get almost anything that you write made into a movie. Almost anything. But not *everything*.

I think, though, that in Hollywood more people have read *Sacred Cow* than any other of my scripts.

Imagine that! You, too, can be best known in the industry for a movie that was never made.

P.S. In the summer of 2006, producer Craig Baumgarten thought that the time was right—George W. Bush's low poll results may have had something to do with it—to try to launch *Sacred Cows* again. They were going to go to Robin Williams, Will Farrell, and Billy Bob Thornton.

INDEX